Microsoft® Excel 2000

Illustrated Intermediate Edition

APPROVED COURSEWARE

ONE MAIN STREET, CAMBRIDGE, MA 02142

Australia • Canada • Denmark • Japan • Mexico • New Zealand • Philippines
Puerto Rico • Singapore • South Africa • Spain • United Kingdom • United States

Microsoft Excel 2000 – Illustrated Intermediate Edition is published by Course Technology

Senior Product Manager: Kathryn H. Schooling
Product Managers: Jennifer A. Duffy, Rebecca VanEsselstine
Associate Product Manager: Emily Heberlein
Authors: Elizabeth Eisner Reding, Tara Lynn O'Keefe
Contributing Author: Barbara Clemens
Editorial Assistant: Stacie Parillo
Marketing Manager: Kristine Murray
Production Editor: Christine Spillett
Development Editor: Rachel Biheller Bunin, India Koopman
Composition House: GEX, Inc.
QA Manuscript Reviewers: Nicole Ashton, Jeff Schwartz, Alex White
Text Designer: Joseph Lee, Joseph Lee Designs
Cover Designer: Doug Goodman, Doug Goodman Designs

For more information contact:

Course Technology
One Main Street
Cambridge, MA 02142
Or find us on the World Wide Web at: www.course.com

ISBN 0-7600-6390-7

Printed in the United States of America

6 7 8 9 B 04 03

The Illustrated Series Offers the Entire Package for your Microsoft Office 2000 Needs

Office 2000 MOUS Certification Coverage

The Illustrated Series offers a growing number of Microsoft-approved titles that cover the objectives required to pass the Office 2000 MOUS exams. After studying with any of the approved Illustrated titles (see list on inside cover), you will have mastered the Core and Expert skills necessary to pass any Office 2000 MOUS exam with flying colors. In addition, **Excel 2000 MOUS Certification Objectives** at the end of the book map to where specific MOUS skills can be found in each lesson and where students can find additional practice.

Helpful New Features

The Illustrated Series responded to Customer Feedback by adding a **Project Files list** in the Readme file on the Project Disk for easy reference, Changing the red font in the Steps to green for easier reading, and Adding New Conceptual lessons to units to give students the extra information they need when learning Office 2000.

New Exciting Case and Innovative On-Line Companion

There is an exciting new case study used throughout our textbooks, a fictitious company called MediaLoft, designed to be "real-world" in nature by introducing the kinds of activities that students will encounter when working with Microsoft Office 2000. The **MediaLoft Web site**, available at www.course.com/illustrated/medialoft, is an innovative Student Online Companion which enhances and augments the printed page by bringing students onto the Web for a dynamic and continually updated learning experience. The MediaLoft site mirrors the case study used throughout the book, creating a real-world intranet site for this chain of bookstore cafés. This Companion is used to complete the WebWorks exercise in each unit of this book, and to allow students to become familiar with the business application of an intranet site.

Enhance Any Illustrated Text with these Exciting Products!

Course CBT

Enhance your students' Office 2000 classroom learning experience with self-paced computer-based training on CD-ROM. Course CBT engages students with interactive multimedia and hands-on simulations that reinforce and complement the concepts and skills covered in the textbook. All the content is aligned with the MOUS (Microsoft Office User Specialist) program, making it a great preparation tool for the certification exams. Course CBT also includes extensive pre- and post-assessments that test students' mastery of skills.

SAM 2000

How well do your students *really* know Microsoft Office? SAM 2000 is a performance-based testing program that measures students' proficiency in Microsoft Office 2000. SAM 2000 is available for Office 2000 in either a live or simulated environment. You can use SAM 2000 to place students into or out of courses, monitor their performance throughout a course, and help prepare them for the MOUS certification exams.

Create Your Ideal Course Package with CourseKits™

If one book doesn't offer all the coverage you need, create a course package that does. With Course Technology's CourseKits—our mix-and-match approach to selecting texts—you have the freedom to combine products from more than one series. When you choose any two or more Course Technology products for one course, we'll discount the price and package them together so your students can pick up one convenient bundle at the bookstore.

For more information about any of these offerings or other Course Technology products, contact your sales representative or visit our web site at:

www.course.com

Preface

Welcome to *Microsoft Excel 2000 – Illustrated Intermediate Edition!* This book in our highly visual design offers users a hands-on introduction to Microsoft Excel 2000 and also serves as an excellent reference for future use. This book is part of an integrated learning system consisting of three manuals providing progressive training in Microsoft Excel 2000. If you would like additional coverage of Excel 2000, we also offer *Microsoft Excel 2000- Illustrated Basic Edition* and Microsoft *Excel 2000- Illustrated Advanced Edition.* These three manuals, when used in conjunction with one another, serve as courseware for the Microsoft Office User Specialist (MOUS) program. After completing the units in these three books, you will be prepared to take the core and expert level MOUS exams for Microsoft Excel 2000. By passing the certification exams, you demonstrate to employers your proficiency in Excel 2000. See more information on MOUS exams and where to find them on the inside cover.

▶ Organization and Coverage

This text contains five units that teach introductory Excel skills. In these units students learn how to build, edit and format worksheets and charts.

▶ About this Approach

The Illustrated approach is designed to make your workers more productive. It also works to help them retain useful information. The skills your employees learn from these manuals can be immediately applied to their daily tasks. The manuals are an ideal reference tool for after the training is completed, and when used as such, can lower the demands on your internal technical support staff.

Each skill is presented on two facing pages, with the step-by-step instructions on the left page, and large screen illustrations on the right. Students can focus on a single skill without having to turn the page. This unique design makes information extremely accessible and easy to absorb, and provides a great reference after the course. This hands-on approach also makes it ideal for both self-paced or instructor-led classes.

Each lesson, or "information display," contains the following elements:

Each 2-page spread focuses on a single skill.

Clear step-by-step directions explain how to complete the specific task, with what students are to type in green. When students follow the numbered steps, they quickly learn how each procedure is performed and what the results will be.

Concise text that introduces the basic principles discussed in the lesson. Procedures are easier to learn when concepts fit into a framework.

Excel 2000

Editing a Chart

Once you've created a chart, it's easy to modify it. You can change data values in the worksheet, and the chart will automatically be updated to reflect the new data. You can also easily change chart types using the buttons on the Chart toolbar. Jim looks over his worksheet and realizes he entered the wrong data for the Kansas City store in November and December. After he corrects this data, he wants to see how the same data looks using different chart types.

Steps

Trouble?
If you cannot see the chart and data together on your monitor, click View on the menu bar, click Zoom, then click 75%.

1. If necessary, scroll the worksheet so that you can see both the chart and row 8, containing the Kansas City sales figures, then place your mouse pointer over the data point to display **Series "Kansas City" Point "December" Value "15,500"**
   As you correct the values, the columns for November and December in the chart automatically change.
2. Click cell **F8**, type **18000** to correct the November sales figure, press [→], type **19500** in cell **G8**, then click
   The Kansas City columns for November and December reflect the increased sales figures. See Figure D-9. The totals are also updated in column H and row 10.
3. Select the chart by clicking anywhere within the chart border, then click the **Chart Type list arrow** on the Chart toolbar
   The chart type buttons appear on the Chart Type palette. Table D-3 describes the chart types available.
4. Click the **Bar Chart button** on the palette
   The column chart changes to a bar chart. See Figure D-10. You look at the bar chart, take some notes, and then decide to convert it back to a column chart. You now want to see if the large increase in sales would be better presented with a three-dimensional column chart.
5. Click the **Chart Type list arrow**, then click the **3-D Column Chart button** on the palette
   A three-dimensional column chart appears. You notice that the three-dimensional column format is more crowded than the two-dimensional format but gives you a sense of volume.
6. Click the **Chart Type list arrow**, then click the **Column Chart button** on the palette
7. Save your work

QuickTip
Experiment with different formats for your charts until you get just the right look.

CLUES TO USE

Rotating a chart

In a three-dimensional chart, columns or bars can sometimes be obscured by other data series within the same chart. You can rotate the chart until a better view is obtained. Double-click the chart, click the tip of one of its axes (select the Corners object), then drag the handles until a more pleasing view of the data series appears. See Figure D-8.

FIGURE D-8: 3-D chart rotated with improved view of data series

MediaLoft Sales - Eastern Division

Click to rotate chart

▶ EXCEL D-8 WORKING WITH CHARTS

Tips as well as trouble-shooting advice right where you need it – next to the step itself.

Clues to Use boxes provide concise information that either expands on one component of the major lesson skill or describes an independent task that is in some way related to the major lesson skill.

Other Features

The two-page lesson format featured in this book provides the new user with a powerful learning experience. Additionally, this book contains the following features:

- **Real-World Case**
  The case study used throughout the textbook, a fictitious company called MediaLoft, is designed to be "real-world" in nature and introduces the kinds of activities that users will encounter when working with Microsoft Excel 2000. With a real-world case, the process of solving problems will be more meaningful.

  Students can also enhance their skills by completing the Web Works exercises in each unit by going to the innovative Student Online Companion, available at www.course.com/illustrated/medialoft. The MediaLoft site mirrors the case study by acting as the company's intranet site, further allowing students to become familiar with applicable business scenarios.

- **Practice**
  Each unit concludes with a Concepts Review that tests students' understanding of what they learned in the unit. The Concepts Review is followed by a Skills Review, which provides students with additional hands-on practice of the skills they learned in the unit. The Skills Review is followed by Independent Challenges, which pose case problems for students to solve. At least one Independent Challenge in each unit asks students to use the World Wide Web to solve the problem as indicated by a Web Work icon. The Visual Workshops that follow the Independent Challenges help students develop critical thinking skills. Students are shown completed Web pages or screens and are asked to recreate them from scratch.

Every lesson features large-size, full-color representations of what the students' screen should look like after completing the numbered steps.

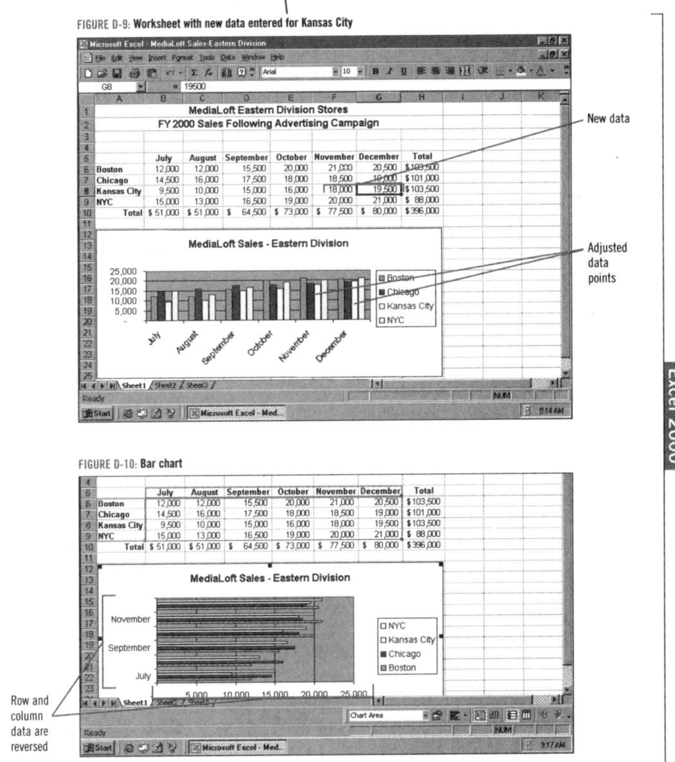

FIGURE D-9: Worksheet with new data entered for Kansas City

New data

Adjusted data points

Excel 2000

FIGURE D-10: Bar chart

Row and column data are reversed

TABLE D-3: Commonly used chart type buttons

click	to display a	click	to display a	click	to display a	click	to display a
	area chart		pie chart		3-D area chart		3-D pie chart
	bar chart		(xy) scatter chart		3-D bar chart		3-D surface chart
	column chart		doughnut chart		3-D column chart		3-D cylinder chart
	line chart		radar chart		3-D line chart		3-D cone chart

WORKING WITH CHARTS EXCEL D-9

Quickly accessible summaries of key terms, toolbar buttons, or keyboard alternatives connected with the lesson material. Students can refer easily to this information when working on their own projects at a later time.

The page numbers are designed like a road map. Excel indicates the Excel section, D indicates the fourth unit, and 9 indicates the page within the unit.

Instructor's Resource Kit

MediaLoft Web site Available at www.course.com/illustrated/medialoft, this innovative Student Online Companion enhances and augments the printed page by bringing students onto the Web for a dynamic and continually updated learning experience. The MediaLoft site mirrors the case study used throughout the book, creating a real-world intranet site for this fictional national chain of bookstore cafes. This Companion is used to complete the WebWorks exercise in each unit of this book, and to allow students to become familiar with the business application of an intranet site.

Instructor's Manual Available as an electronic file, the Instructor's Manual is quality-assurance tested and includes unit overviews, detailed lecture topics for each unit with teaching tips, an Upgrader's Guide, solutions to all lessons and end-of-unit material, and extra Independent Challenges. The Instructor's Manual is available on the Instructor's Resource Kit CD-ROM or you can download it from www.course.com.

Course Test Manager Designed by Course Technology, this Windows-based testing software helps instructors design, administer, and print tests and pre-tests. A full-featured program, Course Test Manager also has an online testing component that allows students to take tests at the computer and have their exams automatically graded.

Course Faculty Online Companion You can browse this text's password-protected site to obtain the Instructor's Manual, Solution Files, Project Files, and any updates to the text. Contact your Customer Service Representative for the site address and password.

Project Files Project Files contain all of the data that students will use to complete the lessons and end-of-unit material. A Readme file includes instructions for using the files. Adopters of this text are granted the right to install the Project Files on any standalone computer or network. The Project Files are available on the Instructor's Resource Kit CD-ROM, the Review Pack, and can also be downloaded from www.course.com.

Solution Files Solution Files contain every file students are asked to create or modify in the lessons and end-of-unit material. A Help file on the Instructor's Resource Kit includes information for using the Solution Files.

Learning Microsoft Outlook 2000 E-mail Learning Microsoft Outlook 2000 E-mail is a simulation program designed to mimic the experience of using the mail capabilities of Microsoft Outlook 2000. Using Learning Microsoft Outlook 2000 E-mail, your students will learn to send, receive, forward, and reply to messages, as well as to manage a mailbox. To complete the Microsoft Outlook 2000 unit your students must use a computer that has the Learning Microsoft Outlook 2000 E-mail program installed from either the Review Pack or the Instructor's Resource Kit. Adopters of this text are granted the right to install Learning Microsoft Outlook 2000 E-mail on any standalone computer or network.

CyberClass CyberClass is a web-based tool designed for on-campus or distance learning. Use it to enhance how you currently run your class by posting assignments and your course syllabus or holding online office hours. Or, use it for your distance learning course, and offer mini-lectures, conduct online discussion groups, or give your mid-term exam. For more information, visit our Web site at: www.course.com/products/cyberclass/index.html.

WebCT WebCT is a tool used to create Web-based educational environments and also uses WWW browsers as the interface for the course-building environment. The site is hosted on your school campus, allowing complete control over the information. WebCT has its own internal communication system, offering internal e-mail, a Bulletin Board, and a Chat room.

Course Technology offers pre-existing supplemental information to help in your WebCT class creation, such as a suggested Syllabus, Lecture Notes, Figures in the Book/ Course Presenter, Student Downloads, and Test Banks in which you can schedule an exam, create reports, and more.

Contents

Exciting New Features and Products III
Preface IV

Excel 2000

Managing Workbooks and Preparing Them for the Web EXCEL F-1
Freezing Columns and Rows EXCEL F-2
Splitting the worksheet into multiple panes EXCEL F-3
Inserting and Deleting Worksheets EXCEL F-4
Specifying headers and footers EXCEL F-5
Consolidating Data with 3-D References EXCEL F-6
Consolidating data from different workbooks using linking EXCEL F-7
Hiding and Protecting Worksheet Areas EXCEL F-8
Changing workbook properties EXCEL F-9
Saving Custom Views of a Worksheet EXCEL F-10
Using a workspace EXCEL F-11
Controlling Page Breaks and Page Numbering EXCEL F-12
Using Page Break Preview EXCEL F-13
Creating a Hyperlink between Excel Files EXCEL F-14
Using hyperlinks to navigate large worksheets EXCEL F-14
Inserting a picture EXCEL F-15
Saving an Excel file as an HTML Document EXCEL F-16
Send a workbook via e-mail EXCEL F-17
Concepts Review EXCEL F-18
Skills Review EXCEL F-19
Independent Challenges EXCEL F-20
Visual Workshop EXCEL F-24

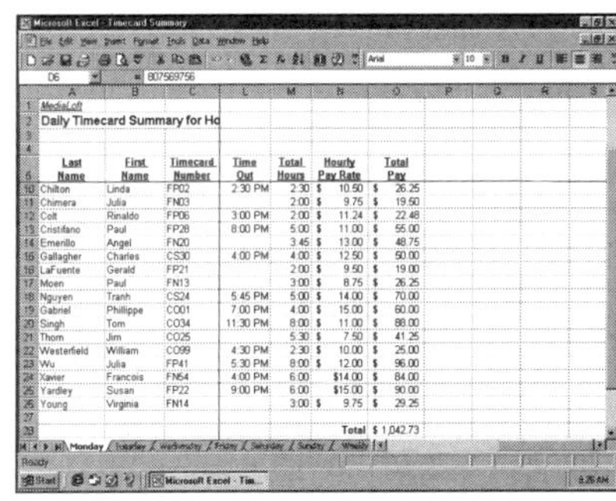

Automating Worksheet Tasks EXCEL G-1
Planning a Macro EXCEL G-2
Macros and viruses EXCEL G-3
Recording a Macro EXCEL G-4
Using Templates to Create a Workbook EXCEL G-5
Running a Macro EXCEL G-6
Editing a Macro EXCEL G-8
Adding comments to code EXCEL G-9
Using Shortcut Keys with Macros EXCEL G-10
Using the Personal Macro Workbook EXCEL G-12
Working with the Personal Macro Workbook EXCEL G-13
Adding a Macro as a Menu Item EXCEL G-14
Creating a Toolbar for Macros EXCEL G-16
Concepts Review EXCEL G-18
Skills Review EXCEL G-20
Independent Challenges EXCEL G-21
Visual Workshop EXCEL G-24

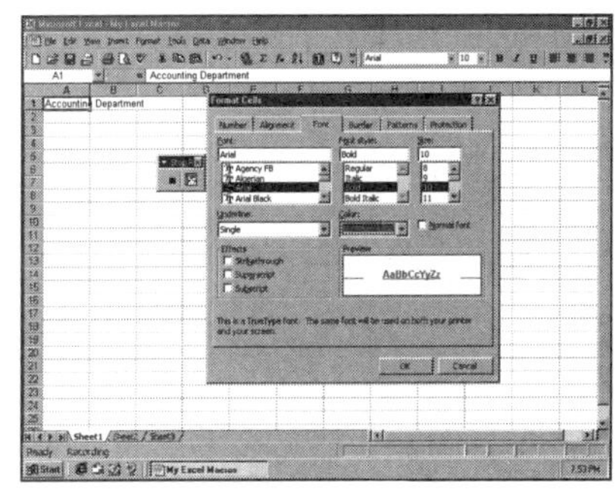

Using Lists EXCEL H-1
Planning a List EXCEL H-2
Lists versus databases EXCEL H-3
Creating a List EXCEL H-4
Maintaining the quality of information in a list EXCEL H-5
Adding Records with the Data Form EXCEL H-6
Finding Records EXCEL H-8
Using wildcards to fine-tune your search EXCEL H-9
Deleting Records EXCEL H-10
Advantage of deleting records from the worksheet EXCEL H-11
Sorting a List by One Field EXCEL H-12
Rotating and indenting to improve label appearance EXCEL H-13
Sorting a List by Multiple Fields EXCEL H-14
Specifying a custom sort order EXCEL H-15
Printing a List EXCEL H-16
Setting a print area EXCEL H-17

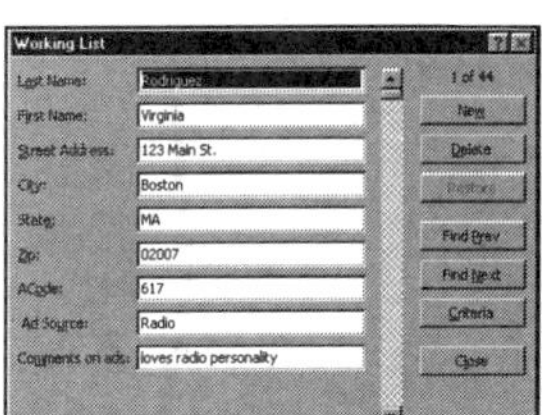

Contents

Concepts Review .... EXCEL H-18
Skills Review .... EXCEL H-19
Independent Challenges .... EXCEL H-20
Visual Workshop .... EXCEL H-24

Analyzing List Data EXCEL I-1

Retrieving Records with AutoFilter .... EXCEL I-2
Creating a Custom Filter .... EXCEL I-4
And and Or logical conditions .... EXCEL I-5
Filtering a List with Advanced Filter .... EXCEL I-6
Understanding the criteria range .... EXCEL I-7
Extracting List Data .... EXCEL I-8
Understanding the criteria range and the copy-to location .... EXCEL I-9
Creating Subtotals Using Grouping and Outlines .... EXCEL I-10
Show or hide details in an Excel outline .... EXCEL I-11
Looking Up Values in a List .... EXCEL I-12
Using the HLOOKUP function .... EXCEL I-13
Summarizing List Data .... EXCEL I-14
Using Data Validation for List Entries .... EXCEL I-16
Concepts Review .... EXCEL I-18
Skills Review .... EXCEL I-19
Independent Challenges .... EXCEL I-21
Visual Workshop .... EXCEL I-24

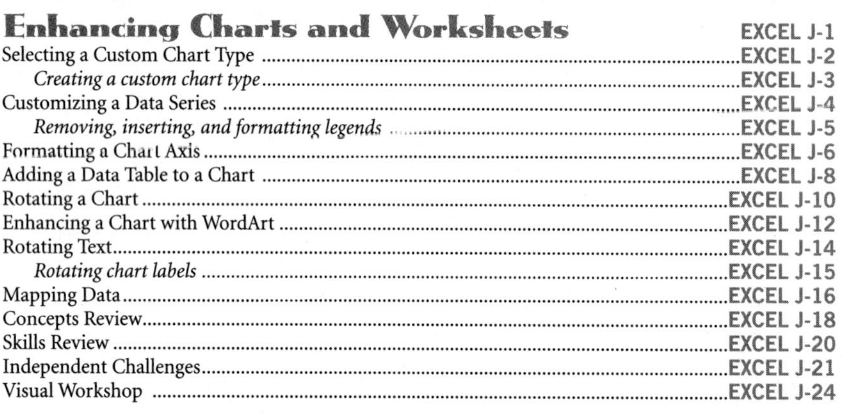

Enhancing Charts and Worksheets EXCEL J-1

Selecting a Custom Chart Type .... EXCEL J-2
Creating a custom chart type .... EXCEL J-3
Customizing a Data Series .... EXCEL J-4
Removing, inserting, and formatting legends .... EXCEL J-5
Formatting a Chart Axis .... EXCEL J-6
Adding a Data Table to a Chart .... EXCEL J-8
Rotating a Chart .... EXCEL J-10
Enhancing a Chart with WordArt .... EXCEL J-12
Rotating Text .... EXCEL J-14
Rotating chart labels .... EXCEL J-15
Mapping Data .... EXCEL J-16
Concepts Review .... EXCEL J-18
Skills Review .... EXCEL J-20
Independent Challenges .... EXCEL J-21
Visual Workshop .... EXCEL J-24

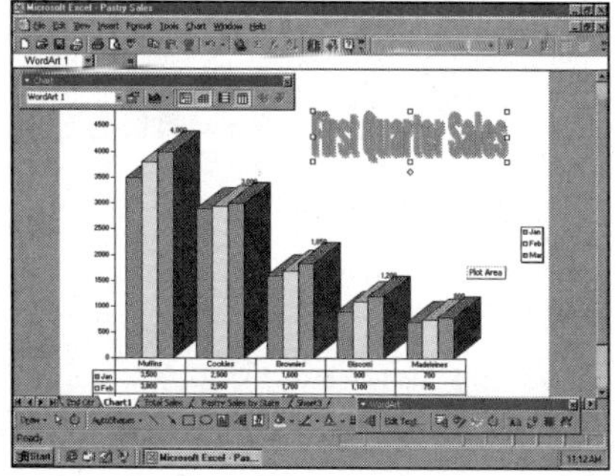

Sharing Excel Files and Incorporating Web Information EXCEL N-1

Sharing Excel Files .... EXCEL N-2
Setting Up a Shared Workbook .... EXCEL N-4
Tracking Changes in a Shared Workbook .... EXCEL N-6
Merging workbooks .... EXCEL N-7
Applying and Removing Passwords .... EXCEL N-8
Removing passwords .... EXCEL N-9
Creating an Interactive Worksheet for an Intranet or the Web .... EXCEL N-10
Managing HTML files on an intranet or Web site .... EXCEL N-11
Creating an Interactive PivotTable for an Intranet or the Web .... EXCEL N-12
Adding fields to a PivotTable list using the Web browser .... EXCEL N-13
Creating Hyperlinks between Excel Files and the Web .... EXCEL N-14
Using hyperlinks to navigate large worksheets .... EXCEL N-15
Running Queries to Retrieve Data on the Web .... EXCEL N-16
Finding stock symbols .... EXCEL N-16
Creating a new query to retrieve Web page data .... EXCEL N-17
Concepts Review .... EXCEL N-18
Skills Review .... EXCEL N-19
Independent Challenges .... EXCEL N-21
Visual Workshop .... EXCEL N-24

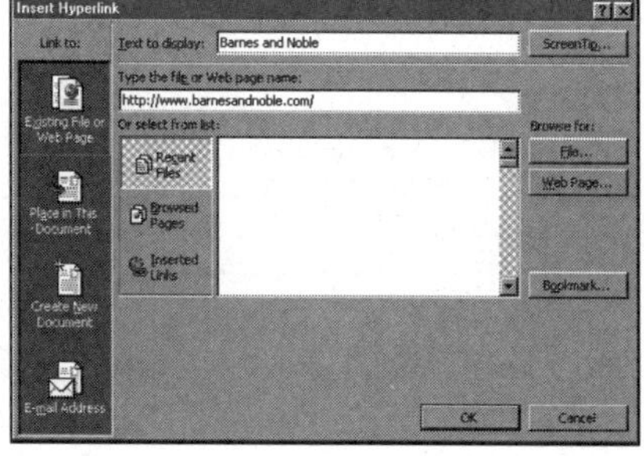

Word 2000 MOUS Certification Objectives 1
Glossary 1
Index 3

Excel 2000

Unit F

Managing Workbooks and Preparing Them for the Web

Objectives

- MOUS ► Freeze columns and rows
- MOUS ► Insert and delete worksheets
- MOUS ► Consolidate data with 3-D references
- MOUS ► Hide and protect worksheet areas
- ► Save custom views of a worksheet
- MOUS ► Control page breaks and page numbering
- MOUS ► Create a hyperlink between Excel files
- MOUS ► Save an Excel file as an HTML document

In this unit you will learn several Excel features to help you manage and print workbook data. You will also learn how to prepare workbooks for publication on the World Wide Web. MediaLoft's accounting department asks Jim Fernandez to design a timecard summary worksheet to track salary costs for hourly workers. He designs a worksheet using some employees from the MediaLoft Houston store. When the worksheet is complete, the accounting department will add the rest of the employees and place it on the MediaLoft intranet site for review by store managers. Jim will save the worksheet in HTML format for viewing on the site.

Excel 2000

Freezing Columns and Rows

As rows and columns fill up with data, you might need to scroll through the worksheet to add, delete, modify, and view information. Looking at information without row or column labels can be confusing. In Excel, you can temporarily freeze columns and rows, which enables you to view separate areas of your worksheets at the same time. **Panes** are the columns and rows that **freeze**, or remain in place, while you scroll through your worksheet. The freeze feature is especially useful when you're dealing with large worksheets. Sometimes, though, even freezing is not sufficient. In those cases, you can create as many as four areas, or panes, on the screen at one time and move freely within each of them. Jim needs to verify the total hours worked, hourly pay rate, and total pay for salespeople Paul Cristifano and Virginia Young. Because the worksheet is becoming more difficult to read as its size increases, Jim needs to freeze the column and row labels.

QuickTip

To return personalized toolbars and menus to their default state, click Tools on the menu bar, click Customize, click Reset my usage data on the Options tab, click Yes, then click Close.

1. **Start Excel if necessary, open the workbook titled EX F-1, save it as Timecard Summary, scroll through the Monday worksheet to view the data and click cell D6**
   You move to cell D6 because you want to freeze columns A, B, and C. By doing so, you will be able to see each employee's last name, first name, and timecard number on the screen when you scroll to the right. Because you want to scroll down the worksheet and still be able to read the column headings, you also freeze the labels in rows 1 through 5. Excel freezes the columns to the left and the rows above the cell pointer.

2. **Click Window on the menu bar, then click Freeze Panes**
   A thin line appears along the column border to the left of the active cell, and another line appears along the row above the active cell indicating that columns A through C and rows 1 through 5 are frozen.

QuickTip

To easily change worksheet data without manual scrolling, click Edit on the menu bar, click Replace, then enter text you want to find and text you want to replace it with. Use the Find Next, Replace, and Replace All buttons to find and replace occurrences of the found text with the replacement text.

3. **Scroll to the right until columns A through C and L through O are visible**
   Because columns A, B, and C are frozen, they remain on the screen; columns D through K are temporarily hidden from view. Notice that the information you are looking for in row 13 (last name, total hours, hourly pay rate, and total pay for Paul Cristifano) is readily available. You jot down Paul's data but still need to verify Virginia Young's information.

4. **Scroll down until row 26 is visible**
   Notice that in addition to columns A through C, rows 1 through 5 remain on the screen as well. See Figure F-1. Jim jots down the information for Virginia Young. Even though a pane is frozen, you can click in the frozen area of the worksheet and edit the contents of the cells there, if necessary.

QuickTip

When you open an existing workbook, the cell pointer is in the cell it was in when you last saved the workbook. Press [Ctrl][Home] to return to cell A1 prior to saving and closing a workbook.

5. **Press [Ctrl][Home]**
   Because the panes are frozen, the cell pointer moves to cell D6, not A1.

6. **Click Window on the menu bar, then click Unfreeze Panes**
   The panes are unfrozen.

7. **Return to cell A1, then save the workbook**

FIGURE F-1: Scrolled worksheet with frozen rows and columns

Microsoft Excel - Timecard Summary

D6 = 807569756

	A	B	C	L	M	N	O
1	MediaLoft						
2	Daily Timecard Summary for Ho						
3							
4							
5	Last Name	First Name	Timecard Number	Time Out	Total Hours	Hourly Pay Rate	Total Pay
10	Chilton	Linda	FP02	2:30 PM	2:30	$ 10.50	$ 26.25
11	Chimera	Julia	FN03		2:00	$ 9.75	$ 19.50
12	Colt	Rinaldo	FP06	3:00 PM	2:00	$ 11.24	$ 22.48
13	Cristifano	Paul	FP28	8:00 PM	5:00	$ 11.00	$ 55.00
14	Emerillo	Angel	FN20		3:45	$ 13.00	$ 48.75
15	Gallagher	Charles	CS30	4:00 PM	4:00	$ 12.50	$ 50.00
16	LaFuente	Gerald	FP21		2:00	$ 9.50	$ 19.00
17	Moen	Paul	FN13		3:00	$ 8.75	$ 26.25
18	Nguyen	Tranh	CS24	5:45 PM	5:00	$ 14.00	$ 70.00
19	Gabriel	Phillippe	CO01	7:00 PM	4:00	$ 15.00	$ 60.00
20	Singh	Tom	CO34	11:30 PM	8:00	$ 11.00	$ 88.00
21	Thorn	Jim	CO25		5:30	$ 7.50	$ 41.25
22	Westerfield	William	CO99	4:30 PM	2:30	$ 10.00	$ 25.00
23	Wu	Julia	FP41	5:30 PM	8:00	$ 12.00	$ 96.00
24	Xavier	Francois	FN54	4:00 PM	6:00	$14.00	$ 84.00
25	Yardley	Susan	FP22	9:00 PM	6:00	$15.00	$ 90.00
26	Young	Virginia	FN14		3:00	$ 9.75	$ 29.25
27							
28						Total	$ 1,042.73

Monday / Tuesday / Wednesday / Friday / Saturday / Sunday / Weekly

Break in row numbers due to frozen rows 1-5

Break in column letters due to frozen columns A-C

Excel 2000

CLUES TO USE

Splitting the worksheet into multiple panes

Excel provides a way to split the worksheet area into vertical and/or horizontal panes, so that you can click inside any one pane and scroll to locate desired information in that pane while the other panes remain in place. See Figure F-2. To split a worksheet area into multiple panes, drag the split box (the small box at the top of the vertical scroll bar or at the right end of the horizontal scroll bar) in the direction you want the split to appear. To remove the split, move the mouse over the split until the pointer changes to a double pointed arrow ⇕, then double-click.

FIGURE F-2: Worksheet split into two horizontal panes

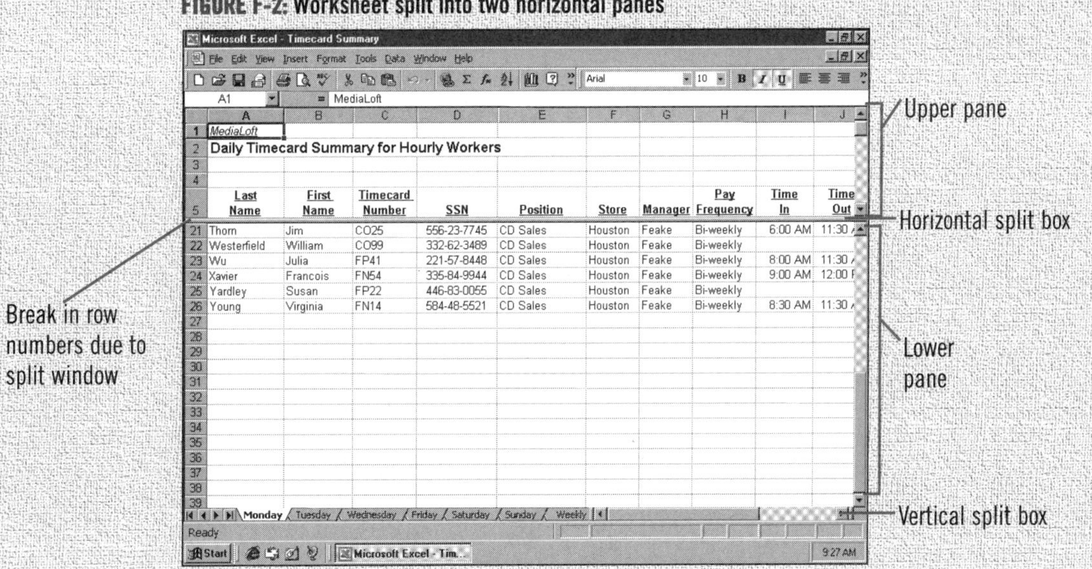

	A	B	C	D	E	F	G	H	I	J
1	MediaLoft									
2	Daily Timecard Summary for Hourly Workers									
5	Last Name	First Name	Timecard Number	SSN	Position	Store	Manager	Pay Frequency	Time In	Time Out
21	Thorn	Jim	CO25	556-23-7745	CD Sales	Houston	Feake	Bi-weekly	6:00 AM	11:30
22	Westerfield	William	CO99	332-62-3489	CD Sales	Houston	Feake	Bi-weekly		
23	Wu	Julia	FP41	221-57-8448	CD Sales	Houston	Feake	Bi-weekly	8:00 AM	11:30
24	Xavier	Francois	FN54	335-84-9944	CD Sales	Houston	Feake	Bi-weekly	9:00 AM	12:00
25	Yardley	Susan	FP22	446-83-0055	CD Sales	Houston	Feake	Bi-weekly		
26	Young	Virginia	FN14	584-48-5521	CD Sales	Houston	Feake	Bi-weekly	8:30 AM	11:30

Inserting and Deleting Worksheets

You can insert and delete worksheets in a workbook as needed. For example, because new workbooks open with only three sheets available (Sheet1, Sheet2, and Sheet3), you need to insert at least one more sheet if you want to have four quarterly worksheets in an annual financial budget workbook. You can do this by using commands on the menu bar or pop-up menu. Jim was in a hurry when he added the sheet tabs to the Timecard Summary workbook. He needs to insert a sheet for Thursday and delete the sheet for Sunday because these Houston workers do not work on Sundays.

Steps

QuickTip

You also can copy the active worksheet by clicking Edit on the menu bar, then clicking Move or Copy Sheet. Choose the sheet the copy will precede, then select the Create a copy check box.

1. Click the **Friday sheet tab**, click **Insert** on the menu bar, then click **Worksheet**
   Excel automatically inserts a new sheet tab labeled Sheet1 to the left of the Friday sheet.
2. Rename the Sheet1 tab **Thursday**
   Now the tabs read Monday, Tuesday, Wednesday, Thursday, Friday, and Saturday. The tab for the Weekly Summary is not visible, but you still need to delete the Sunday worksheet.
3. Click the **Sunday sheet tab**, move the pointer over the **Sunday tab**, then click the **right mouse button**
   A pop-up menu appears. See Figure F-3. The pop-up menu allows you to insert, delete, rename, move, or copy sheets, select all the sheets, or view any Visual Basic programming code in a workbook.
4. Click **Delete** on the pop-up menu
   A message box warns that the selected sheet will be deleted permanently. You must acknowledge the message before proceeding.
5. Click **OK**
   The Sunday sheet is deleted. Next, to check your work, you view a menu of worksheets in the workbook.

QuickTip

You can scroll several tabs at once by pressing [Shift] while clicking one of the middle tab scrolling buttons.

6. Move the mouse pointer over any tab scrolling button, then **right-click**
   When you right-click a tab scrolling button, Excel automatically opens a menu of the worksheets in the active workbook. Compare your list with Figure F-4.
7. Click **Monday**, return to cell A1, then save the workbook

FIGURE F-3: Worksheet pop-up menu

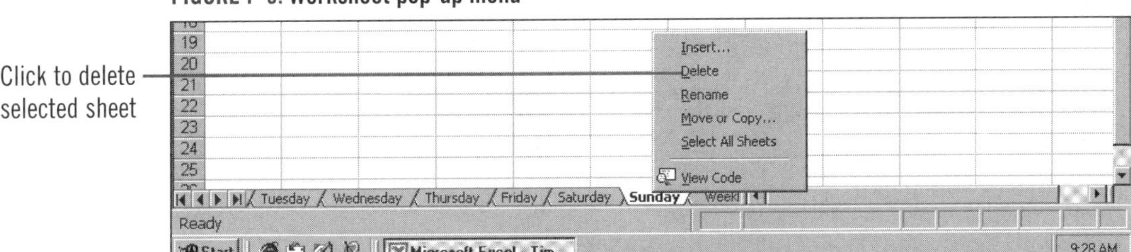

FIGURE F-4: Workbook with menu of worksheets

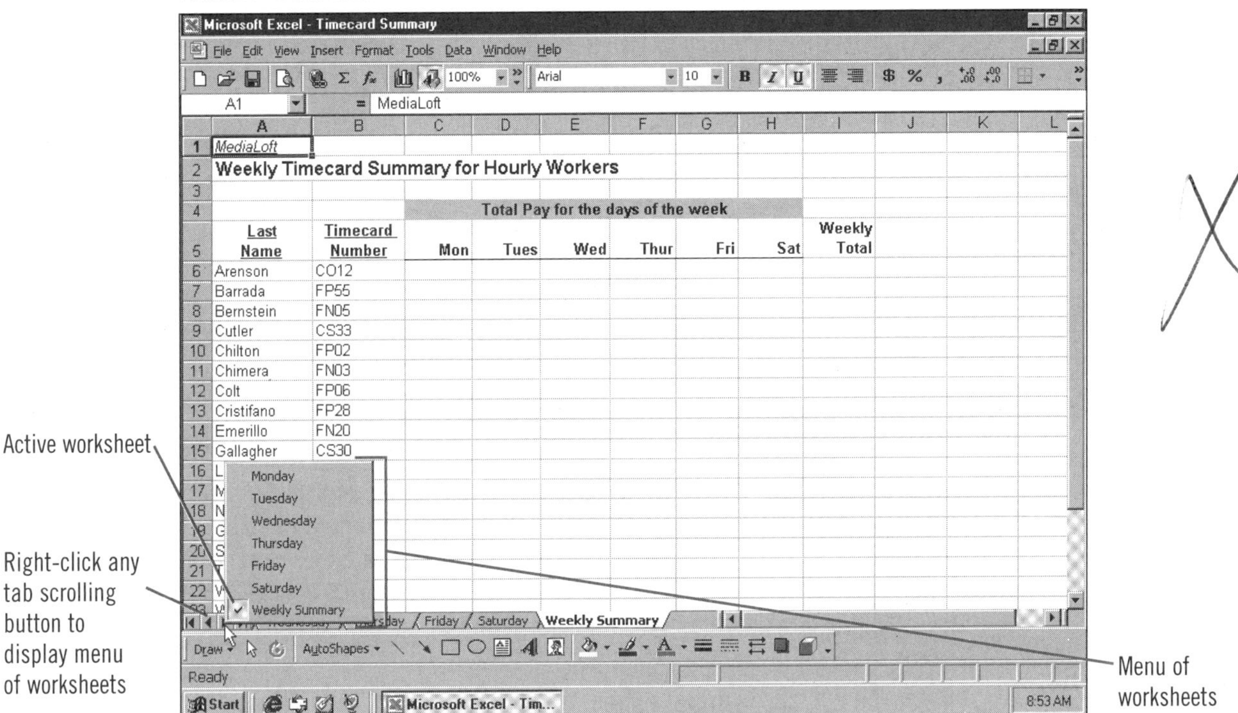

Excel 2000

Specifying headers and footers

As you prepare a workbook for others to view, it is helpful to give them as much data as possible about the worksheet—how many pages, who created it on what date, and the like. You can do this easily in a **header** or **footer**, information that prints at the top or bottom of each printed page. Headers and footers are visible on screen only in Print Preview. To add a header, for example, click View on the menu bar, click Header and Footer, click Custom Header, and you see a dialog box similar to that in Figure F-5. Both the header and the footer are divided into three sections, and you can enter information in any or all of them. Type information such as your name and click the icons to enter the page number, total pages, date, time, filename, or sheet name to enter codes that represent these items. Click OK, view the preview on the Header and Footer tab, then click OK again.

FIGURE F-5: Header dialog box

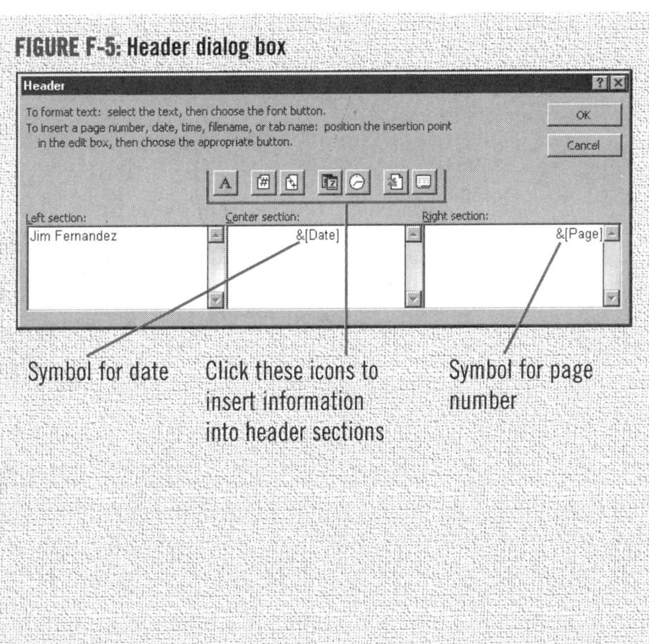

Excel 2000

Consolidating Data with 3-D References

When you want to summarize similar data that exists in different sheets or workbooks, you can combine and display it in one sheet. For example, you might have departmental sales figures on four different store sheets that you want to add together, or **consolidate**, on one summary sheet that shows total departmental sales for all stores. The best way to consolidate data is to use cell references to the various sheets on a consolidation, or summary, sheet. Because they reference other sheets that are usually behind the summary sheet, such references effectively create another dimension in the workbook and are called **3-D references**. You can reference data in other sheets and in other workbooks. Referencing cells is a better method than retyping calculated results because the data values on which calculated totals depend might change. If you reference the values instead, any changes to the original values are automatically reflected in the consolidation sheet. Although Jim does not have timecard data for the remaining days of the week, he wants to test the Weekly Summary sheet that will consolidate the timesheet data. He does this by creating a reference from the total pay data in the Monday sheet to the Weekly Summary sheet. First, he freezes panes to improve the view of the worksheets prior to initiating the reference between them.

1. On the Monday sheet, click cell **D6**, click **Window** on the menu bar, click **Freeze Panes**, then scroll horizontally to bring columns L through O into view
2. Right-click a **tab scrolling button**, then click **Weekly Summary**

   Because the Weekly Summary sheet (which is the consolidation sheet) will contain the reference, the cell pointer must reside there when you initiate the reference. To make a simple **reference** within the same sheet or between sheets, position the cell pointer in the cell to contain the reference, type = (equal sign), position the cell pointer in the cell to be referenced, and then enter the information.

Trouble?

If you have difficulty referencing cells between sheets, press [Esc] and begin again.

3. While in the Weekly Summary sheet, click cell **C6**, type **=**, activate the Monday sheet, click cell **O6**, then click the **Enter button** on the formula bar

   The formula bar reads =Monday!O6. See Figure F-6. *Monday* references the Monday sheet. The ! (exclamation point) is an **external reference indicator** meaning that the cell referenced is outside the active sheet; O6 is the actual cell reference in the external sheet. The result, $33.00, appears in cell C6 of the Weekly Summary sheet, showing the reference to the value displayed in cell O6 of the Monday sheet.
4. While in the Weekly Summary sheet, copy cell **C6** into cells **C7:C26**

   Excel copies the contents of cell C6 with its relative reference down the column. You can test a reference by changing one cell that it is based on and seeing if the reference changes.
5. Activate the Monday sheet, edit cell L6 to read **6:30 PM**, then activate the Weekly Summary sheet

   Cell C6 now shows $41.25. Changing Beryl Arenson's "time out" from 5:30 to 6:30 increased her pay from $33.00 to $41.25. This makes sense because Beryl's hours went from four to five, and her hourly salary is $8.25. The reference to Monday's total pay was automatically updated in the Weekly Summary sheet. See Figure F-7.
6. Preview, then print the Weekly Summary sheet

   To preview and print an entire workbook, click File on the menu bar, click Print, click to select the Entire Workbook option button, then click Preview. In the Preview window, you can page through the entire workbook. When you click Print, the entire workbook will print.
7. Activate the Monday sheet, then unfreeze the panes
8. Save the workbook

FIGURE F-6: Worksheet showing referenced cell

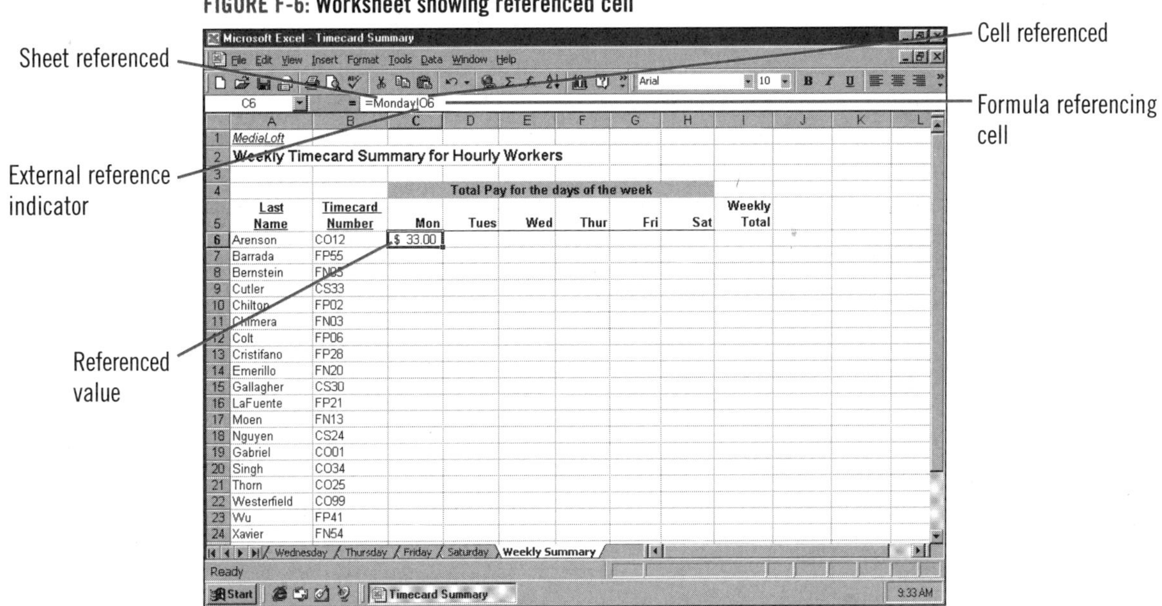

FIGURE F-7: Weekly Summary worksheet with updated reference

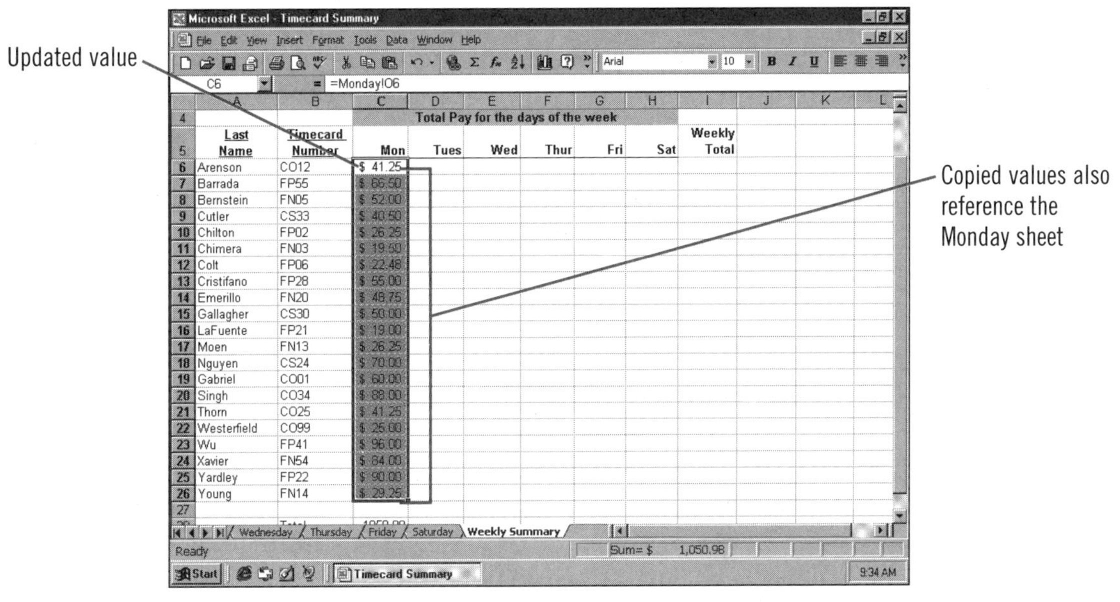

Consolidating data from different workbooks using linking

Just as you can reference data between cells in a worksheet and between sheets, you can reference data between workbooks dynamically so that changes made in referenced cells in one workbook are reflected in the consolidation sheet in the other workbook. This dynamic referencing is called **linking**. To link a single cell between workbooks, open both workbooks, select the cell to receive the linked data, press = (equal sign), select the cell in the other workbook containing the data to be linked, then press [Enter]. Excel automatically inserts the name of the referenced workbook in the cell reference. To perform calculations, enter formulas on the consolidation sheet using cells in the supporting sheets. If you are linking more than one cell, you can copy the linked data to the Clipboard, select in the other workbook the upper-left cell to receive the link, click Edit on the menu bar, click Paste Special, then click Paste Link.

Excel 2000

Hiding and Protecting Worksheet Areas

Worksheets can contain sensitive information that you don't want others to view or alter. To protect such information, Excel gives you two basic options. You can **hide** the formulas in selected cells (or rows, columns, or entire sheets), and you can **lock** selected cells, in which case other people will be able to view the data (values, numbers, labels, formulas, etc.) in those cells but not to alter it in any way. See Table F-1 for a list of options you can use to protect a worksheet. You set the lock and hide options in the Format Cells dialog box. You lock and unlock cells by clicking the Locked check box in the Format Cells dialog box Protection tab, and hide and "unhide" cell formulas by clicking the Hidden check box. The lock and hide options will not function unless an Excel protection feature, which you access via the Tools menu, is also activated. A common worksheet protection strategy is to unlock cells in which data will be changed, sometimes referred to as the **data entry area**, and to lock cells in which the data should not be changed. Then, when you protect the worksheet, the unlocked areas can still be changed. Because Jim will assign someone to enter the sensitive timecard information into the worksheet, he plans to hide and lock selected areas of the worksheet.

Steps

1. **Make sure the Monday sheet is active, select range I6:L27, click Format on the menu bar, click Cells, then click the Protection tab**
   You include row 27, even though it does not contain data, in the event that new data is added to the row later. Notice that the Locked box in the Protection tab is already checked, as shown in Figure F-8. The Locked check box is selected by default, meaning that all the cells in a new workbook start out locked. (Note, however, that cell locking is not applied unless the protection feature is also activated. The protection feature is inactive by default.)
2. **Click the Locked check box to deselect it, then click OK**
   Excel stores time as a fraction of a 24-hour day. In the formula for total pay, hours must be multiplied by 24. This concept might be confusing to the data entry person, so you hide the formulas.
3. **Select range O6:O26, click Format on the menu bar, click Cells, click the Protection tab, click the Hidden check box to select it, then click OK**
   The screen data remains the same (unhidden and unlocked) until you set the protection in the next step.
4. **Click Tools on the menu bar, point to Protection, then click Protect Sheet**
   The Protect Sheet dialog box opens. You choose not to use a password.
5. **Click OK**
   You are ready to test the new worksheet protection.
6. **Click cell O6**
   Notice that the formula bar is empty because of the hidden formula setting.
7. **In cell O6, type T to confirm that locked cells cannot be changed, then click OK**
   When you attempt to change a locked cell, a message box reminds you of the protected cell's read-only status. See Figure F-9.
8. **Click cell I6, type 9, and notice that Excel allows you to begin the entry, press [Esc] to cancel the entry, then save the workbook**
   Because you unlocked the cells in columns I through L before you protected the worksheet, you can make changes to these cells. Jim is satisfied that the Time In and Time Out data can be changed as necessary.

QuickTip

To turn off worksheet protection, click Tools on the menu bar, point to Protection, then click Unprotect Sheet. If prompted for a password, type the password, then click OK. To remove passwords, open the workbook or worksheet using the password, then go to the window where you entered the password, highlight the password, and press [Delete]. Remember that passwords are case sensitive.

FIGURE F-8: Protection tab in Format Cells dialog box

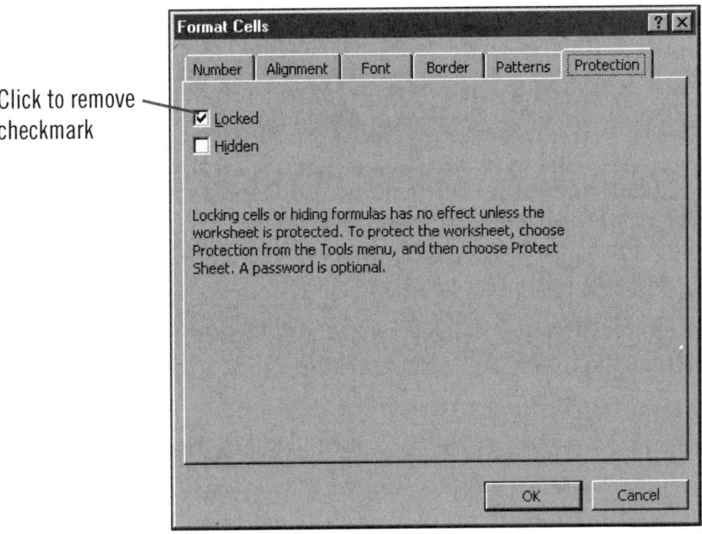

FIGURE F-9: Reminder of protected cell's read-only status

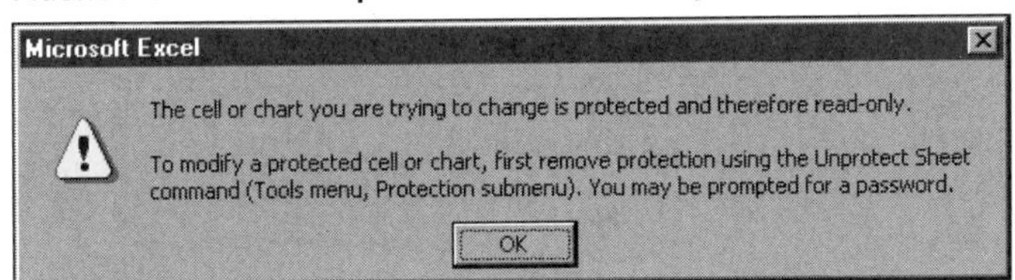

TABLE F-1: Options for hiding and protecting worksheet elements

task	menu commands
Hide/Unhide a column	Format, Column, Hide or Unhide
Hide/Unhide a formula	Format, Cells, Protection tab, select/deselect Hidden check box
Hide/Unhide a row	Format, Row, Hide or Unhide
Hide/Unhide a sheet	Format, Sheet, Hide or Unhide
Protect workbook	Tools, Protection, Protect Workbook, assign optional password
Protect worksheet	Tools, Protection, Protect Sheet, assign optional password
Unlock/Relock cells	Format, Cells, Protection tab, deselect/select Locked check box

***Note:** Some of the hide and protect options do not take effect until protection is enabled.*

Changing workbook properties

You can also password-protect an entire workbook from being opened or modified by changing its file properties. Click File, click Save As, click Tools, then click General Options. Specify the password(s) for opening or modifying the workbook. You can also use this dialog box to offer users an option to open the workbook in read-only format. To make an entire workbook read-only so that users can open but not change it, click Start on the Taskbar, point to Programs, then click Windows Explorer. Locate and click the filename, click File on the menu bar, click Properties, click the General tab, then, under Attributes, select the Read-only check box.

Excel 2000

Saving Custom Views of a Worksheet

A **view** is a set of display and/or print settings that you can name and save, then access at a later time. By using the Excel Custom Views feature, you can create several different views of a worksheet without having to create separate sheets. For example, if you often switch between portrait and landscape orientations when printing different parts of a worksheet, you can create two views with the appropriate print settings for each view. You set the display and/or print settings first, then name the view. Because Jim will generate several reports from his data, he saves the current print and display settings as a custom view. To better view the data to be printed, he decides to use the Zoom box to display the entire worksheet on one screen. The Zoom box has a default setting of 100% magnification and appears on the Standard toolbar.

Trouble?

If the Zoom box does not appear on your Standard toolbar, click the More Buttons button to view it.

QuickTip

To delete views from the active worksheet, select the view in the Views list box, then click Delete.

Trouble?

If you receive the message, "Some view settings could not be applied," repeat Step 5 to ensure worksheet protection is turned off.

QuickTip

With Report Manager add-in on the View menu, you can group worksheets and their views to be printed in sequence as one large report. If Report Manager is not on your View menu, click Tools/Add-Ins to add it.

1. With the Monday sheet active, select range **A1:O28**, click the **Zoom box list arrow** on the Standard toolbar, click **Selection**, then press **[Ctrl][Home]** to return to cell A1
   Excel automatically adjusts the display magnification so that the data selected fits on one screen. See Figure F-10. After selecting the **Zoom box**, you also can pick a magnification percentage from the list or type the desired percentage.
2. Click **View** on the menu bar, then click **Custom Views**
   The Custom Views dialog box opens. Any previously defined views for the active worksheet appear in the Views box. In this case, Jim had created a custom view named Generic containing default print and display settings. See Figure F-11.
3. Click **Add**
   The Add View dialog box opens, as shown in Figure F-12. Here, you enter a name for the view and decide whether to include print settings and hidden rows, columns, and filter settings. You want to include the selected options.
4. In the Name box, type **Complete Daily Worksheet**, then click **OK**
   After creating a custom view of the worksheet, you return to the worksheet area. You are ready to test the two custom views. In case the views require a change to the worksheet, it's a good idea to turn off worksheet protection.
5. Click **Tools** on the menu bar, point to **Protection**, then click **Unprotect Sheet**
6. Click **View** on the menu bar, then click **Custom Views**
   The Custom Views dialog box opens, listing both the Complete Daily Worksheet and Generic views.
7. Click **Generic** in the Views list box, click **Show**, preview the worksheet, then close the Preview
   The Generic custom view returns the worksheet to the Excel default print and display settings. Now you are ready to test the new custom view.
8. Click **View** on the menu bar, click **Custom Views**, click **Complete Daily Worksheet** in the Views list box, click **Show**
   The entire worksheet fits on the screen.
9. Return to the Generic view, then save your work
   Jim is satisfied with the custom view of the worksheet he created.

FIGURE F-10: Selected data fit to one screen

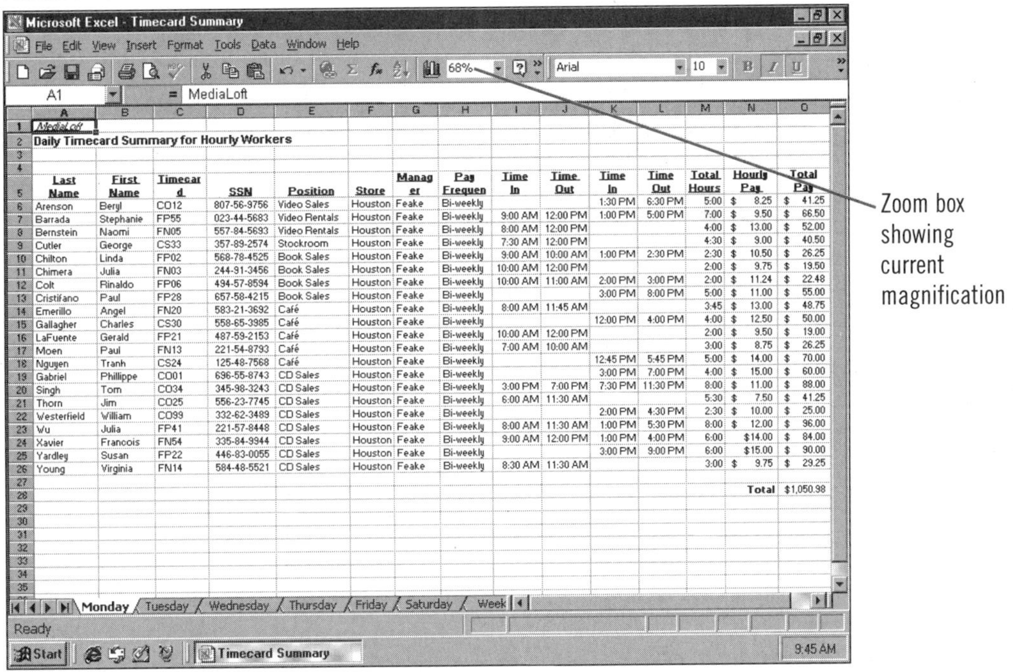

FIGURE F-11: Custom Views dialog box

FIGURE F-12: Add View dialog box

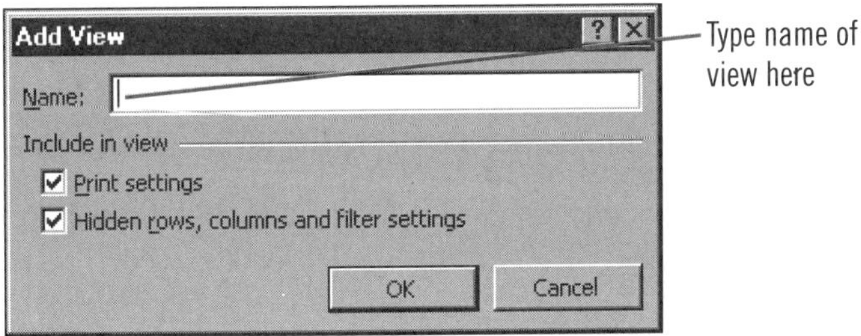

Using a workspace

If you work with several workbooks at a time in a particular arrangement, you can create a **workspace** containing information about their location and window sizes. Then, instead of opening each workbook individually, you can just open the workspace, which will automatically display the workbooks in the sizes and locations saved in the workspace. To create a workspace, open the workbooks and locate and size them as you would like them to appear. Click File on the menu bar, click Save Workspace, then type a name for the workspace file. Then open the workspace file and open the workbooks in their saved locations and sizes. Remember, however, that the workspace file does not contain the workbooks themselves, so you still have to back up the original workbook files. To start the workspace automatically when you turn on your computer, place the workspace file only in your XLStart folder.

Excel 2000

Controlling Page Breaks and Page Numbering

The vertical and horizontal dashed lines in worksheets indicate page breaks. Excel automatically inserts a page break when your worksheet data doesn't fit on one page. These page breaks are **dynamic**, which means they adjust automatically when you insert or delete rows and columns and when you change column widths or row heights. Everything to the left of the first vertical dashed line and above the first horizontal dashed line is printed on the first page. You can override the automatic breaks by choosing the Page Break command on the Insert menu. Table F-2 describes the different types of page breaks you can use. Jim wants another report displaying no more than half the hourly workers on each page. To accomplish this, he must insert a manual page break.

1. Click cell **A16**, click **Insert** on the menu bar, then click **Page Break**
   A dashed line appears between rows 15 and 16, indicating a horizontal page break. See Figure F-13. After you set page breaks, it's a good idea to preview each page.
2. Preview the worksheet, then click **Zoom**
   Notice that the status bar reads "Page 1 of 4" and that the data for the employees up through Charles Gallagher appears on the first page. Jim decides to place the date in the footer.
3. While in the Print Preview window, click **Setup**, click the **Header/Footer tab**, click **Custom Footer**, click the **Right section box**, click the **Date button**
4. Click the **Left section box**, type your name, then click **OK**
   Your name, the page number, and the date appear in the Footer preview area.
5. In the Page Setup dialog box, click **OK**, and, still in Print Preview, check to make sure all the pages show your name and the page numbers, click **Print**, then click **OK**
6. Click **View** on the menu bar, click **Custom Views**, click **Add**, type **Half N Half**, then click **OK**
   Your new custom view has the page breaks and all current print settings.
7. Make sure cell H16 is selected, then click **Insert** on the menu bar and click **Remove Page Break**
8. Save the workbook

QuickTip

To insert the page number in a header or footer section yourself, click [#] in the Header or Footer dialog box.

QuickTip

To remove a manual page break, select any cell directly below or to the right of the page break, click Insert on the menu bar, then click Remove Page Break.

TABLE F-2: Page break options

type of page break	where to position cell pointer
Both horizontal and vertical page breaks	Select the cell below and to the right of the gridline where you want the breaks to occur
Only a horizontal page break	Select the cell in column A that is directly below the gridline where you want the page to break
Only a vertical page break	Select a cell in row 1 that is to the right of the gridline where you want the page to break

FIGURE F-13: Worksheet with horizontal page break

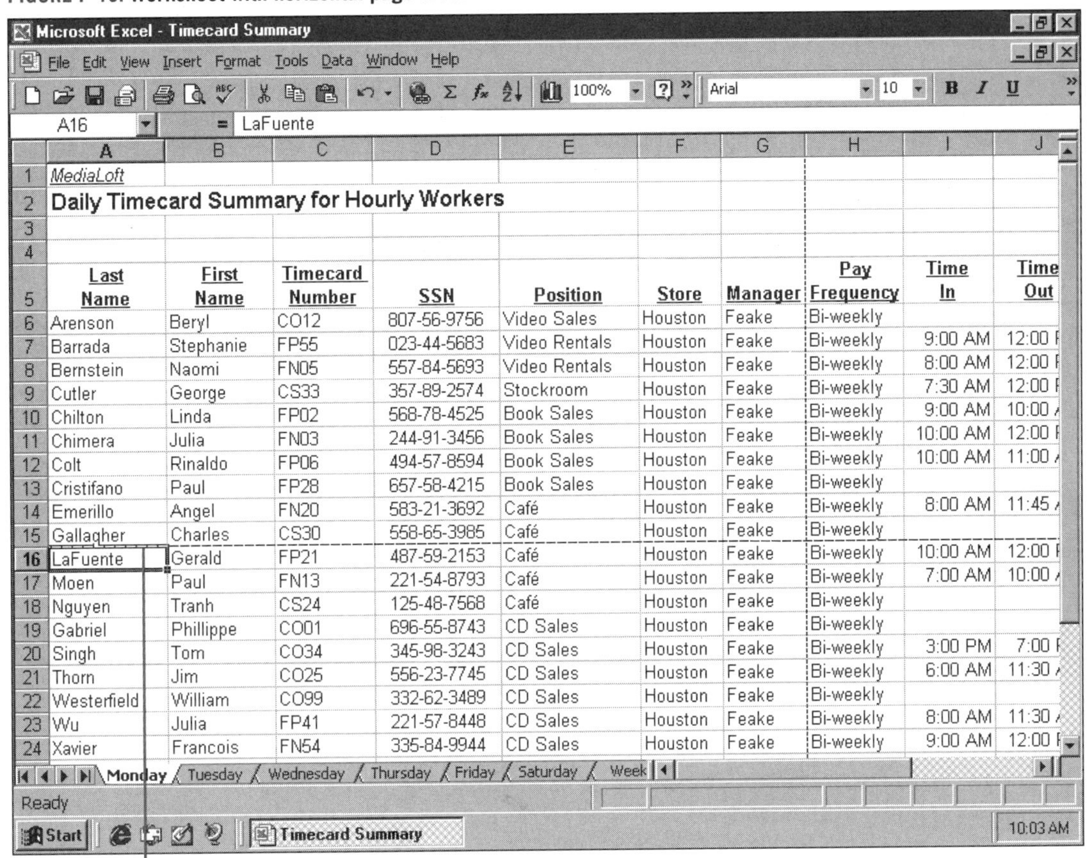

	A	B	C	D	E	F	G	H	I	J
1	MediaLoft									
2	Daily Timecard Summary for Hourly Workers									
3										
4										
5	Last Name	First Name	Timecard Number	SSN	Position	Store	Manager	Pay Frequency	Time In	Time Out
6	Arenson	Beryl	CO12	807-56-9756	Video Sales	Houston	Feake	Bi-weekly		
7	Barrada	Stephanie	FP55	023-44-5683	Video Rentals	Houston	Feake	Bi-weekly	9:00 AM	12:00 I
8	Bernstein	Naomi	FN05	557-84-5693	Video Rentals	Houston	Feake	Bi-weekly	8:00 AM	12:00 I
9	Cutler	George	CS33	357-89-2574	Stockroom	Houston	Feake	Bi-weekly	7:30 AM	12:00 I
10	Chilton	Linda	FP02	568-78-4525	Book Sales	Houston	Feake	Bi-weekly	9:00 AM	10:00 /
11	Chimera	Julia	FN03	244-91-3456	Book Sales	Houston	Feake	Bi-weekly	10:00 AM	12:00 I
12	Colt	Rinaldo	FP06	494-57-8594	Book Sales	Houston	Feake	Bi-weekly	10:00 AM	11:00 /
13	Cristifano	Paul	FP28	657-58-4215	Book Sales	Houston	Feake	Bi-weekly		
14	Emerillo	Angel	FN20	583-21-3692	Café	Houston	Feake	Bi-weekly	8:00 AM	11:45 /
15	Gallagher	Charles	CS30	558-65-3985	Café	Houston	Feake	Bi-weekly		
16	LaFuente	Gerald	FP21	487-59-2153	Café	Houston	Feake	Bi-weekly	10:00 AM	12:00 I
17	Moen	Paul	FN13	221-54-8793	Café	Houston	Feake	Bi-weekly	7:00 AM	10:00 /
18	Nguyen	Tranh	CS24	125-48-7568	Café	Houston	Feake	Bi-weekly		
19	Gabriel	Phillippe	CO01	696-55-8743	CD Sales	Houston	Feake	Bi-weekly		
20	Singh	Tom	CO34	345-98-3243	CD Sales	Houston	Feake	Bi-weekly	3:00 PM	7:00 I
21	Thorn	Jim	CO25	556-23-7745	CD Sales	Houston	Feake	Bi-weekly	6:00 AM	11:30 /
22	Westerfield	William	CO99	332-62-3489	CD Sales	Houston	Feake	Bi-weekly		
23	Wu	Julia	FP41	221-57-8448	CD Sales	Houston	Feake	Bi-weekly	8:00 AM	11:30 /
24	Xavier	Francois	FN54	335-84-9944	CD Sales	Houston	Feake	Bi-weekly	9:00 AM	12:00 I

Dashed line indicates horizontal break after row 15

Using Page Break Preview

By clicking View on the menu bar, then clicking Page Break Preview, or clicking Page Break Preview in the Print Preview window, you can view and change page breaks manually. (If you see a dialog box asking if you want help, just click OK to close it.) Simply drag the page break lines to the desired location. See Figure F-14. To exit Page Break Preview, click View on the menu bar, then click Normal.

FIGURE F-14: Page Break Preview window

	Last Name	First Name	Timecard	SSN	Position	Store	Manager	Pay Frequen	Time In	Time Out	Time In	Time Out	Total Hours	Hourly Pay	Total Pay
6	Arenson	Beryl	CO12	807-56-9756	Video Sales	Houston	Feake	Bi-weekly			1:30 PM	6:30 PM	5:00	$ 8.25	$ 41.25
7	Barrada	Stephanie	FP55	023-44-5683	Video Rentals	Houston	Feake	Bi-weekly	9:00 AM	######	1:00 PM	6:00 PM	7:00	$ 9.50	$ 66.50
8	Bernstein	Naomi	FN05	557-84-5693	Video Rentals	Houston	Feake	Bi-weekly	8:00 AM	######			4:00	$ 13.00	$ 52.00
9	Cutler	George	CS33	357-89-2574	Stockroom	Houston	Feake	Bi-weekly	7:30 AM	######			4:30	$ 9.00	$ 40.50
10	Chilton	Linda	FP02	568-78-4525	Book Sales	Houston	Feake	Bi-weekly	9:00 AM	######	1:00 PM	2:30 PM	2:30	$ 10.50	$ 26.25
11	Chimera	Julia	FN03	244-91-3456	Book Sales	Houston	Feake	Bi-weekly	######	######			2:00	$ 9.75	$ 19.50
12	Colt	Rinaldo	FP06	494-57-8594	Book Sales	Houston	Feake	Bi-weekly	######	######	2:00 PM	3:00 PM	2:00	$ 11.24	$ 22.48
13	Cristifano	Paul	FP28	657-58-4215	Book Sales	Houston	Feake	Bi-weekly			3:00 PM	8:00 PM	5:00	$ 11.00	$ 55.00
14	Emerillo	Angel	FN20	583-21-3692	Café	Houston	Feake	Bi-weekly	8:00 AM	######			3:45	$ 13.00	$ 48.75
15	Gallagher	Charles	CS30	558-65-3985	Café	Houston	Feake	Bi-weekly			######	4:00 PM	4:00	$ 12.50	$ 50.00
16	LaFuente	Gerald	FP21	487-59-2153	Café	Houston	Feake	Bi-weekly	######	######			2:00	$ 9.50	$ 19.00
17	Moen	Paul	FN13	221-54-8793	Café	Houston	Feake	Bi-weekly	7:00 AM	######			3:00	$ 8.75	$ 26.25
18	Nguyen	Tranh	CS24	125-48-7568	Café	Houston	Feake	Bi-weekly			######	5:45 PM	5:00	$ 14.00	$ 70.00
19	Gabriel	Phillippe	CO01	696-55-8743	CD Sales	Houston	Feake	Bi-weekly			3:00 PM	7:00 PM	4:00	$ 15.00	$ 60.00
20	Singh	Tom	CO34	345-98-3243	CD Sales	Houston	Feake	Bi-weekly	3:00 PM	7:00 PM	7:30 PM	######	8:00	$ 11.00	$ 88.00
21	Thorn	Jim	CO25	556-23-7745	CD Sales	Houston	Feake	Bi-weekly	6:00 AM	######			5:30	$ 7.50	$ 41.25
22	Westerfield	William	CO99	332-62-3489	CD Sales	Houston	Feake	Bi-weekly			2:00 PM	4:30 PM	2:30	$ 10.00	$ 25.00
23	Wu	Julia	FP41	221-57-8448	CD Sales	Houston	Feake	Bi-weekly	8:00 AM	######	1:00 PM	5:30 PM	8:00	$ 12.00	$ 96.00
24	Xavier	Francois	FN54	335-84-9944	CD Sales	Houston	Feake	Bi-weekly	9:00 AM	######	1:00 PM	4:00 PM	6:00	$14.00	$ 84.00
25	Yardley	Susan	FP22	446-83-0055	CD Sales	Houston	Feake	Bi-weekly			3:00 PM	9:00 PM	6:00	$15.00	$ 90.00
26	Young	Virginia	FN14	584-48-5521	CD Sales	Houston	Feake	Bi-weekly	8:30 AM	######			3:00	$ 9.75	$ 29.25
27															
28														Total	#####

Page 1 Page 2 Page 3 Page 4

Cell pointer in cell A16

Drag page break lines to change page breaks

Excel 2000

Excel 2000

Creating a Hyperlink between Excel Files

As you manage the content and appearance of your workbooks, you may want the workbook user to have access to information in another workbook. It might be nonessential information or data that is too detailed to place in the workbook itself. In these cases, you can create a **hyperlink**, an object (a filename, a word, a phrase, or a graphic) in a worksheet that, when you click it, will jump to another worksheet, called the **target**. The target can be a document created in another software program or a site on the World Wide Web. For example, in a worksheet that lists customer invoices, at each customer's name, you might create a hyperlink to an Excel file containing payment terms for each customer. You can also use hyperlinks to navigate to other locations in a large worksheet. Jim wants managers who view the Timecard Summary worksheet to be able to view the pay categories for MediaLoft store employees. He creates a hyperlink at the Hourly Pay Rate column heading. Users will click the hyperlink to view the Pay Rate worksheet.

Steps

1. Display the Monday worksheet
2. Click **Edit**, click **Go To**, type **N5** (the cell containing **the text Hourly Pay Rate**), then click **OK**
3. Click the **Insert Hyperlink button** on the Standard toolbar, then click **Existing File or Web Page**, if necessary

   The Insert Hyperlink dialog box opens. See Figure F-15. The icons under Link to: on the left side of the dialog box let you specify the type of location you want the link to jump to: an existing file or Web page, a place in the same document, a new document, or an e-mail address. Since Jim wants users to display a document he has created, the first icon, Existing File or Web Page, is correct and is already selected.
4. Click **File** under Browse for, then in the Link to File dialog box, navigate to your Project Disk and double-click **Pay Rate Classifications**

   The Insert Hyperlink dialog box reappears with the filename you selected in the Type the file or Web page name text box. This document appears when users click this hyperlink. You can also specify the ScreenTip that users will see when they hold the pointer over the hyperlink.
5. Click **ScreenTip**, type **Click here to see MediaLoft pay rate classifications**, click **OK**, then click **OK** again

   Cell N5 now contains underlined blue text, indicating that it is a hyperlink. After you create a hyperlink, you should check it to make sure it jumps to the correct destination.
6. Move the pointer over the **Hourly Pay Rate text**, view the ScreenTip, then click once

   Notice that when you move the pointer over the text, the pointer changes to , indicating that it is a hyperlink, and the ScreenTip appears. After you click, the Pay Rate Classifications worksheet appears. See Figure F-16. The Web toolbar appears beneath the Standard and Formatting toolbars.
7. Click the **Back button** on the Web toolbar, then save the workbook

Using hyperlinks to navigate large worksheets

Hyperlinks are useful in navigating large worksheets or workbooks. You can create a hyperlink from any cell to another cell in the same worksheet, a cell in another worksheet, or a defined name anywhere in the workbook. Under Link to in the Insert Hyperlink dialog box, click Place in This Document. Then type the cell reference and indicate the sheet, or select the named location in the scroll box.

FIGURE F-15: Insert Hyperlink dialog box

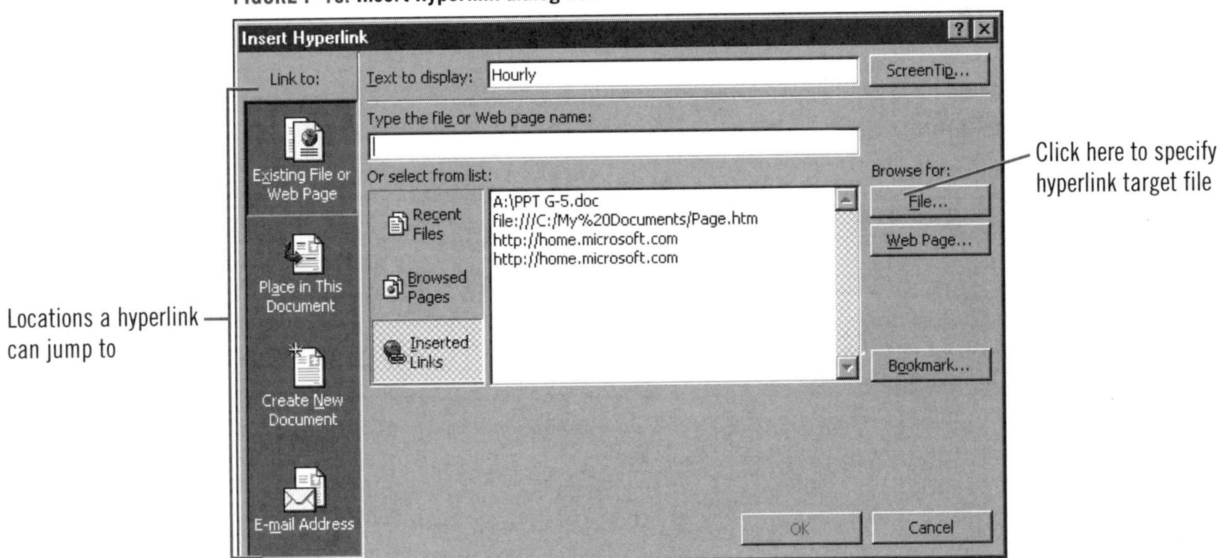

FIGURE F-16: Target document

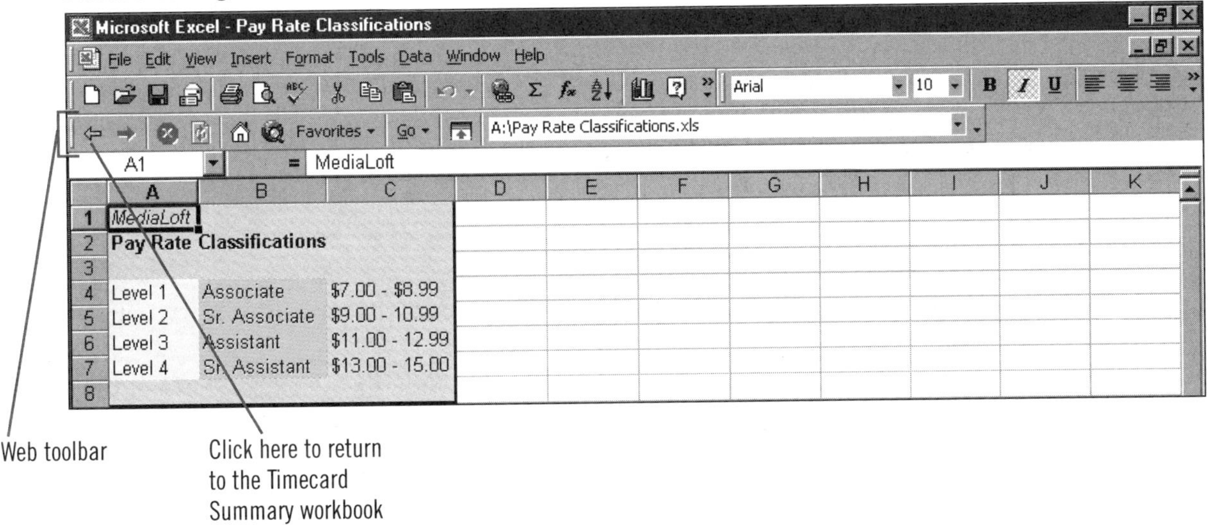

Inserting a picture

As you prepare your workbooks for viewing by others on an intranet or on the Internet, you may want to enhance their appearance by adding pictures. You can easily add your own picture, such as a company logo or a scanned picture, or a picture from the Microsoft Clip Gallery. To insert a Clip Gallery picture on a worksheet, click Insert on the menu bar, point to Picture, then click Clip Art. Click a category, click the image you want to insert, then click the Insert Clip icon. Close the Insert Clip Art window. The picture is an **object** that you can move, resize, or delete. To move a picture, click and then drag it. To resize it, click it once to select it, then drag one of its corners. To delete it, click to select it, then press [Delete].

Excel 2000

Saving an Excel file as an HTML Document

One way to share Excel data is to publish, or **post**, it online over a network so that others can access it using their Web browsers. The network can be an **intranet**, which is an internal network site used by a particular group of people who work together, or the World Wide Web. The **World Wide Web** is a structure of documents, or pages, connected electronically over a large computer network called the **Internet**, which is made up of smaller networks and computers. If you save and post an entire workbook, users can click worksheet tabs to view each sheet. If you save a single worksheet, you can make the Web page interactive, meaning that users can enter, format, and calculate worksheet data. To post an Excel document to an intranet or the World Wide Web, you must first save it in **HTML (Hypertext Markup Language)**, which is the format that a Web browser can read. Jim saves the entire Timecard Summary workbook in HTML format so it can be posted on the MediaLoft intranet for managers' use.

Steps 1 2 3 4

1. **Click File on the menu bar, then click Save as Web Page**
   The Save As dialog box opens. See Figure F-17. By default, the Entire Workbook option button is selected, which is what Jim wants. However, he wants the title bar of the Web page to be more descriptive than the filename.
2. **Click Change Title**
   The Set Page Title dialog box opens.
3. **Type MediaLoft Houston Timecard Summary, then click OK**
   The Page title area displays the new title. The Save as type list box indicates that the workbook will be saved as a Web page, which is in HTML format.
4. **Change the filename to Timecard Summary - Web, then click the Save in list arrow and locate your Project Disk**
5. **Click Save**
   A dialog box appears, indicating that the custom views you saved earlier will not be part of the HTML file.
6. **Click Yes**
   Excel saves the Web page version as an HTML file in the folder location you specified in the Save As dialog box, and in the same place creates a folder in which it places associated files, such as a file for each worksheet. To make the workbook available to others, you would post all these files on a network server. When the save process is complete, the original XLS file closes and the HTML file opens on your screen.
7. **Click File on the menu bar, click Web Page Preview, then maximize the browser window**
   The workbook opens in your default Web browser, which could be Internet Explorer or Netscape, showing you what it would look like if you opened it on an intranet or on the Internet. See Figure F-18. The Monday worksheet appears as it would if it were on a Web site or intranet, with tabs at the bottom of the screen for each daily sheet. If you wanted to use this document online, you would also need to save the target document (Pay Rate Classifications) in HTML format and post it to the Web site.
8. **Click the Weekly Summary tab**
   The Weekly Summary worksheet appears just as it would in Excel.
9. **Close the Web browser window, then close the Timecard Summary - Web workbook and the Pay Rate Classifications workbook, then exit Excel**

QuickTip

If you want, you can create a folder in the Save As dialog box. Click the Create new folder button and in the Save As dialog box, type the name of the new folder and click OK. The new folder automatically opens and appears in the Save in list. When you click Save, the HTML files will be saved in your new folder.

FIGURE F-17: Save As dialog box

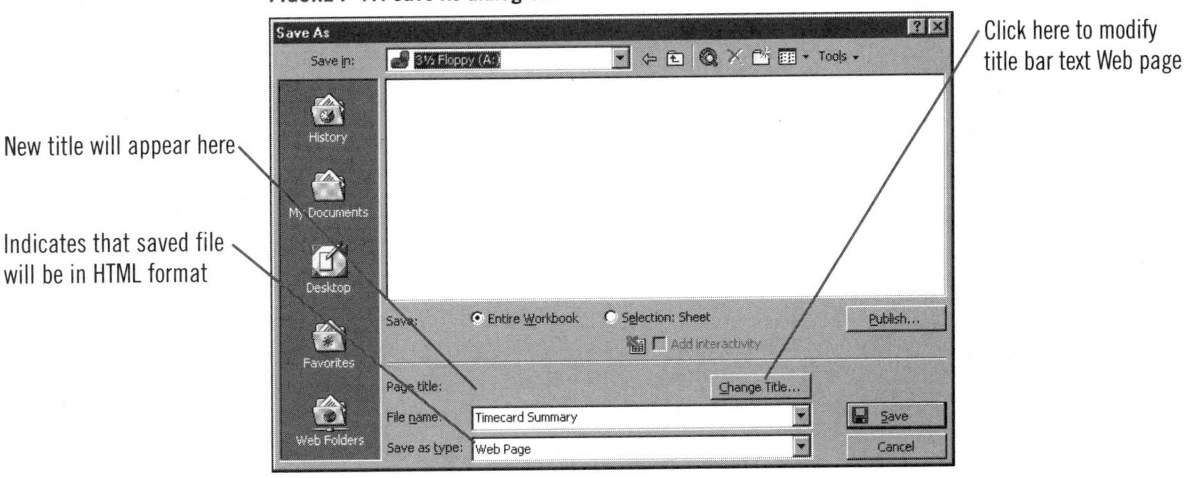

FIGURE F-18: Workbook in Web page preview

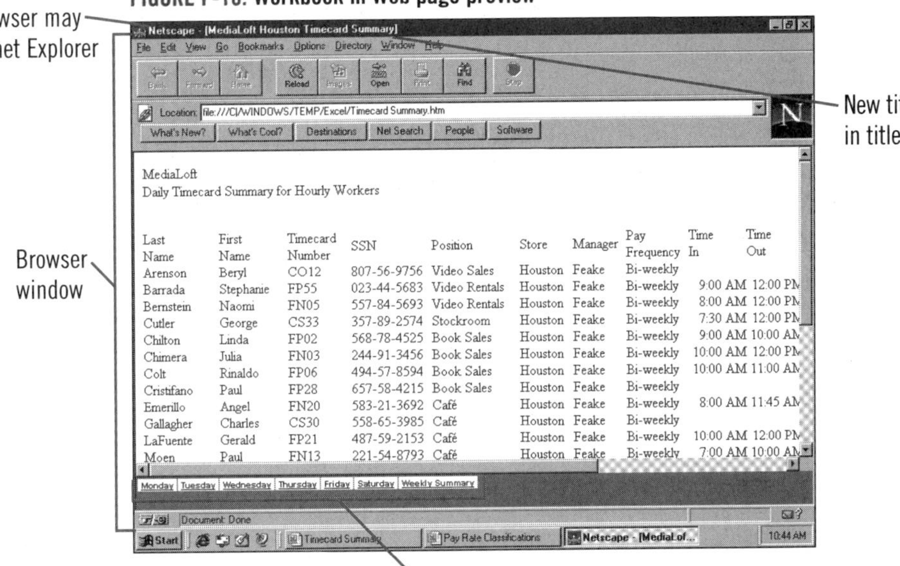

Send a workbook via e-mail

You can send an entire workbook or a worksheet to any e-mail recipient from within Excel. To send a workbook as an attachment to an e-mail message, click File, point to Send to, then click Mail Recipient (as attachment). Fill in the To and Cc information and click Send. See Figure F-19. (If Internet Explorer is not your default Web browser, you may need to respond to additional dialog boxes.) You can also route a workbook to one or more recipients on a routing list that you create. Click File, point to Send to, then click Routing Recipient. Click Create New Contact and enter contact information, then fill in the Routing slip. Depending on your e-mail program, you may have to follow a different procedure. See your instructor or lab resource person for help.

FIGURE F-19: E-mailing an Excel file as an attachment

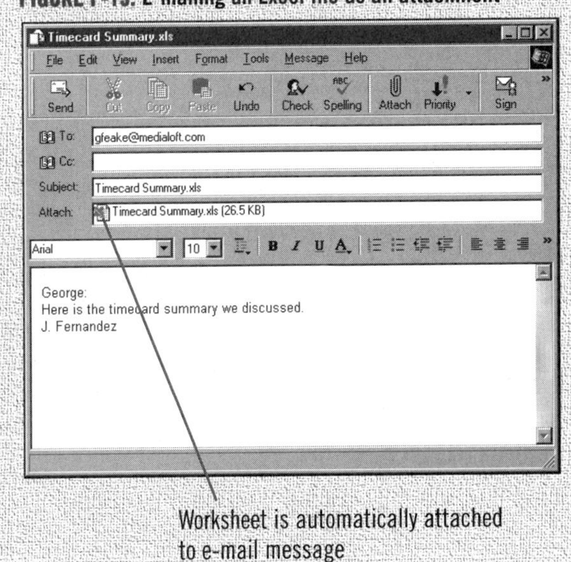

Practice

► Concepts Review

Label each element of the Excel screen shown in Figure F-20.

FIGURE F-20

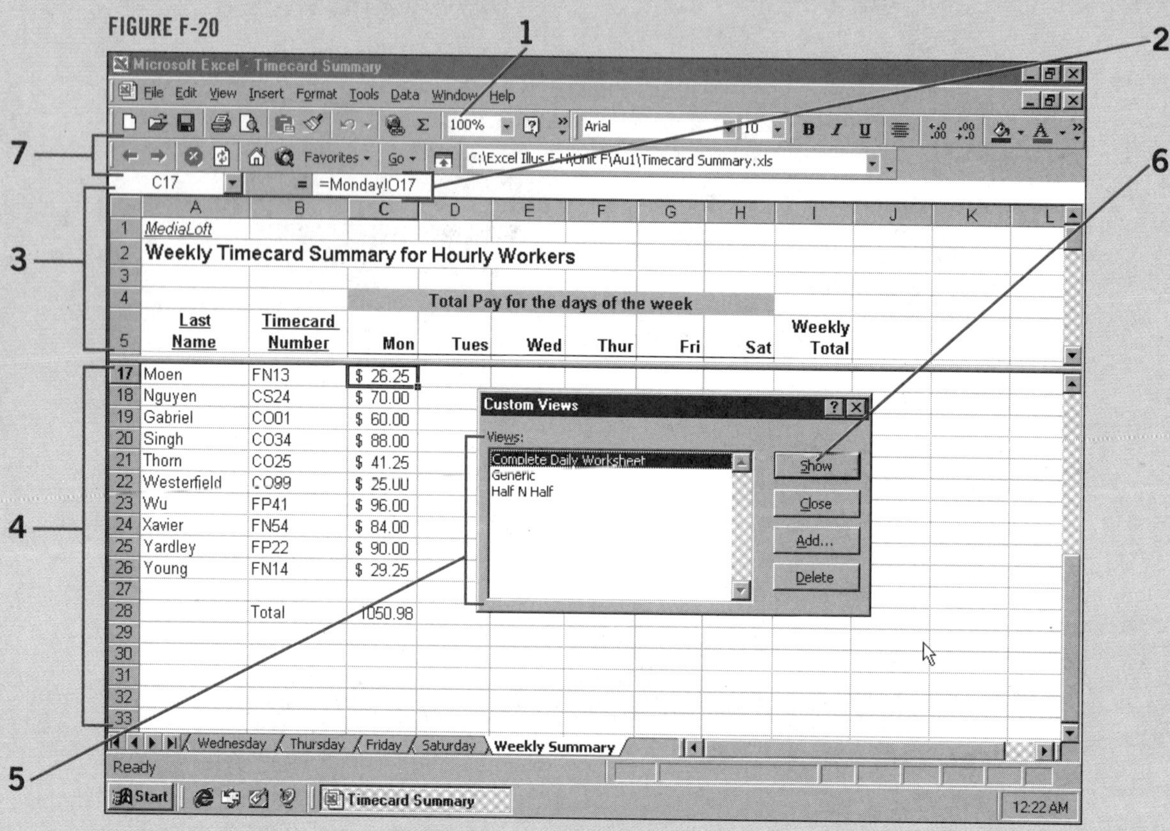

Match each of the terms with the statement that describes its function.

a. **Dashed line**
b. **Hyperlink**
c. **3-D reference**
d. [icon]
e. [icon]

8. Inserts a code to print the total number of pages
9. Uses values from different workbooks
10. Indicates a page break
11. Inserts a code to print the sheet name in a header or footer
12. An object you click to display a target

Select the best answer from the list of choices.

13. You can save frequently used display and print settings by using the ____________ feature.
- **a.** HTML
- **b.** View menu
- **c.** Custom Views
- **d.** Save command

14. You freeze areas of the worksheet to
- **a.** Freeze data and unlock formulas.
- **b.** Lock column and row headings in place while you scroll through the worksheet.
- **c.** Freeze all data in place so that you can see it.
- **d.** Lock open windows in place.

15. To protect a worksheet, you must first unlock those cells that ____________, and then issue the Protect Sheet command.
- **a.** never change
- **b.** the user will be allowed to change
- **c.** have hidden formulas
- **d.** are locked

Skills Review

1. Freeze columns and rows.
- **a.** Open the workbook titled EX F-2, then save it as "Quarterly Household Budget".
- **b.** Freeze columns A and B and rows 1 through 3 for improved viewing. (*Hint:* Click cell C4 prior to issuing the Freeze Panes command.)
- **c.** Scroll until columns A and B and F through H are visible.
- **d.** Press [Ctrl][Home] to return to cell C4.
- **e.** Unfreeze the panes.

2. Insert and delete worksheets.
- **a.** With the 2001 sheet active, use the sheet pop-up menu to insert a new Sheet1 to its left.
- **b.** Delete Sheet1.
- **c.** Add a custom footer to the 2001 sheet with your name on the left side and the page number on the right side.
- **d.** Add a custom header with the worksheet name on the left side.
- **e.** Preview and print the worksheet.

3. Consolidate data with 3-D references.
- **a.** In cell C22, enter a reference to cell G7.
- **b.** In cell C23, enter a reference to cell G18.
- **c.** Activate the 2002 worksheet.
- **d.** In cell C4, enter a reference to cell C4 on the 2001 worksheet.
- **e.** In the 2002 worksheet, copy the contents of cell C4 into cells C5:C6.
- **f.** Preview the 2002 worksheet, view the Page Break Preview, and drag the page break so all the data fits on one page.
- **g.** Print the 2002 worksheet and save your work.

4. **Hide and protect worksheet areas.**
   a. On the 2001 sheet, unlock the expense data in the range C10:F17.
   b. Protect the sheet without using a password.
   c. To make sure the other cells are locked, attempt to make an entry in cell D4.
   d. Confirm the message box warning.
   e. Change the first-quarter mortgage expense to $3,400.
   f. Unprotect the worksheet.
   g. Save the workbook.
5. **Save custom views of a worksheet.**
   a. Set the zoom on the 2001 worksheet so all the data fits on your screen.
   b. Make this a new view called "Entire 2001 Budget".
   c. Use the Custom Views dialog box to return to Generic view.
   d. Save the workbook.
6. **Control page breaks and page numbering.**
   a. Insert a page break above cell A9.
   b. Save the view as "Halves".
   c. Preview and print the worksheet, then preview and print the entire workbook.
   d. Save the workbook.
7. **Create a hyperlink between Excel files.**
   a. On the 2001 worksheet, make cell A9 a hyperlink to thc file Expense Details, with a ScreenTip that reads "Click here to see expense assumptions".
   b. Test the link, then print the Expense Details worksheet.
   c. Return to the Household Budget worksheet using the Web toolbar.
   d. On the 2002 worksheet, enter the text "Based on 2001 budget" in cell A2.
   e. Make the text in cell A2 a hyperlink to cell A1 in the 2001 worksheet. (*Hint:* Use the Place in this document button.)
   f. Test the hyperlink.
   g. Add any clip art picture to your worksheet, then move and resize it so it doesn't obscure any worksheet information.
8. **Save an Excel file as an HTML document.**
   a. Save the entire budget workbook as a Web page with a title bar that reads "Our Budget" and the file named Quarterly Household Budget - Web.
   b. Preview the Web page in your browser.
   c. Test the worksheet tabs in the browser to make sure they work.
   d. Return to Excel, then close the HTML document.
   e. Close the Expense Details worksheet, then exit Excel.

► Independent Challenges

1. You own PC Assist, a software training company. You have added several new entries to the August check register and are ready to enter September's check activity. Because the sheet for August will include much of the same information you need for September, you decide to copy it. Then you will edit the new sheet to fit your needs for September check activity. You will use sheet referencing to enter the beginning balance and beginning check number. Using your own data, you will complete five checks for the September register.

To complete this independent challenge:

a. Open the workbook entitled EX F-3, then save it as "Update to Check Register".
b. Delete Sheet 2 and Sheet 3, then create a worksheet for September by copying the August sheet.
c. With the September sheet active, delete the data in range A6:E24.

d. To update the balance at the beginning of the month, use sheet referencing from the last balance entry in the August sheet.
e. Generate the first check number. (*Hint:* Use a formula that references the last check number in August and adds one.)
f. Enter data for five checks.
g. Add a footer to the September sheet that includes your name left-aligned on the printout and the system date right-aligned on the printout. Add a header that displays the sheet name centered on the printout.
h. Save the workbook.
i. Preview the entire workbook, then close the Preview window.
j. Preview the September worksheet, then print it in landscape orientation on a single page.
k. Save and close the workbook, then exit Excel.

2. You are a new employee for a computer software manufacturer. You are responsible for tracking the sales of different product lines and determining which computer operating system generates the most software sales each month. Although sales figures vary from month to month, the format in which data is entered does not. Use Table F-3 as a guide to create a worksheet tracking sales across personal computer (PC) platforms by month. Use a separate sheet for each month and create data for three months. Use your own data for the number of software packages sold in the Windows and Macintosh columns for each product. Create a summary sheet with all the sales summary information.

To complete this independent challenge:

a. Create a new workbook, then save it as "Software Sales Summary".
b. Enter row and column labels, your own data, and formulas for the totals.
c. Create a summary sheet that totals the information in all three sheets. Customize the header to include your name and the date. Set the footer to (none). In Page Setup, center the page both horizontally and vertically.
d. Save the workbook, then preview and print the four worksheets.

TABLE F-3

	Windows	Macintosh	Total
Games Software			
Space Wars 99			
Safari			
Flight School			
Total			
Business Software			
Word Processing			
Spreadsheet			
Presentation			
Graphics			
Page Layout			
Total			
Utilities Products			
Antivirus			
File recovery			
Total			

3. You are a college student with two roommates. Each month you receive your long-distance telephone bill. Because no one wants to figure out who owes what, you split the bill three ways. You are sure that one of your roommates makes two-thirds of the long-distance calls. To make the situation more equitable, you decide to create a spreadsheet to track the long-distance phone calls each month. Create a workbook with a separate sheet for each roommate. Track the following information for each month's long-distance calls: date of call, time of call (AM or PM), call minutes, location called, state called, area code, phone number, and call charge. Total the charges for each roommate. Create a summary sheet of all three roommates' charges for the month.

To complete this independent challenge:

a. Create a new workbook, then save it as "Monthly Long Distance" to the appropriate folder on your Project Disk.
b. Enter column headings and row labels to track each call.
c. Use your own data, entering at least three long-distance calls for each roommate.
d. Create totals for minutes and charges on each roommate's sheet.
e. Create a summary sheet that shows each name and uses cell references to display the total minutes and total charges for each person.
f. On the summary sheet, create a hyperlink from each person's name to cell A1 of their respective worksheet.
g. Create a workbook with the same type of information for the two people in the apartment next door. Save it as "Next Door".
h. Use linking to create a 3-D reference that displays that information on your summary sheet so your roommates can compare their expenses with the neighbors'.
i. Change the workbook properties to Read only.
j. Save the Monthly Long Distance workbook in HTML format and preview it in your Web browser.

4. Maria Abbott, general sales manager at MediaLoft, has asked you to create a projection of MediaLoft advertising expenditures for 1999–2002 that she can put on the company intranet. She wants managers to review this information for an advertising discussion at the next managers meeting. The categories and 1999 figures are already on the site.

a. Connect to the Internet, go to the MediaLoft intranet site at http://www.course.com/illustrated/MediaLoft, click the Marketing link, then locate and print the Ad Campaign Summary. Close your browser and disconnect from the Internet.
b. Start Excel and create a workbook titled "Ad Campaign Projection". Name Sheet1 "1999", enter the categories and numbers from your printout, and use a formula to calculate the total.
c. Add an appropriate worksheet name in cell A1.
d. Create figures for the years 2000–2002 and put them in the columns to the right of the 1999 figures, then use font and fill colors to make the worksheet attractive.
e. Format all numbers in an appropriate format.
f. Use formulas to create totals for each year and for each ad type. Format the totals so they stand out from the other figures and use cell borders as appropriate.
g. Create a custom view of the worksheet and save the view using a descriptive name.
h. Delete the unused sheets.
i. Add your name to the footer, then save and print the worksheet.
j. Save your workbook as a Web page, using the filename Ad Campaign Projection - Web, adding descriptive text to the title bar.
k. Preview the resulting file in your Web Browser, and test the chart tab.
l. Close your browser and Excel.

 Visual Workshop

Create the worksheet shown in Figure F-21. Save the workbook as "Martinez Agency". Preview, then print, the worksheet. (*Hint:* Notice the hyperlink target on the sheet name at the bottom of the figure.)

FIGURE F-21

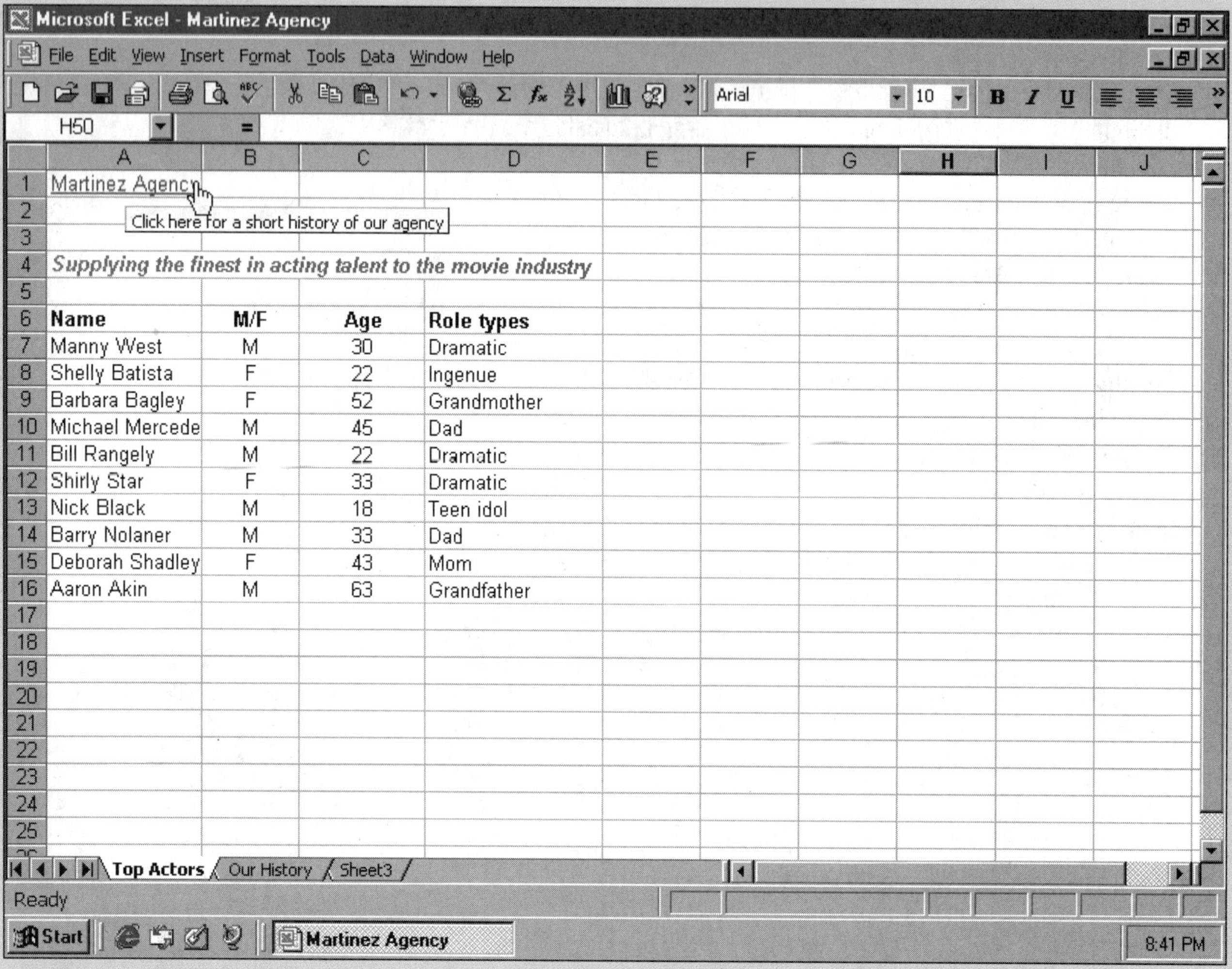

Microsoft Excel - Martinez Agency

File Edit View Insert Format Tools Data Window Help

Arial 10

H50 =

	A	B	C	D
1	Martinez Agency			
2				
3				
4	*Supplying the finest in acting talent to the movie industry*			
5				
6	**Name**	**M/F**	**Age**	**Role types**
7	Manny West	M	30	Dramatic
8	Shelly Batista	F	22	Ingenue
9	Barbara Bagley	F	52	Grandmother
10	Michael Mercede	M	45	Dad
11	Bill Rangely	M	22	Dramatic
12	Shirly Star	F	33	Dramatic
13	Nick Black	M	18	Teen idol
14	Barry Nolaner	M	33	Dad
15	Deborah Shadley	F	43	Mom
16	Aaron Akin	M	63	Grandfather

Click here for a short history of our agency

Top Actors / Our History / Sheet3

Ready

Start | Martinez Agency | 8:41 PM

Automating Worksheet Tasks

Objectives

- Plan a macro
- MOUS Record a macro
- MOUS Run a macro
- MOUS Edit a macro
- Use shortcut keys with macros
- Use the Personal Macro Workbook
- Add a macro as a menu item
- Create a toolbar for macros

A **macro** is a set of instructions that performs tasks in the order you specify. You create macros to automate frequently performed Excel tasks that require a series of steps. For example, if you usually type your name and date in a worksheet footer, Excel can record the keystrokes in a macro that types the text and inserts the current date automatically. In this unit, you will plan and design a simple macro, then record and run it. Then you will edit the macro. You will also create a macro to run when you use shortcut keys, store a macro in the Personal Macro Workbook, add a macro option to the Tools menu, and create a new toolbar for macros. Jim is creating a macro for the accounting department. The macro will automatically insert text that will identify the worksheet as originating in the accounting department.

Excel 2000

Planning a Macro

You create macros for tasks that you perform on a regular basis. For example, you can create a macro to enter and format text or to save and print a worksheet. To create a macro, you record the series of actions or write the instructions in a special format. Because the sequence of actions is important, you need to plan the macro carefully before you record it. You use commands on the Tools menu to record, run, and modify macros. Jim creates a macro for the accounting department that inserts the text "Accounting Department" in the upper-left corner of any worksheet. He plans the macro using the following guidelines:

Steps

1. **Assign the macro a descriptive name, and write out the steps the macro will perform**
   This planning helps eliminate careless errors. Jim decides to name the macro "DeptStamp". He writes a description of the macro, as shown in Figure G-1. See Table G-1 for a list of macros Jim might create to automate other tasks.

2. **Decide how you will perform the actions you want to record**
   You can use the mouse, the keyboard, or a combination of the two. Jim decides to use both the mouse and keyboard.

3. **Practice the steps you want Excel to record and write them down**
   Jim wrote down the sequence of actions as he performed them, and he is now ready to record and test the macro.

4. **Decide where to locate the description of the macro and the macro itself**
   Macros can be stored in an unused area of the active workbook, in a new workbook, or in the Personal Macro Workbook. Jim stores the macro in a new workbook.

FIGURE G-1: Paper description of planned macro

Macro to create stamp with the department name

Name:	DeptStamp
Description:	Adds a stamp to the top left of worksheet identifying it as an accounting department worksheet
Steps:	1. Position the cell pointer in cell A1 2. Type Accounting Department, then click the Enter button 3. Click Format on the menu bar, click Cells 4. Click Font tab, under Font style click Bold, under Underline click Single, and under Color click Red, then click OK

Excel 2000

TABLE G-1: Possible macros and their descriptive names

description of macro	descriptive name
Enter a frequently used proper name, such as Jim Fernandez	JimFernandez
Enter a frequently used company name, such as MediaLoft	CompanyName
Print the active worksheet on a single page, in landscape orientation	FitToLand
Turn off the header and footer in the active worksheet	HeadFootOff
Show a frequently used custom view, such as a generic view of the worksheet, setting the print and display settings back to the Excel defaults	GenericView

Macros and viruses

When you open an Excel Workbook that has macros, you will see a message asking you if you want to enable or disable macros. This is because macros can contain viruses, destructive software programs that can damage your computer files. If you know your workbook came from a trusted source, click Enable macros. If you are not sure of the workbook's source, click Disable macros. If you disable the macros in a workbook, you will not be able to use them in the workbook. For more information, see the Excel Help topic About Viruses and workbook macros.

Excel 2000

Recording a Macro

The easiest way to create a macro is to record it using the Excel Macro Recorder. You simply turn the Macro Recorder on, enter the keystrokes, select the commands you want the macro to perform, then stop the recorder. As you record the macro, each action is translated into programming code that you can later view and modify. Jim wants to create a macro that enters a department stamp in cell A1 of the active worksheet. He creates this macro by recording his actions.

Steps

QuickTip

To return personalized toolbars and menus to a default state, click Tools on the menu bar, click Customize, click Reset my usage data on the Options tab, click Yes, then click Close.

QuickTip

If information in a text box is selected, you can simply type new information to replace it. This saves you from having to delete the existing entry before typing the new entry.

Trouble?

If your results differ from Figure G-4, clear the contents of cell A1, then slowly and carefully repeat Steps 2 through 9. When prompted to replace the existing macro at the end of step 5, click Yes.

1. Start Excel if necessary, click the **New button** on the Standard toolbar, then save the blank workbook as **My Excel Macros**
   Now you are ready to start recording the macro.
2. Click **Tools** on the menu bar, point to **Macro**, then click **Record New Macro**
   The Record Macro dialog box opens. See Figure G-2. Notice the default name Macro1 is selected. You can either assign this name or type a new name. The first character of a macro name must be a letter; the remaining characters can be letters, numbers, or underscores; (spaces are not allowed in macro names; use underscores in place of spaces). This dialog box also allows you to assign a shortcut key for running the macro and to instruct Excel where to store the macro.
3. Type **DeptStamp** in the Macro name box
4. If the Store macro in list arrow box does not read "This Workbook", click the **list arrow** and select **This Workbook**
5. If the Description text box does not contain your name, select the existing name, type your own name, then click **OK**
   The dialog box closes. Excel displays the small Stop Recording toolbar containing the Stop Recording button, and the word "Recording" appears on the status bar. Take your time performing the steps below. Excel records every keystroke, menu option, and mouse action that you make.
6. Press **[Ctrl][Home]**
   The cell pointer moves to cell A1. When you begin an Excel session, macros record absolute cell references. By beginning the recording in cell A1, you ensure that the macro includes the instruction to select cell A1 as the first step.
7. Type **Accounting Department** in cell A1, then click the **Enter button** on the formula bar
8. Click **Format** on the menu bar, then click **Cells**
9. Click the **Font tab**, in the Font style list box click **Bold**, click the **Underline list arrow** and click **Single**, then click the **Color list arrow** and click **red** (third row, first color on left)
   See Figure G-3.
10. Click **OK**, click the **Stop Recording button** on the Stop Recording toolbar, click **cell D1** to deselect cell A1, then save the workbook
    Compare your results with Figure G-4.

FIGURE G-2: **Record Macro dialog box**

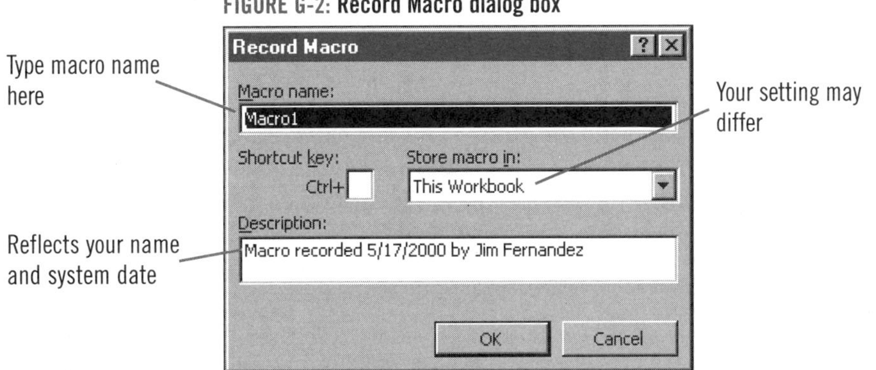

FIGURE G-3: **Font tab of the Format Cells dialog box**

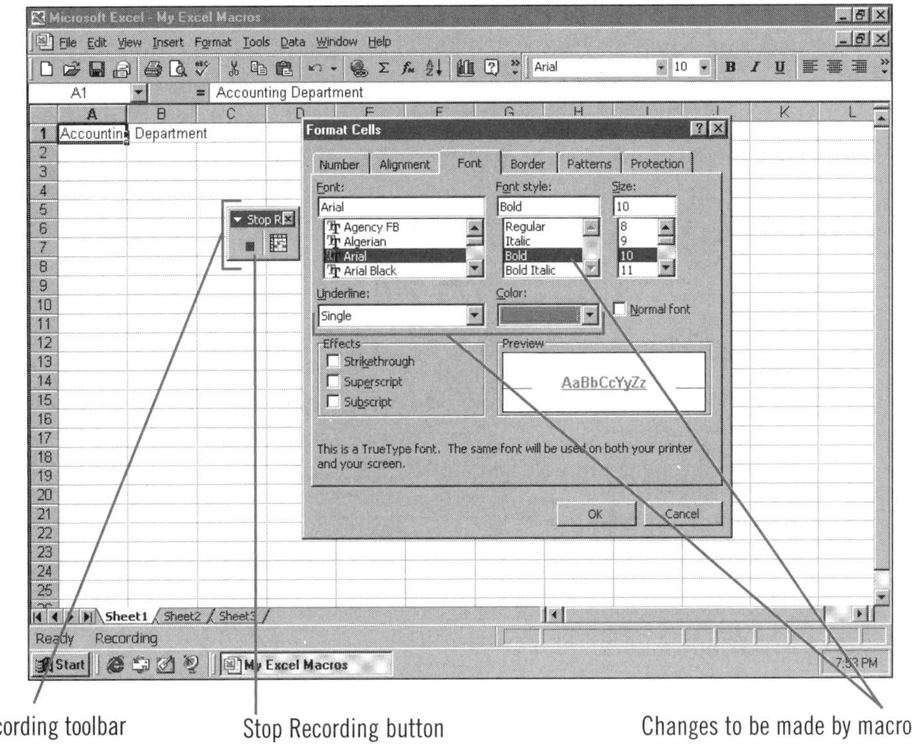

FIGURE G-4: **Personalized department stamp**

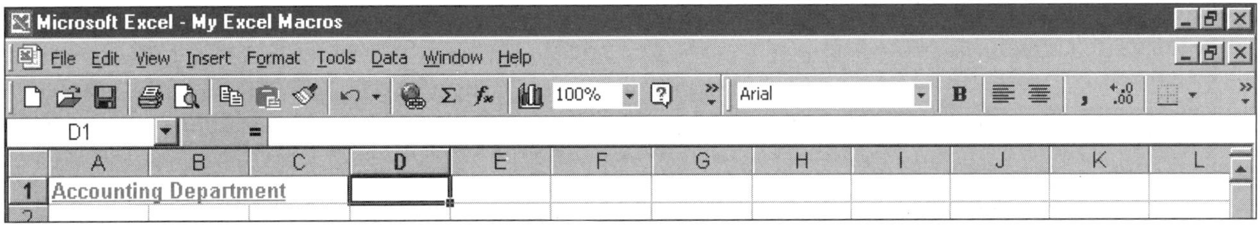

Using templates to create a workbook

You can create a workbook using an Excel **template**, a special-purpose workbook with formatting and formulas, such as an invoice or income statement. Click File on the menu bar, click New, click the Spreadsheet Solutions or Business planner templates tab, then double-click any template. Excel opens a workbook using that template design.

Excel 2000

Excel 2000

Running a Macro

Once you record a macro, you should test it to make sure that the actions performed are correct. To test a macro, you **run**, or execute, it. One way to run a macro is to select the macro in the Macros dialog box, then click Run. Jim clears the contents of cell A1 and then tests the DeptStamp macro. After he runs the macro from the My Excel Macros workbook, he decides to test the macro once more from a newly opened workbook.

Steps

1. Click **cell A1**, click **Edit** on the menu bar, point to **Clear**, click **All**, then click any other cell to deselect cell A1

   When you delete only the contents of a cell, any formatting still remains in the cell. By using the Clear All option on the Edit menu, you can be sure that the cell is free of contents and formatting.

QuickTip

To delete a macro, select the macro name in the Macro dialog box, click Delete, then click Yes to confirm.

2. Click **Tools** on the menu bar, point to **Macro**, then click **Macros**

   The Macro dialog box, shown in Figure G-5, lists all the macros contained in the open workbooks.

3. Make sure **DeptStamp** is selected, click **Run**, then deselect cell A1

   Watch your screen as the macro quickly plays back the steps you recorded in the previous lesson. When the macro is finished, your screen should look like Figure G-6. As long as the workbook containing the macro remains open, you can run the macro from any open workbook.

4. Click the **New button** on the Standard toolbar

   Because the new workbook automatically fills the screen, it is difficult to be sure that the My Excel Macros workbook is still open.

5. Click **Window** on the menu bar

   A list of open workbooks appears underneath the menu options. The active workbook name (in this case, Book2) appears with a check mark to its left. The My Excel Macros workbook appears on the menu, so you know it's open. See Figure G-7.

QuickTip

To stop a macro while it is running, press [Esc].

6. Deselect cell A1 if necessary, click **Tools** on the menu bar, point to **Macro**, click **Macros**, make sure **'My Excel Macros.xls'!DeptStamp** is selected, click **Run**, then deselect cell A1

   Cell A1 should look like Figure G-6. Notice that when multiple workbooks are open, the macro name includes the workbook name between single quotation marks, followed by an exclamation point, indicating that the macro is outside the active workbook. Since you use this workbook only to test the macro, you don't need to save it.

7. Close Book2 without saving changes

   The My Excel Macros workbook reappears.

FIGURE G-5: Macro dialog box

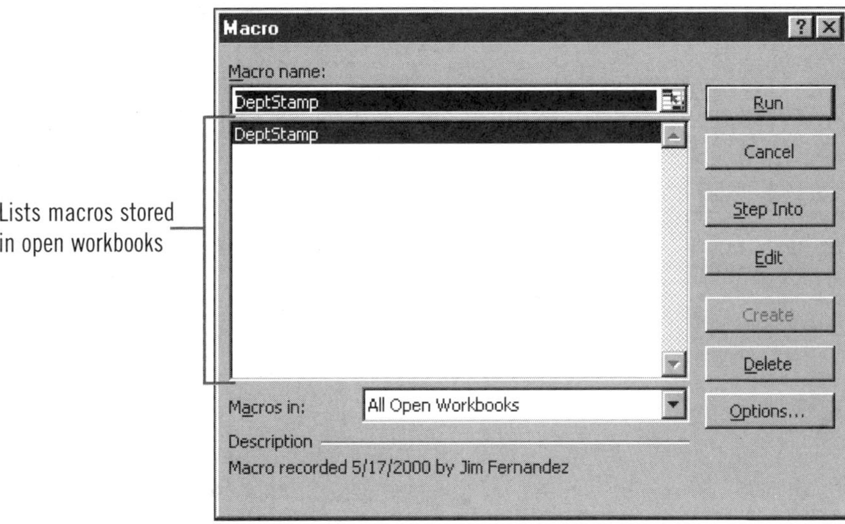

FIGURE G-6: Result of running DeptStamp macro

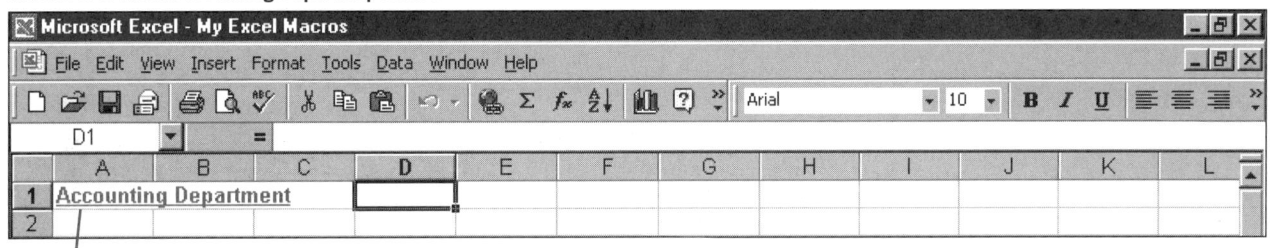

FIGURE G-7: Window menu showing list of open workbooks

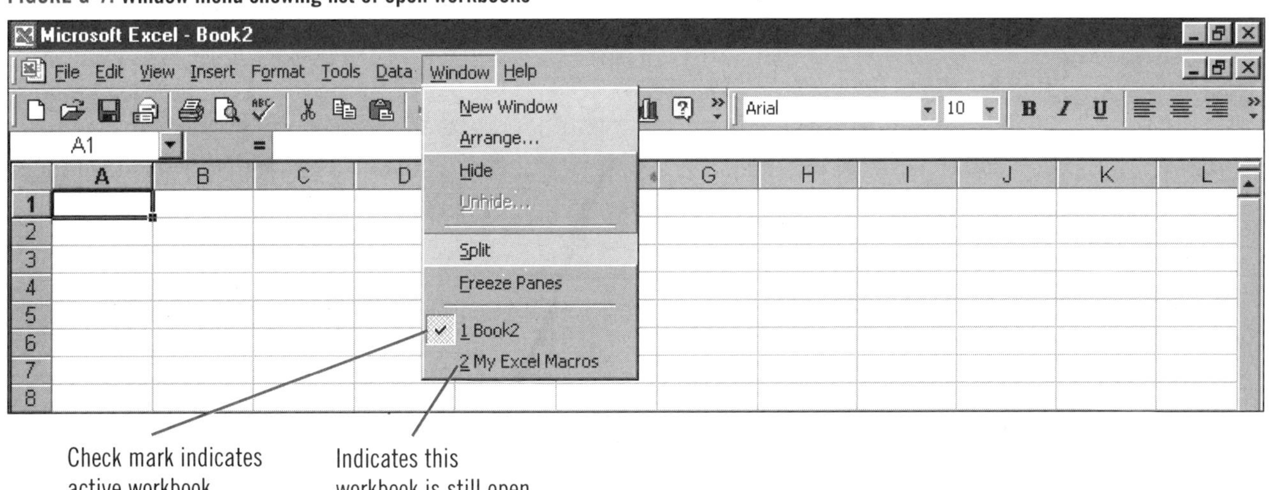

Excel 2000

Excel 2000

Editing a Macro

When you use the Macro Recorder to create a macro, the instructions are recorded automatically in Visual Basic for Applications programming language. Each macro is stored as a **module**, or program code container, attached to the workbook. Once you record a macro, you might need to change it. If you have a lot of changes to make, it might be best to re-record the macro. If you need to make only minor adjustments, you can edit the macro code, or program instructions, directly using the Visual Basic Editor. Jim wants to modify his macro to change the point size of the department stamp to 12.

Steps

QuickTip

Another way to start the Visual Basic Editor is to click Tools on the menu bar, point to Macro, then click Visual Basic Editor, or press [Alt][F11].

1. **Make sure the My Excel Macros workbook is open, click Tools on the menu bar, point to Macro, click Macros, make sure DeptStamp is selected, then click Edit**
   The Visual Basic Editor starts showing the DeptStamp macro steps in a numbered module window (in this case, Module1).
2. **Maximize the window titled My Excel Macros.xls – [Module1 (Code)], then examine the steps in the macro**
   See Figure G-8. The name of the macro and the date it was recorded appear at the top of the module window. Notice that Excel translates your keystrokes and commands into words, known as macro code. For example, the line .FontStyle = "Bold" was generated when you clicked Bold in the Format Cells dialog box. When you make changes in a dialog box during macro recording, Excel automatically stores all the dialog box settings in the macro code. You also see lines of code that you didn't generate directly while recording the DeptStamp macro; for example, .Name = "Arial".
3. **In the line .Size = 10, double-click 10 to select it, then type 12**
   Because Module1 is attached to the workbook and not stored as a separate file, any changes to the module are saved automatically when the workbook is saved.
4. **In the Visual Basic Editor, click File on the menu bar, click Print, then click OK to print the module**
   Review the printout of Module1.
5. **Click File on the menu bar, then click Close and Return to Microsoft Excel**
   You want to rerun the DeptStamp macro to view the point size edit you made using the Visual Basic Editor.
6. **Click cell A1, click Edit on the menu bar, point to Clear, click All, deselect cell A1, click Tools on the menu bar, point to Macro, click Macros, make sure DeptStamp is selected, click Run, then deselect cell A1**
   Compare your results with Figure G-9.
7. **Save the workbook**

FIGURE G-8: **Visual Basic Editor showing Module1**

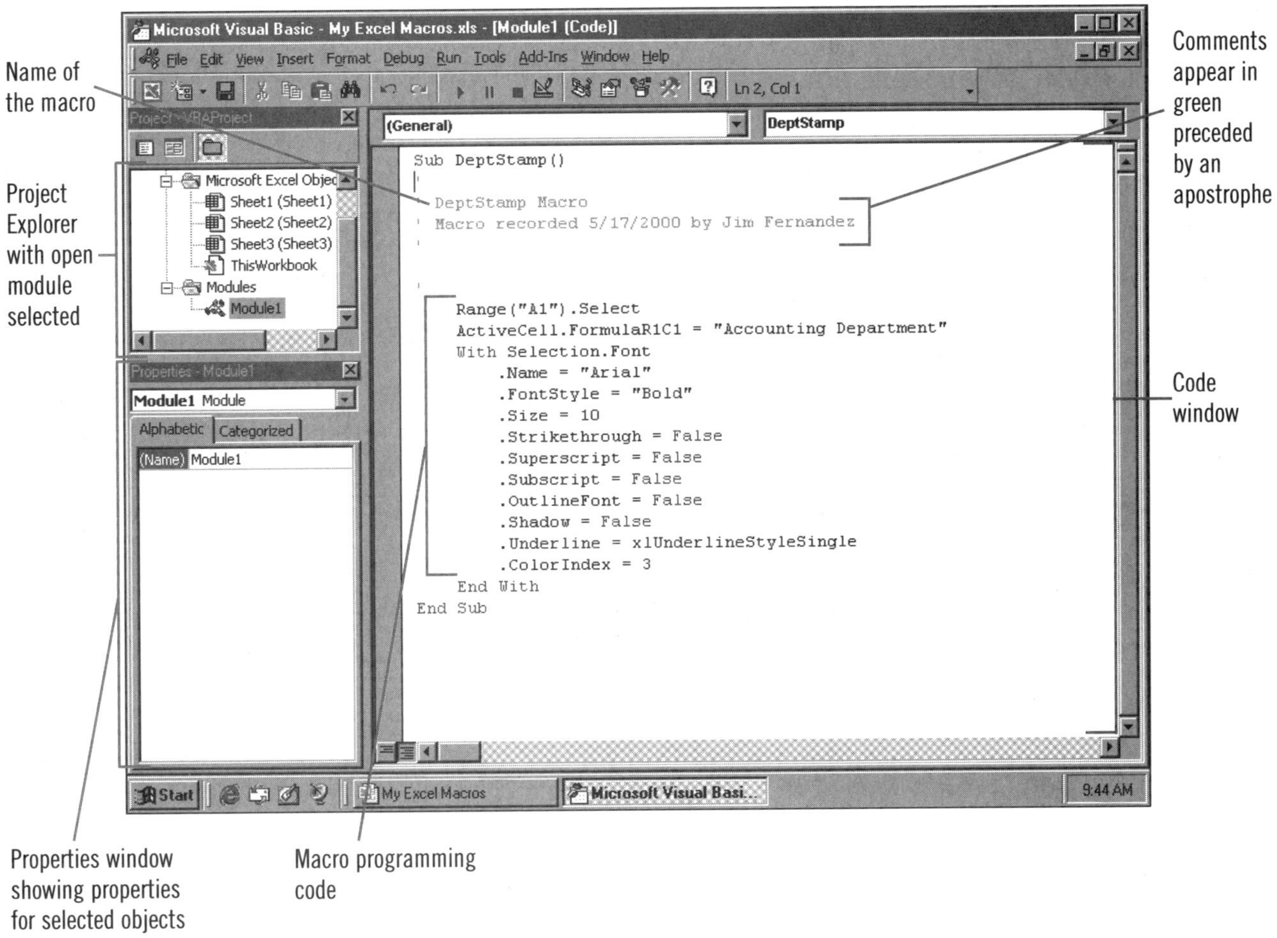

Microsoft Visual Basic - My Excel Macros.xls - [Module1 (Code)]

```
Sub DeptStamp()
'
' DeptStamp Macro
' Macro recorded 5/17/2000 by Jim Fernandez
'

'
    Range("A1").Select
    ActiveCell.FormulaR1C1 = "Accounting Department"
    With Selection.Font
        .Name = "Arial"
        .FontStyle = "Bold"
        .Size = 10
        .Strikethrough = False
        .Superscript = False
        .Subscript = False
        .OutlineFont = False
        .Shadow = False
        .Underline = xlUnderlineStyleSingle
        .ColorIndex = 3
    End With
End Sub
```

Name of the macro

Project Explorer with open module selected

Comments appear in green preceded by an apostrophe

Code window

Properties window showing properties for selected objects

Macro programming code

FIGURE G-9: **Result of running edited DeptStamp macro**

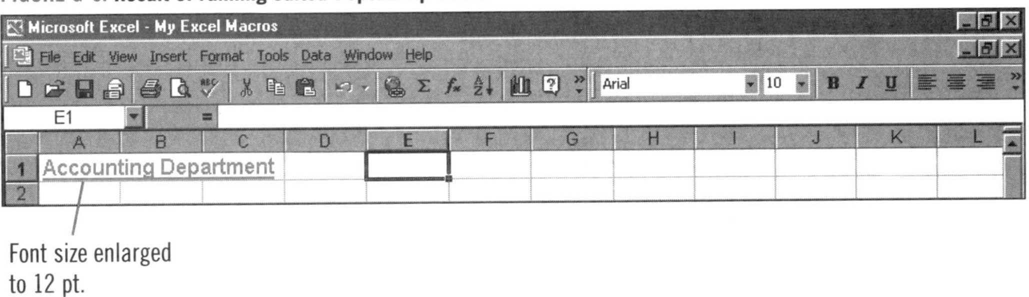

Font size enlarged to 12 pt.

Adding comments to code

With practice, you will be able to interpret the lines of code within your macro. Others who use your macro, however, might want to know the function of a particular line. You can explain the code by adding comments to the macro. Comments are explanatory text added to the lines of code. When you enter a comment, you must type an apostrophe (') before the comment text. Otherwise, Excel thinks you have entered a command. On a color monitor, comments appear in green after you press [Enter]. See Figure G-8. You also can insert blank lines in the macro code to make the code more readable. To do this, type an apostrophe, then press [Enter].

Excel 2000

Using Shortcut Keys with Macros

In addition to running a macro from the Macro dialog box, you can run a macro by assigning a shortcut key combination. Using shortcut keys to run macros reduces the number of keystrokes required to begin macro playback. You assign shortcut key combinations in the Record Macro dialog box. Jim also wants to create a macro called CompanyName to enter the company name into a worksheet. He assigns a shortcut key combination to run the macro.

Steps

1. Click **cell B2**

   You will record the macro in cell B2. You want to be able to enter the company name anywhere in a worksheet. Therefore, you will not begin the macro with an instruction to position the cell pointer, as you did in the DeptStamp macro.

2. Click **Tools** on the menu bar, point to **Macro**, then click **Record New Macro**

   The Record Macro dialog box opens. Notice the option Shortcut key: Ctrl+ followed by a blank box. You can type a letter (A-Z) in the Shortcut key box to assign the key combination of [Ctrl] plus that letter to run the macro. You use the key combination [Ctrl][Shift] plus a letter to avoid overriding any of the Excel's assigned [Ctrl] [letter] shortcut keys, such as [Ctrl][C] for Copy.

3. With the default macro name selected, type **CompanyName**, click the **Shortcut key text box**, press and hold **[Shift]**, type **C**, then, if necessary, replace the name in the Description box with your name

   Compare your screen with Figure G-10. You are ready to record the CompanyName macro.

4. Click **OK** to close the dialog box

   By default, Excel records absolute cell references in macros. Beginning the macro in cell B2 causes the macro code to begin with a statement to select cell B2. Because you want to be able to run this macro in any active cell, you need to instruct Excel to record relative cell references while recording the macro.

> **QuickTip**
>
> When you begin an Excel session, the Relative Reference button is toggled off, indicating that Excel is recording absolute cell references in macros. Once selected, and until it is toggled off again, the Relative Reference setting remains in effect during the current Excel session.

5. Click the **Relative Reference button** on the Stop Recording toolbar

   The Relative Reference button is now indented to indicate that it is selected. See Figure G-11. This button is a toggle and retains the relative reference setting until you click it again to turn it off.

6. Type **MediaLoft** in cell B2, click the **Enter button** on the formula bar, press **[Ctrl][I]** to italicize the text, click the **Stop Recording button** on the Stop Recording toolbar, then deselect cell B2

   MediaLoft appears in italics in cell B2. You are ready to run the macro in cell A5 using the shortcut key combination.

7. Click cell **A5**, press and hold **[Ctrl][Shift]**, type **C**, then deselect the cell

   The result appears in cell A5. See Figure G-12. Because the macro played back in the selected cell (A5) instead of the cell where it was recorded (B2), Jim is convinced that the macro recorded relative cell references.

8. Save the workbook

FIGURE G-10: Record Macro dialog box with shortcut key assigned

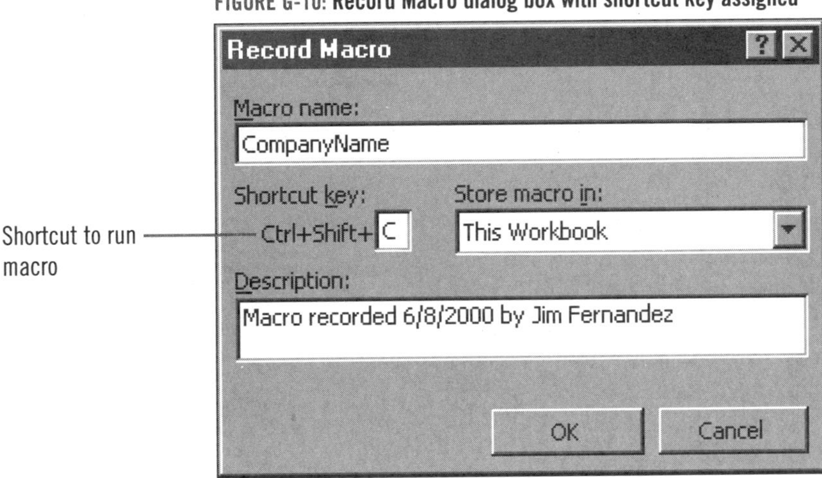

FIGURE G-11: Stop Recording toolbar with Relative Reference button selected

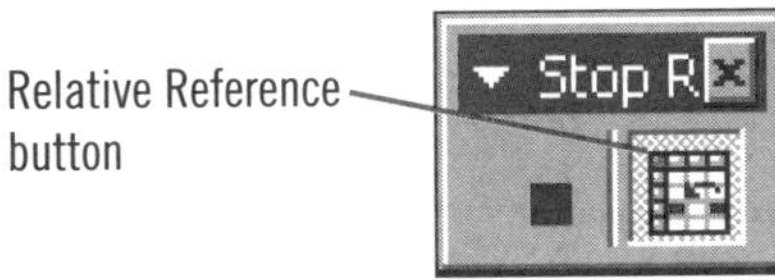

FIGURE G-12: Result of running the CompanyName macro

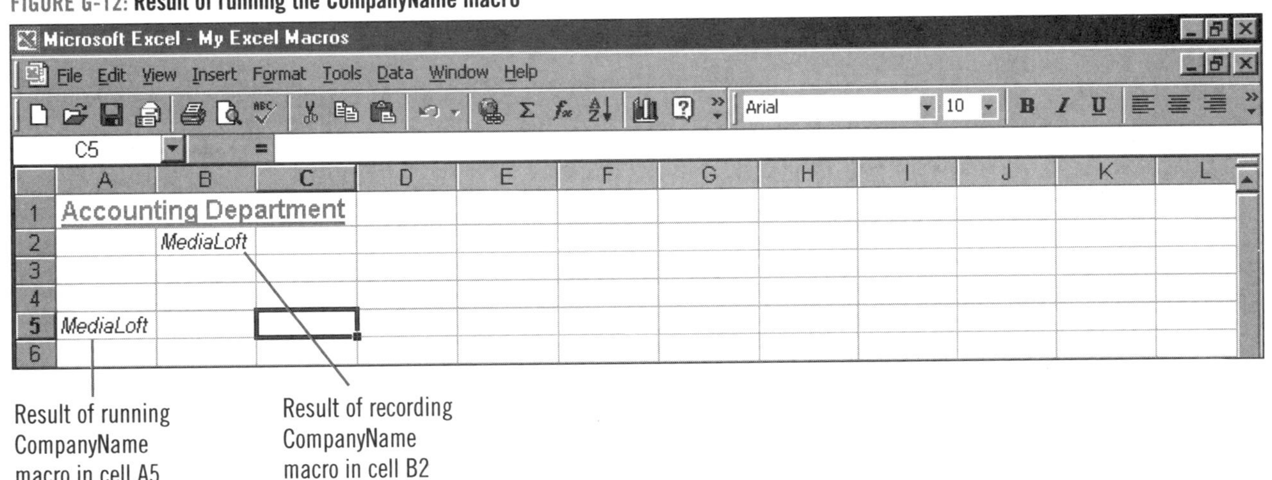

Excel 2000

Excel 2000

Using the Personal Macro Workbook

You can store commonly used macros in a **Personal Macro Workbook**. The Personal Macro Workbook is always available, unless you specify otherwise, and gives you access to all the macros it contains, regardless of which workbooks are open. The Personal Macro Workbook file is created automatically the first time you choose to store a macro in it. Additional macros are added to the Personal Macro Workbook when you store them there. Jim often adds a footer to his worksheets identifying his department, the workbook name, the worksheet name, the page number, and the current date. He saves time by creating a macro that automatically inserts this footer. Because he wants this macro to be available whenever he uses Excel, Jim decides to store this macro in the Personal Macro Workbook.

1. From any cell in the active worksheet, click **Tools** on the menu bar, point to **Macro**, then click **Record New Macro**
   The Record Macro dialog box opens.

Trouble?

If you are prompted to replace an existing macro named FooterStamp, click Yes.

2. Type **FooterStamp** in the Macro name box, click the **Shortcut key box**, press and hold **[Shift]**, type **F**, then click the **Store macro in list arrow**
   You have named the macro FooterStamp and assigned it the shortcut combination [Ctrl][Shift][F]. Notice that This Workbook is selected by default, indicating that Excel automatically stores macros in the active workbook. See Figure G-13. You also can choose to store the macro in a new workbook or in the Personal Macro Workbook.

QuickTip

If you see a message saying that the Personal Macro Workbook needs to be opened, open it, and then begin again from step 1. Once created, the Personal Macro Workbook file is usually stored in the Windows/Application Data/ Microsoft/Excel/XLSTART folder under the name "Personal".

3. Click **Personal Macro Workbook**, replace the existing name in the Description text box with your own name, if necessary, then click **OK**
   The recorder is on, and you are ready to record the macro keystrokes. (If there is already a macro assigned to this shortcut, display the Personal Macro workbook and delete the FooterStamp macro. Then return to the My Excel Macro workbook and begin again from step 1.)
4. Click **File** on the menu bar, click **Page Setup**, click the **Header/Footer tab** (make sure to do this even if it is already active), click **Custom Footer**, in the Left section box, type **Accounting**, click the **Center section box**, click the **File Name button**, press **[Spacebar]**, type **/**, press **[Spacebar]**, click the **Tab Name button** to insert the sheet name, click the **Right section box**, type your name followed by a comma, press **[Spacebar]**, click the **Date button**, click **OK** to return to the Header/Footer tab
   The footer stamp is set up, as shown in Figure G-14.

QuickTip

You can copy or move macros stored in other workbooks to the Personal Macro Workbook using the Visual Basic Editor.

5. Click **OK** to return to the worksheet, then click the **Stop Recording button** on the Stop Recording toolbar
   You want to ensure that the macro will set the footer stamp in any active worksheet.
6. Activate Sheet2, in cell A1 type **Testing the FooterStamp macro**, press **[Enter]**, press and hold **[Ctrl][Shift]**, then type **F**
   The FooterStamp macro plays back the sequence of commands.
7. Preview the worksheet to verify that the new footer was inserted
8. Print, then save the worksheet
   Jim is satisfied that the FooterStamp macro works in any active worksheet. Next, Jim adds the macro as a menu item on the Tools menu.

FIGURE G-13: **Record Macro dialog box showing Store macro in options**

Record Macro
Macro name:
FooterStamp
Shortcut key:
Ctrl+Shift+ F
Store macro in:
This Workbook
Personal Macro Workbook
New Workbook
This Workbook
Description:
Macro recorded 5/17/
OK
Cancel

Click to store in new blank workbook

Click to store in Personal Macro Workbook

Click to store in active workbook

FIGURE G-14: **Header/Footer tab showing custom footer settings**

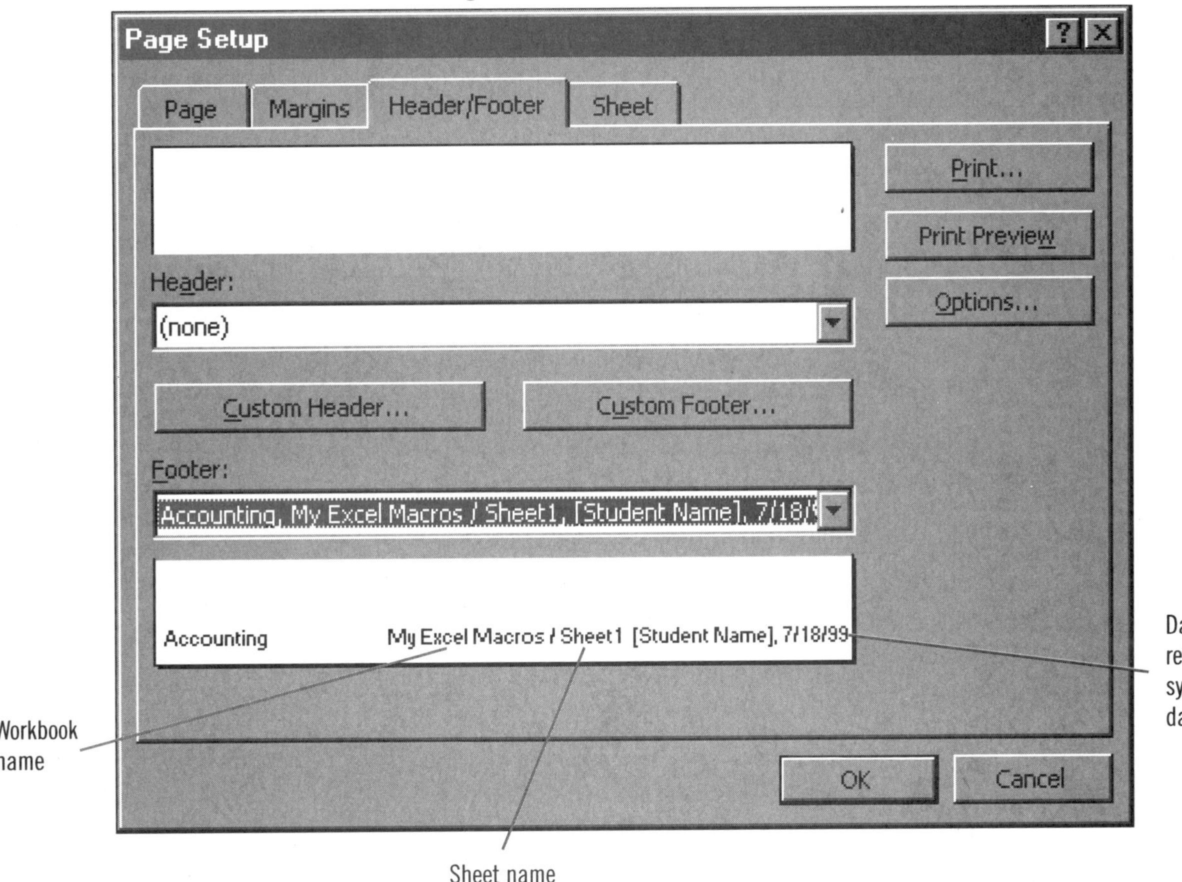

Working with the Personal Macro Workbook

Once created, the Personal Macro Workbook automatically opens each time you start Excel. By default, the Personal Macro Workbook is hidden as a precautionary measure so you don't accidentally add anything to it. When the Personal Macro Workbook is hidden, you can add macros to it but you cannot delete macros from it.

Excel 2000

Adding a Macro as a Menu Item

In addition to storing macros in the Personal Macro Workbook so that they are always available, you can add macros as items on the Excel Worksheet menu bar. The **Worksheet menu bar** is a special toolbar at the top of the Excel screen that you can customize. To increase the availability of the FooterStamp macro, Jim decides to add it as an item on the Tools menu. First, he adds a custom menu item to the Tools menu, then he assigns the macro to that menu item.

Steps

QuickTip

If you want to add a command to a menu bar, first display the toolbar containing the menu to which you want to add the command.

1. Click **Tools** on the menu bar, click **Customize**, click the **Commands tab**, then under Categories, click **Macros**
   See Figure G-15.
2. Click **Custom Menu Item** under Commands, drag the selection to **Tools** on the menu bar (the menu opens), then point just under the last menu option, but do not release the mouse button
   Compare your screen to Figure G-16.
3. Release the mouse button
   Now, Custom Menu item is the last item on the Tools menu.
4. With the Tools menu still open, right-click **Custom Menu Item**, select the text in the Name box (&Custom Menu Item), type **Footer Stamp**, then click **Assign Macro**
   Unlike a macro name, the name of a custom menu item can have spaces between words, as do all standard menu items. The Assign Macro dialog box opens.
5. Click **PERSONAL.XLS!FooterStamp** under Macro name, click **OK**, then click **Close**
6. Click the **Sheet3 tab**, in cell A1 type **Testing macro menu item**, press **[Enter]**, then click **Tools** on the menu bar
   The Tools menu appears with the new menu option at the bottom. See Figure G-17.
7. Click **Footer Stamp**, preview the worksheet to verify that the footer was inserted, then close the Print Preview window
   The Print Preview window appears with the footer stamp. Since others using your machine might be confused by the macro on the menu, it's a good idea to remove it.
8. Click **Tools** on the menu bar, click **Customize**, click the **Toolbars tab**, click **Worksheet Menu Bar** to select it, click **Reset**, click **OK** to confirm, click **Close**, then click **Tools** on the menu bar to make sure that the custom item has been deleted
   Because you did not make any changes to your workbook, you don't need to save it. Next, Jim creates a toolbar for macros and adds macros to it.

Trouble?

If you don't see PERSONAL.XLS!FooterStamp under Macro name, try repositioning the Assign Macro dialog box.

FIGURE G-15: Commands tab of the Customize dialog box

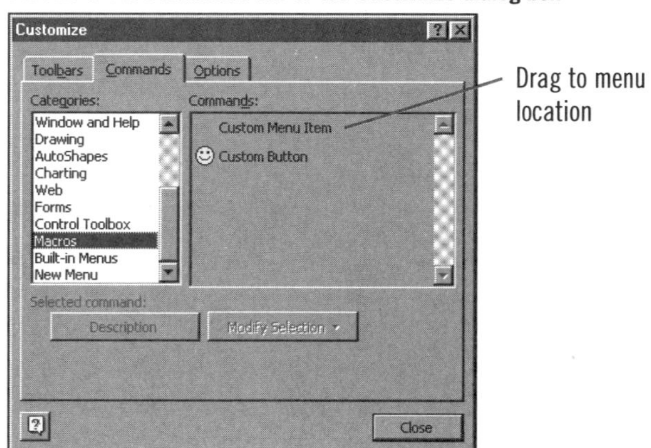

Drag to menu location

FIGURE G-16: Tools menu showing placement of Custom Menu Item

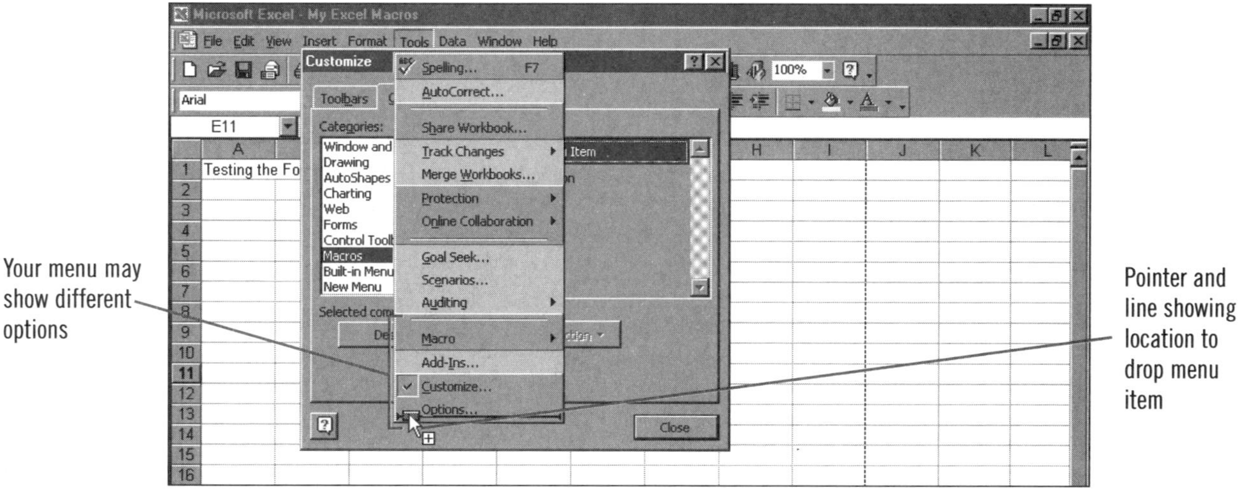

Your menu may show different options

Pointer and line showing location to drop menu item

FIGURE G-17: Tools menu with new Footer Stamp item

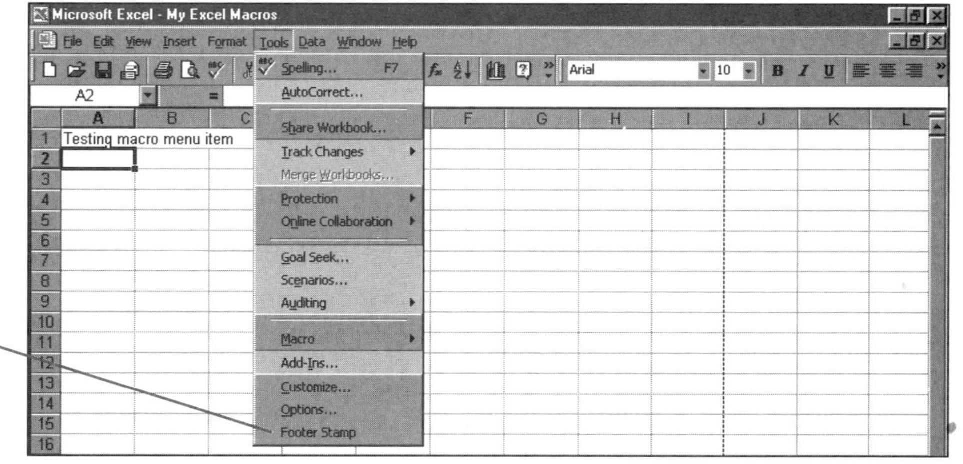

Added menu item

Excel 2000

Excel 2000

Creating a Toolbar for Macros

Toolbars contain buttons that allow you to access commonly used commands. You can create your own custom toolbars to organize commands so that you can find and use them quickly. Once you create a toolbar, you then add buttons to access Excel commands such as macros. Jim has decided to create a custom toolbar called Macros that will contain buttons to run two of his macros.

Steps

QuickTip

Toolbars you create or customize are available to all workbooks on your PC. You also can ensure that a custom toolbar is available with a specific workbook by attaching the toolbar to the workbook using the Toolbar tab in the Customize dialog box.

1. With Sheet3 active, click **Tools** on the menu bar, click **Customize**, click the **Toolbars tab**, if necessary, then click **New**
   The New Toolbar dialog box opens, as shown in Figure G-18. Under Toolbar name, a default name of Custom1 is selected.
2. Type **Macros**, then click **OK**
   Excel adds the new toolbar named Macros to the bottom of the list and a small, empty toolbar named Macros opens. See Figure G-19. Notice that you cannot see the entire toolbar name. A toolbar starts small and automatically expands to fit the buttons you assign to it.
3. Click the **Commands tab** in the Customize dialog box, click **Macros** under Categories, then drag the **Custom Button** over the new Macros toolbar and release the mouse button
   The Macros toolbar now contains one button. You want the toolbar to contain two macros, so you need to add one more button.
4. Drag the **Custom Button** over the Macros toolbar again
   With the two buttons in place, you customize the buttons and assign macros to them.
5. Right-click the left on the Macros toolbar, select **&Custom Button** in the Name box, type **Department Stamp**, click **Assign Macro**, click **DeptStamp**, then click **OK**
   With the first toolbar button customized, you are ready to customize the second button.
6. With the Customize dialog box open, right-click the right on the Macros toolbar, edit the name to read **Company Name**, click **Change Button Image**, click (bottom row, third from the left), right-click , click **Assign Macro**, click **CompanyName** to select it, click **OK**, then close the Customize dialog box
   The Macros toolbar appears with the two customized macro buttons.
7. Move the mouse pointer over on the Macros toolbar to display the macro name (Department Stamp), then click to run the macro; click **cell B2**, move the mouse pointer over on the Macros toolbar to display the macro name (Company Name), click , then deselect the cell
   Compare your screen with Figure G-20. The DeptStamp macro automatically replaces the contents of cell A1.
8. Click **Tools** on the menu bar, click **Customize**, click the **Toolbars tab**, if necessary, under Toolbars click **Macros** to select it, click **Delete**, click **OK** to confirm the deletion, then click **Close**
9. Save, then close the workbooks

Trouble?

If you are prompted to save the changes to the Personal Macro Workbook, click Yes.

FIGURE G-18: New Toolbar dialog box

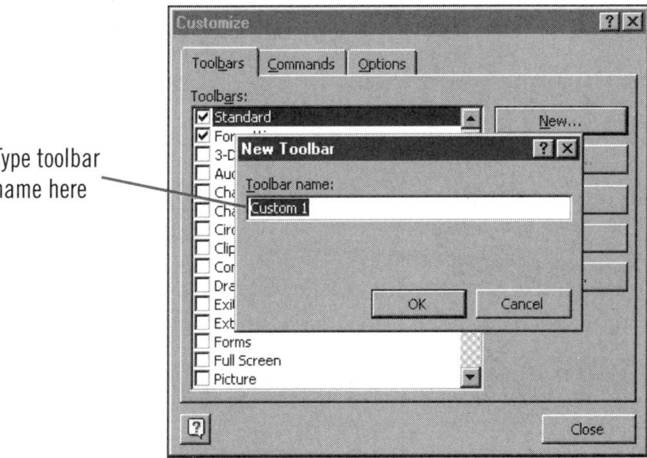

FIGURE G-19: Customize dialog box with new Macros toolbar

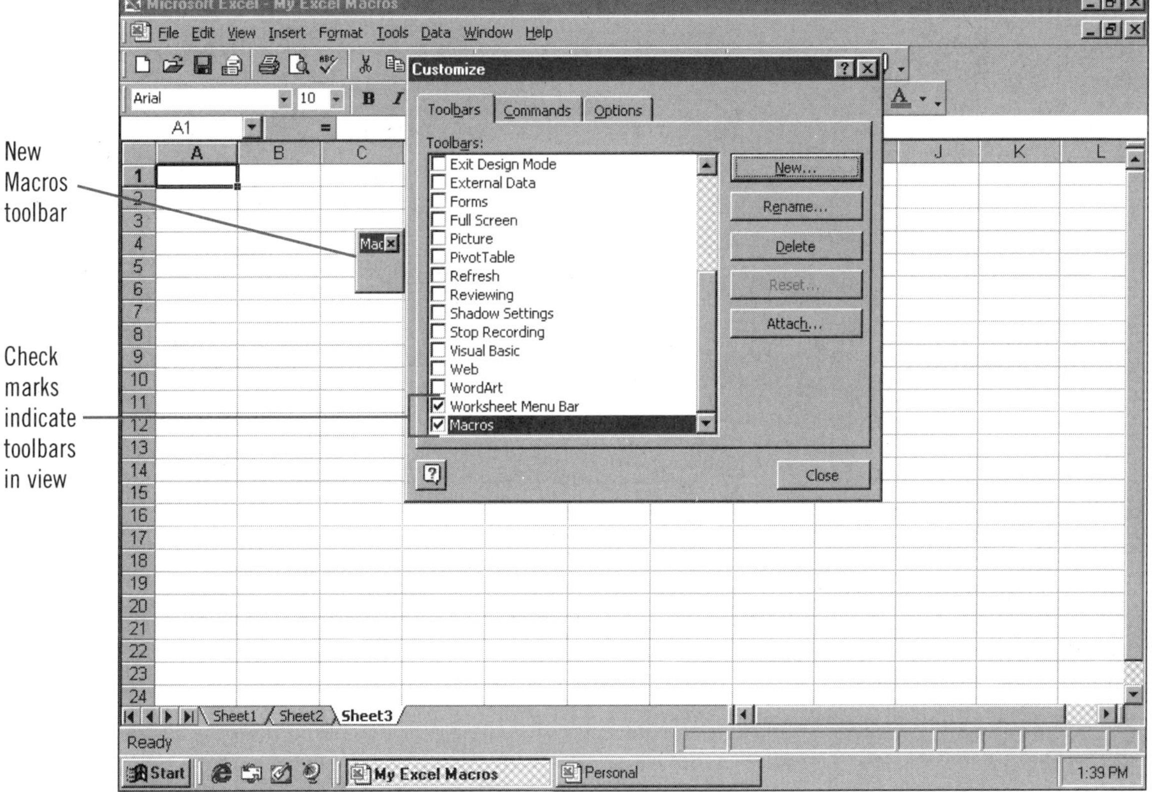

FIGURE G-20: Worksheet showing Macros toolbar with two customized buttons

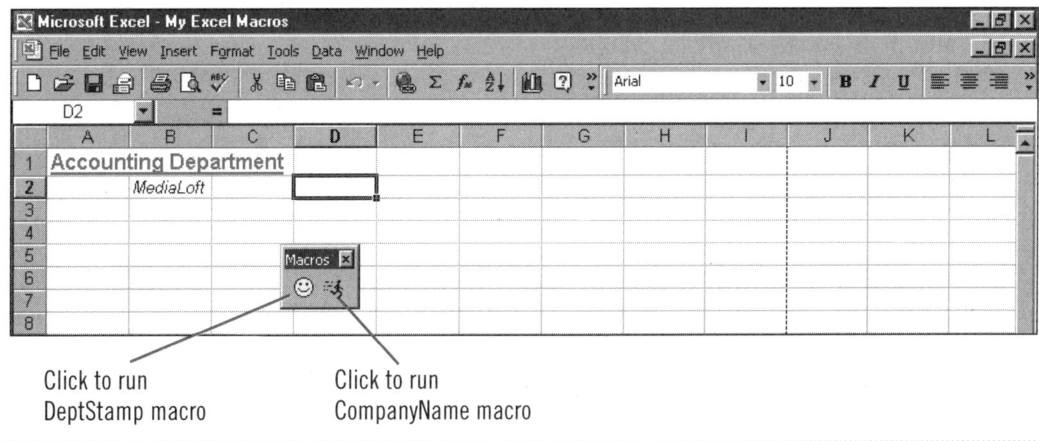

Excel 2000

Practice

► Concepts Review

Label each element of the Excel screen shown in Figure G-21.

FIGURE G-21

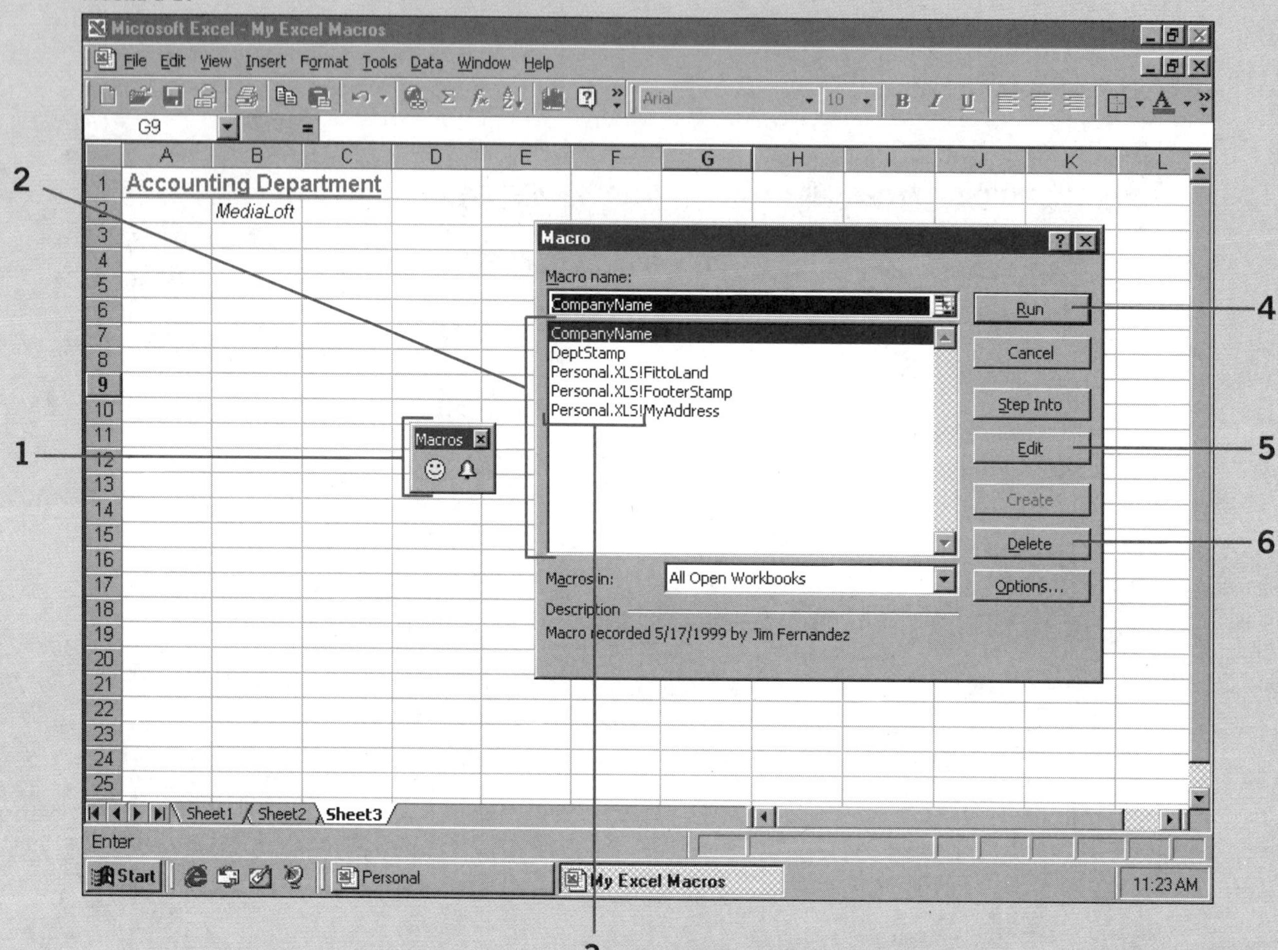

Select the best answer from the list of choices.

7. **Which of the following is the best candidate for a macro?**
   a. One-button or one-keystroke commands
   b. Often-used sequences of commands or actions
   c. Seldom-used commands or tasks
   d. Nonsequential tasks

8. **When you are recording a macro, you can execute commands by using**
   a. Only the keyboard.
   b. Only the mouse.
   c. Any combination of the keyboard and the mouse.
   d. Only menu commands.

9. **A macro is stored in**
   a. The body of a worksheet used for data.
   b. An unused area to the far right or well below the worksheet contents.
   c. A module attached to a workbook.
   d. A Custom Menu Item.

10. **Which of the following is *not* true about editing a macro?**
   a. You edit macros using the Visual Basic Editor.
   b. A macro cannot be edited and must be recorded again.
   c. You can type changes directly in the existing macro code.
   d. You can make more than one editing change in a macro.

11. **Why is it important to plan a macro?**
   a. Macros won't be stored if they contain errors.
   b. Planning helps prevent careless errors from being introduced into the macro.
   c. It is very difficult to correct errors you make in a macro.
   d. Planning ensures that your macro will not contain errors.

12. **Macros are recorded with relative references**
   a. Only if the Relative Reference button is selected.
   b. In all cases.
   c. Only if relative references are chosen while recording the macro.
   d. Only if the Absolute Reference button is not selected.

13. **You can run macros**
   a. From the Macro dialog box.
   b. From shortcut key combinations.
   c. As items on menus.
   d. Using all of the above.

Skills Review

1. Record a macro.

a. Create a new workbook, then save it as "Macros". You will record a macro titled "MyAddress" that enters and formats your name, address, and telephone number in a worksheet.
b. Store the macro in the current workbook.
c. Record the macro, entering your name in cell A1, your street address in cell A2, your city, state, and ZIP code in cell A3, and your telephone number in cell A4.
d. Format the information as 14-point Arial bold.
e. Add a border and make the text the color of your choice.
f. Save the workbook.

2. Run a macro.

a. Clear cell entries in the range affected by the macro.
b. Run the MyAddress macro in cell A1.
c. Clear the cell entries generated by running the MyAddress macro.
d. Save the workbook.

3. Edit a macro.

a. Open the MyAddress macro in the Visual Basic Editor.
b. Locate the line of code that defines the font size, then change the size to 18 point.
c. Edit the selected range to A1:E4, which increases it by three columns to accommodate the changed label size. (*Hint*: It is the second Range line in the macro.)
d. Add a comment line that describes this macro.
e. Save and print the module, then return to Excel.
f. Test the macro in Sheet1.
g. Save the workbook.

4. Use shortcut keys with macros.

a. You will record a macro in the current workbook called "MyName" that records your full name in cell G1.
b. Assign your macro the shortcut key combination [Ctrl][Shift][N] and store it in the current workbook.
c. After you record the macro, clear cell G1.
d. Use the shortcut key combination to run the MyName macro.
e. Save the workbook.

5. Use the Personal Macro Workbook.

a. You will record a new macro called "FitToLand" that sets print orientation to landscape, scaled to fit on a page.
b. Store the macro in the Personal Macro Workbook. If you are prompted to replace the existing FitToLand macro, click Yes.
c. After you record the macro, activate Sheet2, and enter some test data in row 1 that exceeds one page width.
d. In the Page Setup dialog box, return the orientation to portrait and adjust the capital A to 100 percent of normal size.
e. Run the macro.
f. Preview Sheet2 and verify that it's in landscape view and fits on one page.

6. **Add a macro as a menu item.**
   a. On the Commands tab in the Customize dialog box, specify that you want to create a Custom Menu Item.
   b. Place the Custom Menu Item at the bottom of the Tools menu.
   c. Rename the Custom Menu Item "Fit to Landscape".
   d. Assign the macro PERSONAL.XLS!FitToLand to the command.
   e. Go to Sheet3 and change the orientation to portrait, then enter some test data in column A.
   f. Run the Fit to Landscape macro from the Tools menu.
   g. Preview the worksheet and verify that it is in landscape view.
   h. Using the Tools, Customize menu options, select the Worksheet Menu bar, and reset.
   i. Verify that the command has been removed from the Tools menu.
   j. Save the workbook.

7. **Create a toolbar for macros.**
   a. With the Macros workbook still open, you will create a new custom toolbar titled "My Info".
   b. If necessary, drag the new toolbar onto the worksheet.
   c. Display the Macros command category, then drag the Custom Button to the My Info toolbar.
   d. Again, drag the Custom Button to the My Info toolbar.
   e. Rename the first button "My Address", and assign the MyAddress macro to it.
   f. Rename the second button "My Name", and assign the MyName macro to it.
   g. Change the second button image to one of your choice.
   h. On Sheet3, clear the existing cell data, then test both macro buttons on the My Info toolbar.
   i. Use the Toolbars tab of the Customize dialog box to delete the toolbar named My Info.
   j. Save and close the workbook, then exit Excel.

▶ Independent Challenges

1. As a computer-support employee of an accounting firm, you need to develop ways to help your fellow employees work more efficiently. Employees have asked for Excel macros that will do the following:

- Delete the current row and insert a blank row
- Delete the current column and insert a blank column
- Format a selected group of cells with a red pattern, in 12-point Times bold italic

To complete this independent challenge:

a. Plan and write the steps necessary for each macro.
b. Create a new workbook, then save it as "Excel Utility Macros".
c. Create a new toolbar called "Helpers".
d. Create a macro for each employee request described above.
e. Add descriptive comment lines to each module.
f. Add each macro to the Tools menu.
g. On the Helpers toolbar, install buttons to run the macros.
h. Test each macro by using the Run command, the menu command, and the new buttons.
i. Save and then print the module for each macro.
j. Delete the new toolbar, and reset the Worksheet menu bar.

2. You are an analyst in the finance department of a large bank. Every quarter, you produce a number of single-page quarterly budget worksheets. Your manager has informed you that certain worksheets need to contain a footer stamp indicating that the worksheet was produced in the finance department. The footer also should show the date, the current page number of the total pages, and the worksheet filename. You decide that the stamp should not include a header. It's tedious to add the footer stamp and to clear the existing header and footer for the numerous worksheets you produce. You will record a macro to do this.

To complete this independent challenge:

a. Plan and write the steps to create the macro.
b. Create a new workbook, then save it as "Header and Footer Stamp".
c. Create the macro described above. Make sure it adds the footer with the department name and other information, and also clears the existing header.
d. Add descriptive comment lines to the macro code.
e. Add the macro to the Tools menu.
f. Create a toolbar titled "Stamp", then install a button on the toolbar to run the macro.
g. Test the macro to make sure it works from the Run command, menu command, and new button.
h. Save and print the module for the macro.
i. Delete the new toolbar, then reset the Worksheet menu bar.

3. You are an administrative assistant to the marketing vice president at Computers, Inc. A major part of your job is to create spreadsheets that project sales results in different markets. It seems that you are constantly changing the print settings so that workbooks print in landscape orientation and are scaled to fit on one page. You have decided that it is time to create a macro to streamline this process.

To complete this independent challenge:

a. Plan and write the steps necessary for the macro.
b. Create a new workbook, then save it as "Computers Inc Macro".
c. Create a macro that changes the page orientation to landscape and scales the worksheet to fit on a page.
d. Test the macro.
e. Save and print the module sheet.
f. Delete any toolbars you created, and reset the Worksheet menu bar.

4. The MediaLoft New York store has recently instituted a budgeting process for its café operation. At the end of every monthly sales report created in Excel, the staff lists the four largest budget items and then fills in what it expects the figures to be for the next month.

Jim Fernandez at MediaLoft corporate headquarters has asked you to use Excel macros and the MediaLoft intranet site to help automate this task. The New York store staff will then distribute the macro to all stores so they can easily add the budget figures to their monthly reports.

a. Connect to the Internet, go to the MediaLoft intranet site at http://www.course.com/illustrated/MediaLoft, click the Accounting link, then click the Cafe Budget link. Examine the information in the NYC Cafe Expenses chart and note the four largest expense categories. Close your browser and disconnect from the Internet.

b. To complete this independent challenge, start Excel, create a new workbook, then save it as "Cafe Budget Macro". Create a macro named "CafeBudget" in the current workbook (activated by the [Shift][Ctrl][B] key combination) that does the following:

- Inserts the names of the four largest expense categories in contiguous cells in a column, starting with the current cell.
- Inserts the word "Total" in the cell below the last category.
- Inserts the words "Next Month's Budget" in the cell just above and to the right of the categories. The managers will insert their budget figures in the four cells below this heading, to the right of each category name.
- Totals the four figures the managers will insert and places the sum to the right of the Total label, just below the four figures.
- Inserts a bottom border on the Next Month's Budget cell and on the cell containing the last of the four figures.
- Boldfaces the Total text and the cell to its right that will contain the total.
- Places a thick box border around all the information, fills the area with a light green color, and autofits the column information where necessary.
- Makes the cell to the right of the first category the active cell.

c. Clear the worksheet of all contents and formats and test the macro. Edit or rerecord the macro as necessary.

d. Make a custom menu item on the Tools menu called "Cafe Budget" that will run the macro you created.

e. Create a custom toolbar named "Budgets" with a button containing the image of a calculator on it, and assign the button to your CafeBudget macro.

f. Test the custom menu item and the custom toolbar button, clearing the worksheet before running each one.

g. Save your workbook, print the results of the macro, then open the macro in the Visual Basic Editor and print the macro code.

h. Return to Excel, save and close the workbook, then exit Excel.

Visual Workshop

Create the macro shown in Figure G-22. (*Hint:* Save a blank workbook as "File Utility Macros", then create a macro called SaveClose that saves a previously named workbook. Finally, include the line ActiveWorkbook. Close in the module, as shown in the figure.) Print the module. Test the macro. The line "Macro recorded...by..." will reflect your system date and name.

FIGURE G-22

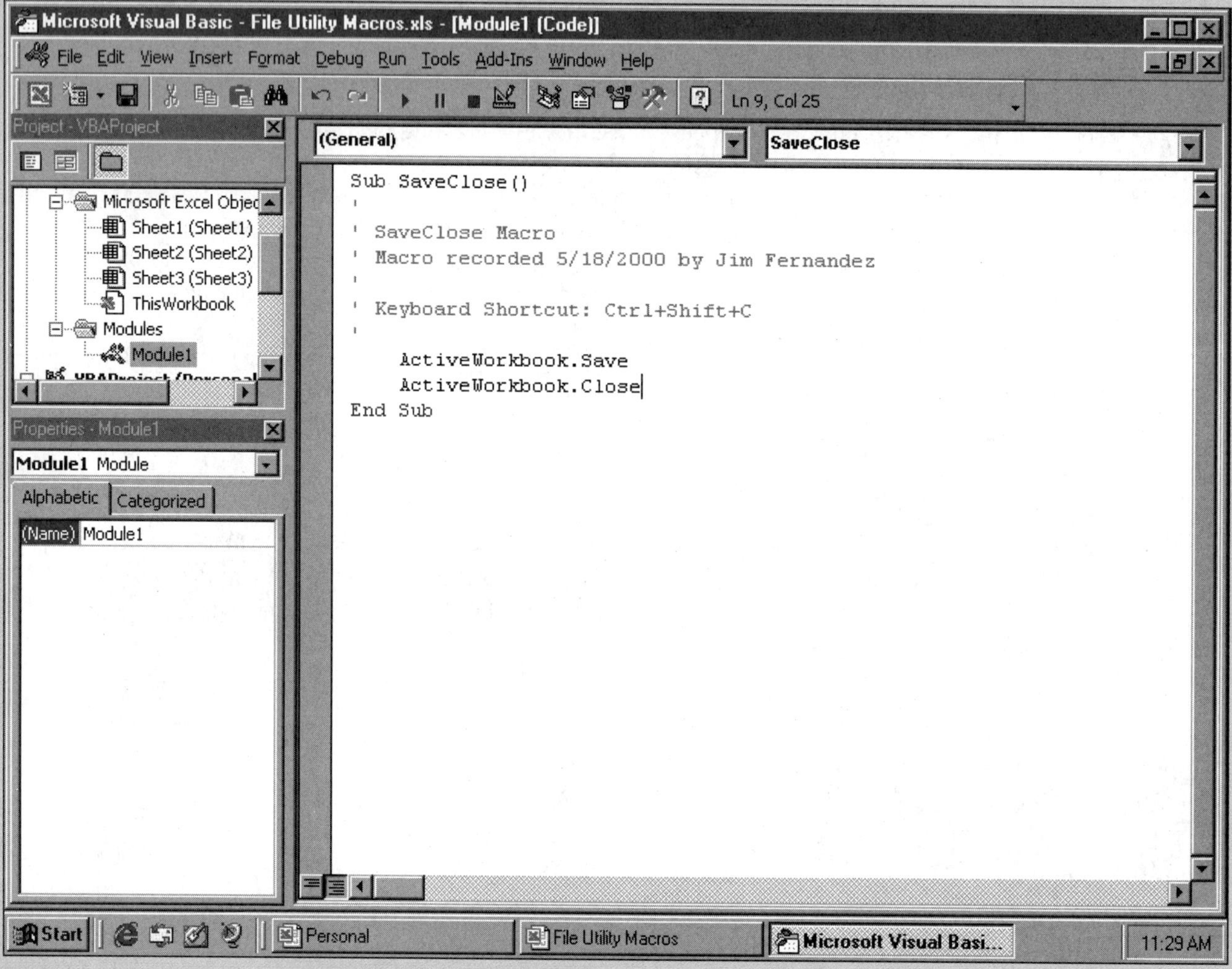

```
Sub SaveClose()
'
' SaveClose Macro
' Macro recorded 5/18/2000 by Jim Fernandez
'
' Keyboard Shortcut: Ctrl+Shift+C
'
    ActiveWorkbook.Save
    ActiveWorkbook.Close
End Sub
```

Excel 2000

Unit H

Using

Lists

Objectives

- Plan a list
- Create a list
- MOUS Add records with the data form
- MOUS Find records
- MOUS Delete records
- MOUS Sort a list by one field
- MOUS Sort a list by multiple fields
- MOUS Print a list

A **database** is an organized collection of related information. Examples of databases include a telephone book, a card catalog, and a roster of company employees. Excel refers to a database as a **list**. Using an Excel list, you can organize and manage worksheet information so that you can quickly find needed data for projects, reports, and charts. In this unit, you'll learn how to plan and create a list; add, change, find, and delete information in a list; and then sort and print a list.

MediaLoft uses lists to analyze new customer information. Jim Fernandez needs to build and manage a list of new customers as part of the ongoing strategy to focus the company's advertising dollars.

Excel 2000

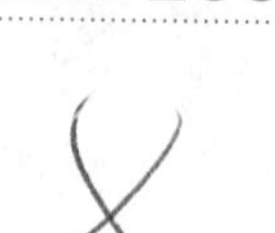

Planning a List

When planning a list, consider what information the list will contain and how you will work with the data now and in the future. Lists are organized into records. A **record** contains data about an object or person. Records, in turn, are divided into fields. **Fields** are columns in the list; each field describes a characteristic about the record, such as a customer's last name or street address. Each field has a **field name**, a column label that describes the field. See Table H-1 for additional planning guidelines. Jim will compile a list of new customers. Before entering the data into an Excel worksheet, he plans his list using the following guidelines:

Details

Identify the purpose of the list

Determine the kind of information the list should contain. Jim will use the list to identify areas of the country in which new customers live.

Plan the structure of the list

Determine the fields that make up a record. Jim has customer cards that contain information about each new customer. Figure H-1 shows a typical card. Each customer in the list will have a record. The fields in the record correspond to the information on the cards.

Write down the names of the fields

Field names can be up to 255 characters in length (the maximum column width), although shorter names are easier to see in the cells. Field names appear in the first row of a list. Jim writes down field names that describe each piece of information shown in Figure H-1.

Determine any special number formatting required in the list

Most lists contain both text and numbers. When planning a list, consider whether any fields require specific number formatting or prefixes. Jim notes that some Zip codes begin with zero. Because Excel automatically drops a leading zero, Jim must type an apostrophe (') when he enters a Zip code that begins with 0 (zero). The apostrophe tells Excel that the cell contains a label rather than a value. If a column contains both numbers and numbers that contain a text character, such as an apostrophe ('), you should format all the numbers as text. Otherwise, the numbers are sorted first, and the numbers that contain text characters are sorted after that; for example, 11542, 60614, 87105, '01810, '02115. To instruct Excel to sort the Zip codes properly, Jim enters all Zip codes with a leading apostrophe.

FIGURE H-1: Customer record and corresponding field names

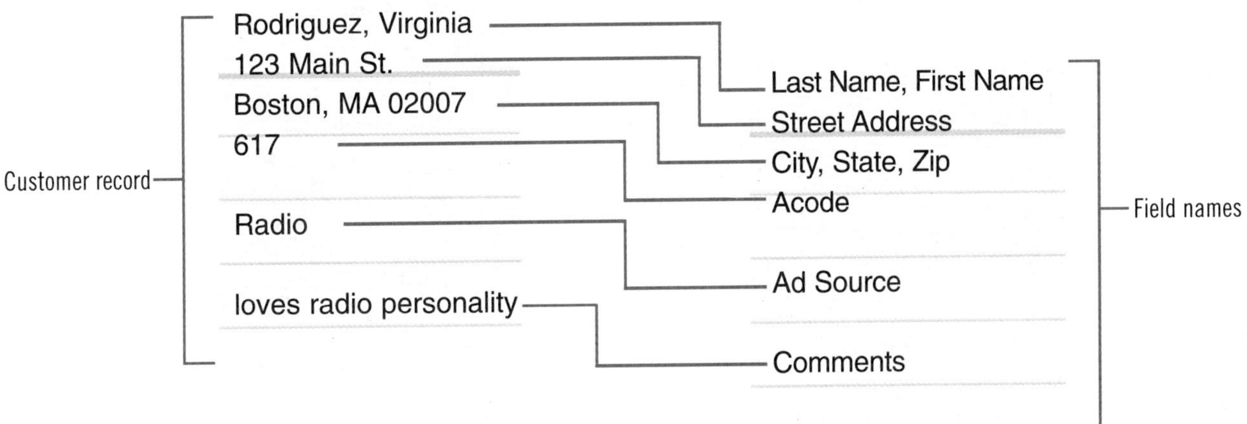

TABLE H-1: Guidelines for planning a list

size and location guidelines	row and column content guidelines
Devote an entire worksheet to your list and list summary information because some list management features can be used on only one list at a time	Plan and design your list so that all rows have similar items in the same column
Leave at least one blank column and one blank row between your list and list summary data. Doing this helps Excel select your list when it performs list management tasks such as sorting	Do not insert extra spaces at the beginning of a cell because that can affect sorting and searching
Avoid placing critical data to the left or right of the list	Use the same format for all cells in a column

Lists versus databases

If your list contains more records than can fit on one worksheet (that is, more than 65,536), you should consider using database software rather than spreadsheet software.

Excel 2000

Creating a List

Once you have planned the list structure, the sequence of fields, and any appropriate formatting, you need to create field names. Table H-2 provides guidelines for naming fields. Jim is ready to create the list using the field names he wrote down earlier.

Steps

QuickTip

To return personalized toolbars and menus to their default state, click Tools on the menu bar, click Customize, click the Options tab in the Customize dialog box, click Reset my usage data to restore the default settings, click Yes, click Close, then close the Drawing toolbar if it is displayed.

Trouble?

If the Bold button or Borders button does not appear on your Formatting toolbar, click the More Buttons button to view it.

QuickTip

If the field name you plan to use is wider than the data in the column, you can turn on Wrap Text to stack the heading in the cell. Doing this allows you to use descriptive field names and still keep the columns from being unnecessarily wide. If you prefer a keyboard shortcut, you can press [Alt][Enter] to force a line break while entering field names.

1. Start Excel if necessary, open the workbook titled **EX H-1**, save it as **New Customer List**, rename Sheet1 as **Practice**, then if necessary maximize the Excel window
   It is a good idea to devote an entire worksheet to your list.

2. Beginning in cell A1 and moving horizontally, type each field name in a separate cell, as shown in Figure H-2
   Always put field names in the first row of the list. Don't worry if your field names are wider than the cells; you will fix this later.

3. Select the field headings in range **A1:I1**, then click the **Bold button** on the Formatting toolbar; with range A1:I1 still selected, click the **Borders list arrow**, then click the **thick bottom border** (second item from left in the second row)

4. Enter the information from Figure H-3 in the rows immediately below the field names, using a leading apostrophe (') for all Zip codes; do not leave any blank rows
   If you don't type an apostrophe, Excel deletes the leading zero (0) in the Zip code. The data appears in columns organized by field name.

5. Select the range **A1:I4**, click **Format** on the menu bar, point to **Column**, click **AutoFit Selection**, click anywhere in the worksheet to deselect the range, then save the workbook
   Automatically resizing the column widths this way is faster than double-clicking the column divider lines between each pair of columns. Compare your screen with Figure H-4.

TABLE H-2: Guidelines for naming fields

guideline	explanation
Use labels to name fields	Numbers can be interpreted as parts of formulas
Do not use duplicate field names	Duplicate field names can cause information to be incorrectly entered and sorted
Format the field names to stand out from the list data	Use a font, alignment, format, pattern, border, or capitalization style for the column labels that are different from the format of your list data
Use descriptive names	Avoid names that might be confused with cell addresses, such as Q4

FIGURE H-2: Field names entered and formatted in row 1

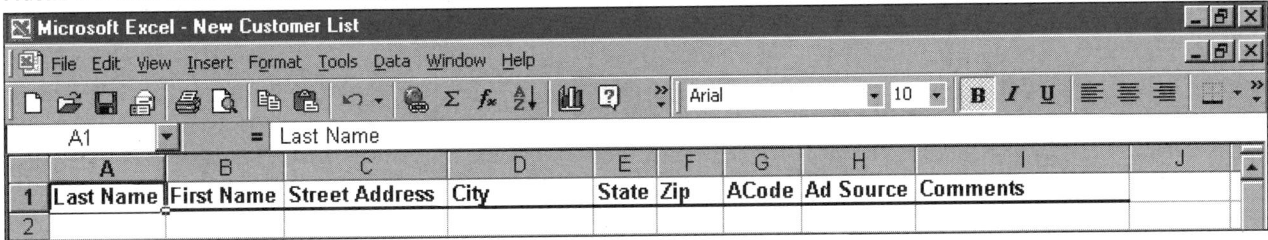

FIGURE H-3: Cards with customer information

Rodriguez, Virginia
123 Main St.
Boston, MA 02007
617

Radio

loves radio personality

Wong, Sam
2120 Central NE.
San Francisco, CA 93772
415

Newspaper

graphics caught eye

Smith, Carol
123 Elm St.
Watertown, MA 02472
617

Newspaper

no comments

FIGURE H-4: List with three records

Microsoft Excel - New Customer List

F2 = '02007

	A	B	C	D	E	F	G	H	I	J
1	Last Name	First Name	Street Address	City	State	Zip	ACode	Ad Source	Comments	
2	Rodriguez	Virginia	123 Main St.	Boston	MA	02007	617	Radio	loves radio personality	
3	Wong	Sam	2120 Central NE	San Francisco	CA	93772	415	Newspaper	graphics caught eye	
4	Smith	Carol	123 Elm St.	Waterton	MA	02472	617	Newspaper	no comments	
5										
6										

New records
Leading apostrophe

Maintaining the quality of information in a list

To protect the list information, make sure the data is entered in the correct field. Stress care and consistency to all those who enter the list data. Haphazardly entered data can yield invalid results later when it is manipulated.

Excel 2000

Excel 2000

Adding Records with the Data Form

You can add records to a list by typing data directly into the cells within the list range. Once the field names are created, you also can use the data form as a quick, easy method of data entry. A **data form** is a dialog box that displays one record at a time. By naming a list range in the name box, you can select the list at any time, and all new records you add to the list will be included in the list range. Jim has entered all the customer records he had on his cards, but he receives the names of two more customers. He decides to use the Excel data form to add the new customer information.

Steps

1. Make sure the New Customer List file is open, then rename Sheet2 **Working List**
   Working List contains the nearly complete customer list. Before using the data form to enter the new data, you must define the list range.

2. Select the range **A1:I45**, click the **name box** to select the reference to cell **A1** there, type **Database**, then press **[Enter]**
   The Database list range name appears in the name box. When you assign the name Database to the list, the commands on the Excel Data menu apply to the list named "Database".

3. While the list is still selected, click **Data** on the menu bar, then click **Form**
   A data form containing the first record appears, as shown in Figure H-5.

4. Click **New**
   A blank data form appears with the insertion point in the first field.

5. Type **Chavez** in the Last Name box, then press **[Tab]** to move the insertion point to the next field

6. Enter the rest of the information for Jeffrey Chavez, as shown in Figure H-6
   Press [Tab] to move the insertion point to the next field, or click in the next field's box to move the insertion point there.

7. Click **New** to add Jeffrey Chavez's record and open another blank data form, enter the record for Cathy Relman as shown in Figure H-6, then click **Close**
   The list records that you add with the data form are placed at the end of the list and are formatted in the same way as the previous records.

8. Scroll down the worksheet to bring rows 46 and 47 into view, check both new records, return to cell A1, then save the workbook

Trouble?

If you accidentally press [↑] or [↓] while in a data form and find yourself positioned in the wrong record, press [↑] or [↓] until you return to the desired record.

QuickTip

Excel 2000 automatically extends formatting and formulas in lists.

FIGURE H-5: Data form showing first record in the list

Working List
Last Name: Rodriguez
First Name: Virginia
Street Address: 123 Main St.
City: Boston
State: MA
Zip: 02007
ACode: 617
Ad Source: Radio
Comments on ads: loves radio personality
1 of 44
New
Delete
Restore
Find Prev
Find Next
Criteria
Close
Total number or records
Click to open a blank data form for adding a record
Current record number
Leading apostrophe not visible in data form after records are inserted

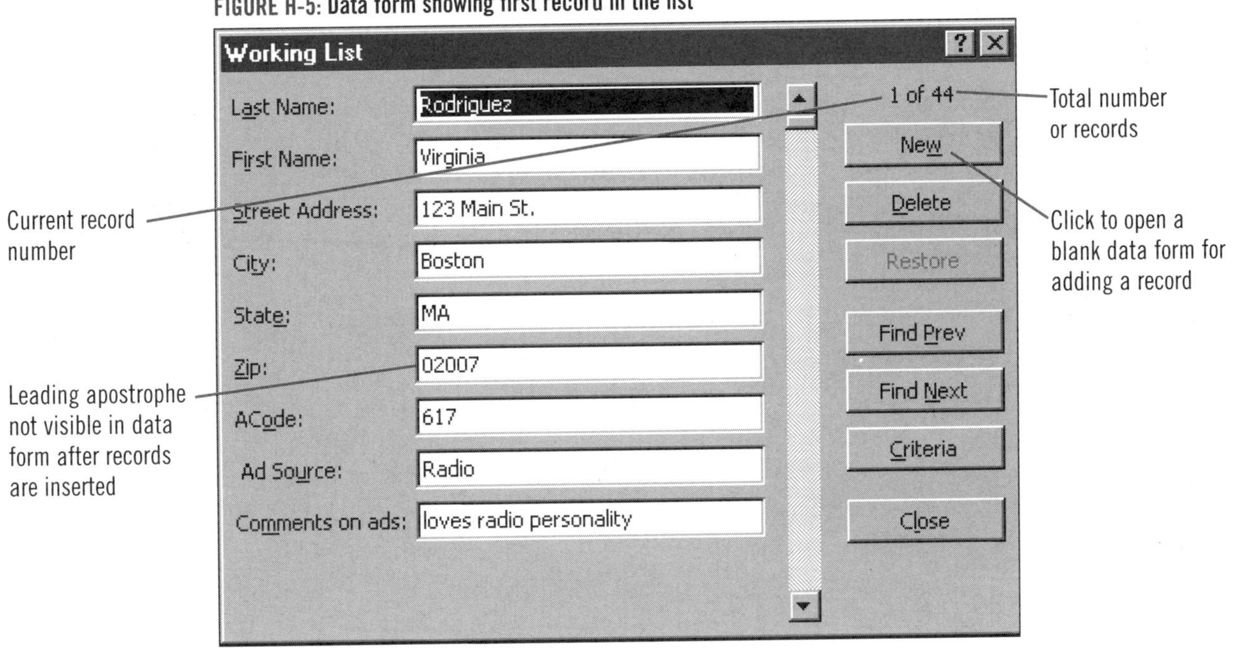

FIGURE H-6: Two data forms with information for two new records

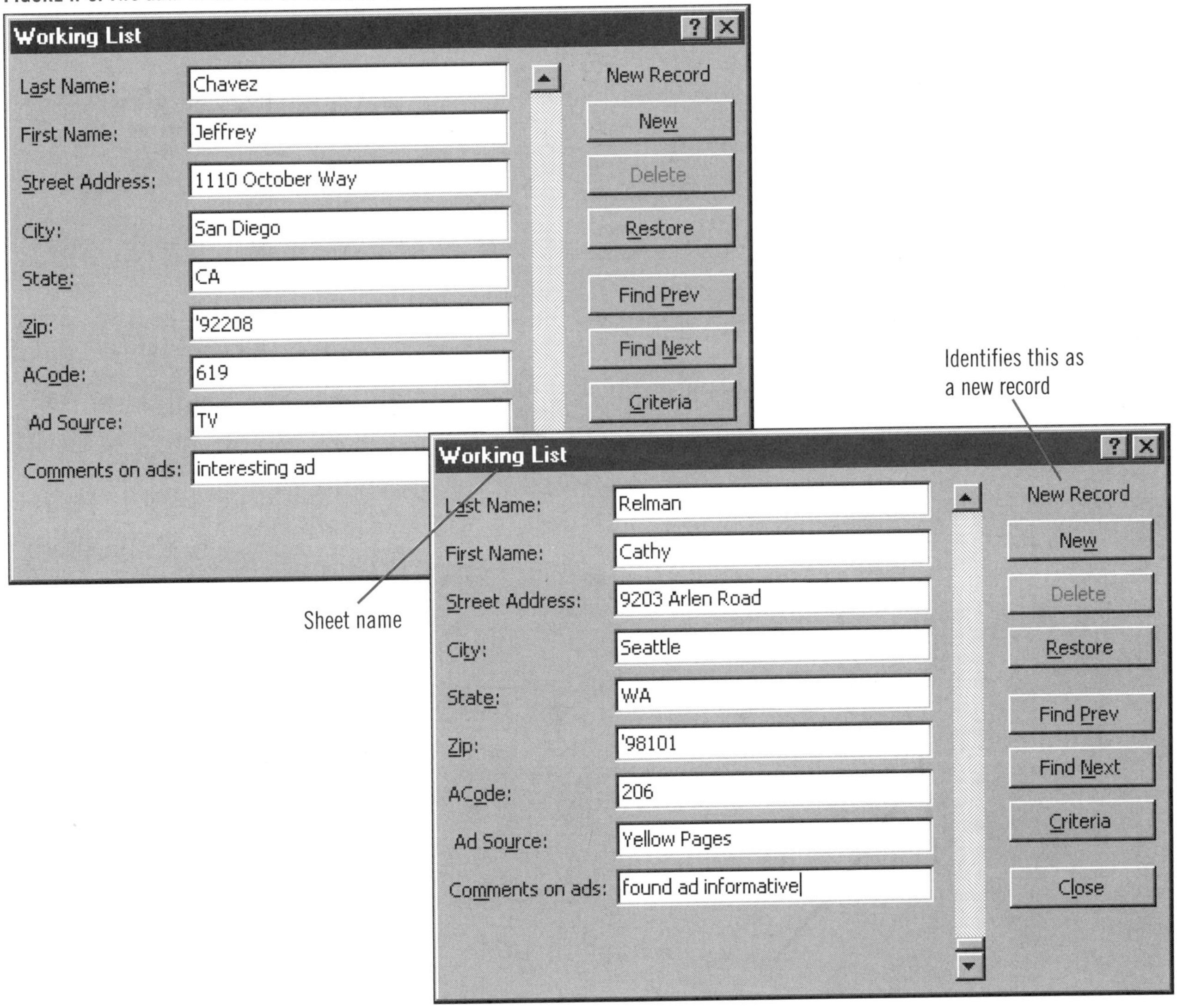

Working List
Last Name: Chavez
First Name: Jeffrey
Street Address: 1110 October Way
City: San Diego
State: CA
Zip: '92208
ACode: 619
Ad Source: TV
Comments on ads: interesting ad
New Record
New
Delete
Restore
Find Prev
Find Next
Criteria
Identifies this as a new record
Working List
Last Name: Relman
First Name: Cathy
Street Address: 9203 Arlen Road
City: Seattle
State: WA
Zip: '98101
ACode: 206
Ad Source: Yellow Pages
Comments on ads: found ad informative
New Record
New
Delete
Restore
Find Prev
Find Next
Criteria
Close
Sheet name

Excel 2000

Finding Records

From time to time, you need to locate specific records in your list. You can use the Excel Find command on the Edit menu or the data form to search your list. Also, you can use the Replace command on the Edit menu to locate and replace existing entries or portions of entries with specified information. Jim wants to be more specific about the radio ad source, so he replaces "Radio" with "KWIN Radio." He also wants to know how many of the new customers originated from the company's TV ads. Jim begins by searching for those records with the ad source "TV".

Trouble?

If you receive the message "No list found", select any cell within the list, then repeat Step 1

1. **From any cell within the list, click Data on the menu bar, click Form, then click Criteria**
   The data form changes so that all fields are blank and "Criteria" appears in the upper-right corner. See Figure H-7. You want to search for records whose Ad Source field contains the label "TV".

2. **Press [Alt][U] to move to the Ad Source box, type TV, then click Find Next**
   Excel displays the first record for a customer who learned about the company through its TV ads. See Figure H-8.

QuickTip

You can also use comparison operators when performing a search using the data form. For example, you could specify >50,000 in a Salary field box to return those records in the Salary field with a value greater than $50,000.

3. **Click Find Next until there are no more matching records, then click Close**
   There are six customers whose ad source is TV. Next, Jim wants to make the radio ad source more specific.

4. **Return to cell A1, click Edit on the menu bar, then click Replace**
   The Replace dialog box opens with the insertion point located in the Find what box. See Figure H-9.

5. **Type Radio in the Find what box, then click the Replace with box**
   Jim wants to search for entries containing "Radio" and replace them with "KWIN Radio".

6. **Type KWIN Radio in the Replace with box**
   You are about to perform the search and replace option specified. Because you notice that there are other list entries containing the word "radio" with a lowercase "r" (in the Comments column), you need to make sure that only capitalized instances of the word are replaced.

7. **Click the Match case box to select it, then click Find Next**
   Excel moves the cell pointer to the first occurrence of "Radio".

8. **Click Replace All**
   The dialog box closes, and you complete the replacement and check to make sure all references to "Radio" in the Ad Source column now read "KWIN Radio". Note that in the Comments column, each instance of the word "radio" remains unchanged.

9. **Make sure there are no entries in the Ad Source column that read "Radio", then save the workbook**

FIGURE H-7: Criteria data form

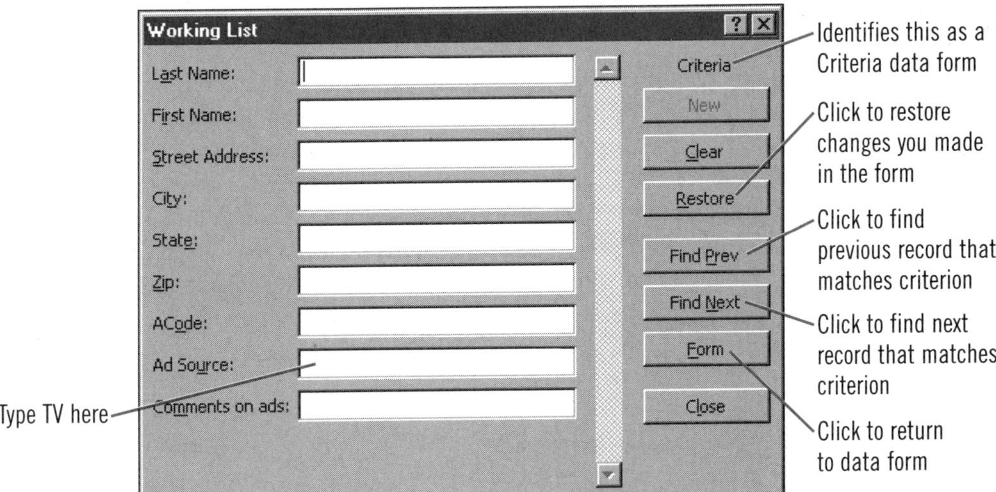

FIGURE H-8: Finding a record using the data form

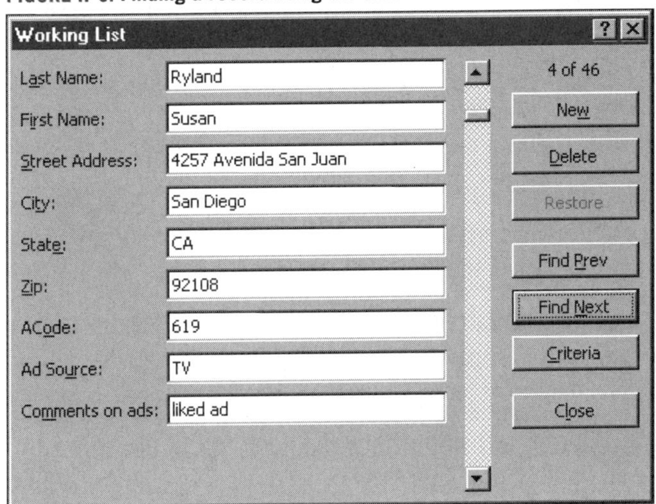

FIGURE H-9: Replace dialog box

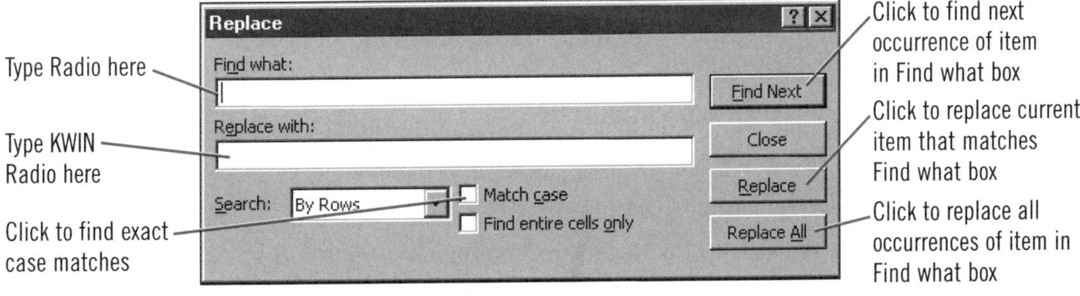

CLUES TO USE

Using wildcards to fine-tune your search

You can use special symbols called **wildcards** when defining search criteria in the data form or Replace dialog box. The question mark (?) wildcard stands for any single character. For example, if you do not know whether a customer's last name is Paulsen or Paulson, you can specify Pauls?n as the search criteria to locate both options. The asterisk (*) wildcard stands for any group of characters. For example, if you specify Jan* as the search criteria in the First Name field, Excel locates all records with first names beginning with Jan (for instance, Jan, Janet, Janice, and so forth).

Excel 2000

Deleting Records

You need to keep your list up to date by removing obsolete records. One way to remove records is to use the Delete button on the data form. You can also delete all records that meet certain criteria—that is, records that have something in common. For example, you can specify a criterion for Excel to find the next record containing Zip code 01879, then remove the record using the Delete button. If specifying one criterion does not meet your needs, you can set multiple criteria. After he notices two entries for Carolyn Smith, Jim wants to check the database for additional duplicate entries. He uses the data form to delete the duplicate record.

Steps

1. Click **Data** on the menu bar, click **Form**, then click **Criteria**
   The Criteria data form appears.

> **QuickTip**
> You can use the data form to edit records as well as to add, search for, and delete them. Just find the desired record and edit the data directly in the appropriate box.

2. Type **Smith** in the **Last Name box**, click the **First Name box**, type **Carolyn**, then click **Find Next**
   Excel displays the first record for a customer whose name is Carolyn Smith. You decide to leave the initial entry for Carolyn Smith (record 5 of 46) and delete the second one, once you confirm it is a duplicate.

3. Click **Find Next**
   The duplicate record for Carolyn Smith, number 40, appears as shown in Figure H-10. You are ready to delete the duplicate entry.

> **QuickTip**
> Clicking Restore on the data form will not restore deleted record(s).

4. Click **Delete**, then click **OK** to confirm the deletion
   The duplicate record for Carolyn Smith is deleted, and all the other records move up one row. The data form now shows the record for Manuel Julio.

5. Click **Close** to return to the worksheet, scroll down until rows 41-46 are visible, then read the entry in row 41
   Notice that the duplicate entry for Carolyn Smith is gone and that Manuel Julio moved up a row and is now in row 41. You also notice a record for K. C. Splint in row 43, which is a duplicate entry.

6. Return to cell A1, and read the record information for K. C. Splint in row 8
   After confirming the duplicate entry, you decide to delete the row.

7. Click cell **A8**, click **Edit** on the menu bar, then click **Delete**
   The Delete dialog box opens, as shown in Figure H-11.

> **QuickTip**
> You can also delete selected cells in a row. Highlight the cells to delete, choose Delete from the Edit menu, and, in the dialog box, indicate if the remaining cells should move up or to the left to replace the selection. Use this command with caution in lists, since with lists you usually delete an entire row.

8. Click the **Entire row option button**, then click **OK**
   You have deleted the entire row. The duplicate record for K. C. Splint is deleted and the other records move up to fill in the gap.

9. Save the workbook
   Recall that you can delete a range name by following these steps: click Insert on the menu bar, point to Name, click Define, highlight the range name, and click delete.

FIGURE H-10: Data form showing duplicate record for Carolyn Smith

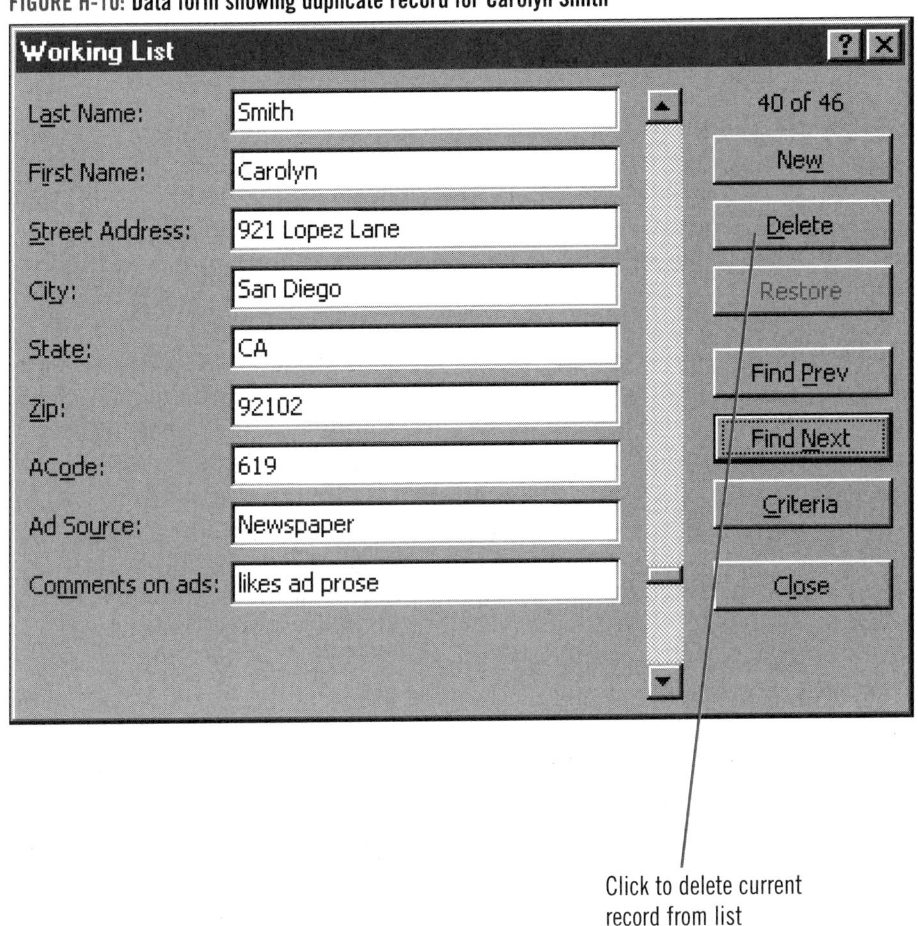

FIGURE H-11: Delete dialog box

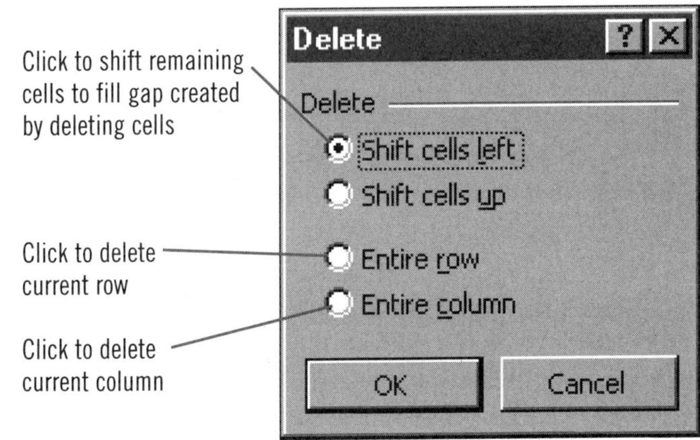

Advantage of deleting records from the worksheet

When you delete a record using the data form, you cannot undo your deletion. When you delete a record by deleting the row in which it resides inside the worksheet area, however, you can immediately restore the record by using the Undo command on the Edit menu, using the Undo button, or pressing [Ctrl][Z].

Excel 2000

Excel 2000

Sorting a List by One Field

Usually, you enter records in the order in which they are received, rather than in alphabetical or numerical order. When you add records to a list using the data form, the records are added to the end of the list. Using the Excel sorting feature, you can rearrange the order of the records. You can use the sort buttons on the Standard toolbar to sort records by one field, or you can use the Sort command on the Data menu to perform more complicated sorts. Alternatively, you can sort an entire list or any portion of a list, or you can arrange sorted information in ascending or descending order. In ascending order, the lowest value (the beginning of the alphabet, for instance, or the earliest date) appears at the top of the list. In a field containing labels and numbers, numbers come first. In descending order, the highest value (the end of the alphabet or the latest date) appears at the top of the list. In a field containing labels and numbers, labels come first. Table H-3 provides examples of ascending and descending sorts. Because Jim wants to be able to return the records to their original order following any sorts, he begins by creating a new field called Entry Order. Then he will perform several single field sorts on the list.

QuickTip

Before you sort records, it is a good idea to make a backup copy of your list or create a field that numbers the records so you can return them to their original order, if necessary.

Trouble?

If your sort does not perform as intended, press [Ctrl][Z] immediately to undo the sort and repeat the step.

1. **Enter the text and format in cell J1 shown in Figure H-12, then AutoFit column J**

2. **Type 1 in cell J2, press [Enter], type 2 in cell J3, press [Enter], select cells J2:J3, drag the fill handle to cell J45**

   With the Entry Order column complete, as shown in Figure H-12, you are ready to sort the list in ascending order by last name. You must position the cell pointer within the column you want to sort prior to issuing the sort command.

3. **Return to cell A1, then click the Sort Ascending button on the Standard toolbar**

   Excel instantly rearranges the records in ascending order by last name, as shown in Figure H-13. You can easily sort the list in descending order by any field.

4. **Click cell G1, then click the Sort Descending button on the Standard toolbar**

   Excel sorts the list, placing those records with higher-digit area codes at the top. Jim wants to update the list range to include original entry order.

5. **Select the range A1:J45, click the name box, type Database, then press [Enter]**

   You are now ready to return the list to original entry order.

6. **Click cell J1, click the Sort Ascending button on the Standard toolbar, then save the workbook**

   The list is back to its original order, and the workbook is saved.

TABLE H-3: Sort order options and examples

option	alphabetic	numeric	date	alphanumeric
Ascending	A, B, C	7, 8, 9	1/1, 2/1, 3/1	12A, 99B, DX8, QT7
Descending	C, B, A	9, 8, 7	3/1, 2/1, 1/1	QT7, DX8, 99B, 12A

FIGURE H-12: List with Entry Order field added

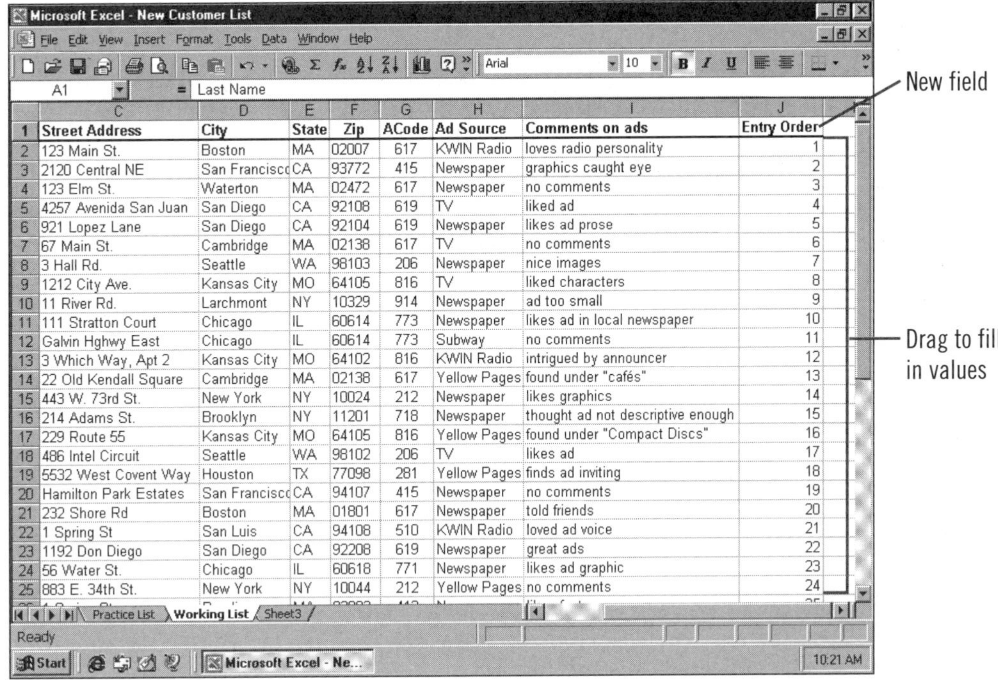

	Street Address	City	State	Zip	ACode	Ad Source	Comments on ads	Entry Order
2	123 Main St.	Boston	MA	02007	617	KWIN Radio	loves radio personality	1
3	2120 Central NE	San Francisc	CA	93772	415	Newspaper	graphics caught eye	2
4	123 Elm St.	Waterton	MA	02472	617	Newspaper	no comments	3
5	4257 Avenida San Juan	San Diego	CA	92108	619	TV	liked ad	4
6	921 Lopez Lane	San Diego	CA	92104	619	Newspaper	likes ad prose	5
7	67 Main St.	Cambridge	MA	02138	617	TV	no comments	6
8	3 Hall Rd.	Seattle	WA	98103	206	Newspaper	nice images	7
9	1212 City Ave.	Kansas City	MO	64105	816	TV	liked characters	8
10	11 River Rd.	Larchmont	NY	10329	914	Newspaper	ad too small	9
11	111 Stratton Court	Chicago	IL	60614	773	Newspaper	likes ad in local newspaper	10
12	Galvin Hghwy East	Chicago	IL	60614	773	Subway	no comments	11
13	3 Which Way, Apt 2	Kansas City	MO	64102	816	KWIN Radio	intrigued by announcer	12
14	22 Old Kendall Square	Cambridge	MA	02138	617	Yellow Pages	found under "cafés"	13
15	443 W. 73rd St.	New York	NY	10024	212	Newspaper	likes graphics	14
16	214 Adams St.	Brooklyn	NY	11201	718	Newspaper	thought ad not descriptive enough	15
17	229 Route 55	Kansas City	MO	64105	816	Yellow Pages	found under "Compact Discs"	16
18	486 Intel Circuit	Seattle	WA	98102	206	TV	likes ad	17
19	5532 West Covent Way	Houston	TX	77098	281	Yellow Pages	finds ad inviting	18
20	Hamilton Park Estates	San Francisc	CA	94107	415	Newspaper	no comments	19
21	232 Shore Rd	Boston	MA	01801	617	Newspaper	told friends	20
22	1 Spring St	San Luis	CA	94108	510	KWIN Radio	loved ad voice	21
23	1192 Don Diego	San Diego	CA	92208	619	Newspaper	great ads	22
24	56 Water St.	Chicago	IL	60618	771	Newspaper	likes ad graphic	23
25	883 E. 34th St.	New York	NY	10044	212	Yellow Pages	no comments	24

FIGURE H-13: List sorted alphabetically by Last Name

	Last Name	First Name	Street Address	City	State	Zip	ACode	Ad Source	Comments on ads
2	Alderson	Bert	12 East Shore Blvd.	White Plains	NY	10288	914	Newspaper	told friends to read
3	Ballard	Adelia	3 Hall Rd.	Seattle	WA	98103	206	Newspaper	nice images
4	Black	John	11 River Rd.	Larchmont	NY	10329	914	Newspaper	ad too small
5	Carter	Yvonne	900 Cam. del Monte Sol	San Diego	CA	92106	619	Newspaper	likes description of product
6	Chavez	Jeffrey	1110 October Way	San Diego	CA	92208	619	TV	interesting ad
7	Dewey	Evan	823 Northside Heights	Houston	TX	77092	281	Newspaper	great ads
8	Dickenson	Tonia	883 E. 34th St.	New York	NY	10044	212	Yellow Pages	no comments
9	Dobbins	Camilla	486 Intel Circuit	Seattle	WA	98102	206	TV	likes ad
10	Duran	Maria	Galvin Hghwy East	Chicago	IL	60614	773	Subway	no comments
11	Fried	Martha	Hamilton Park Estates	San Francisc	CA	94107	415	Newspaper	no comments
12	Gonzales	Fred	5532 West Covent Way	Houston	TX	77098	281	Yellow Pages	finds ad inviting
13	Graham	Shelley	989 26th Street	Chicago	IL	60611	773	Yellow Pages	great store description
14	Green	Latrell	343 3rd Avenue	Brooklyn	NY	11201	718	TV	likes audio track
15	Hesh	Gayle	1192 Don Diego	San Diego	CA	92208	619	Newspaper	great ads
16	Ichikawa	Pam	232 Shore Rd	Boston	MA	01801	617	Newspaper	told friends
17	Janis	Steve	402 9th Street	Seattle	WA	98100	206	Newspaper	found in Restaurant Sectior
18	Julio	Manuel	544 Cameo Place	Belmont	MA	02483	617	Newspaper	no comments
19	Kane	Peter	67 Main St.	Cambridge	MA	02138	617	TV	no comments
20	Kelly	Shawn	22 Old Kendall Square	Cambridge	MA	02138	617	Yellow Pages	found under "cafés"
21	Khalsa	Pip	1100 Vista Road	Santa Fe	NM	87505	505	Newspaper	found in Entertainment sect
22	Kim	Pearlie	9 First St.	San Francisc	CA	94177	415	Newspaper	great ads
23	Lee	Ginny	3 Which Way, Apt 2	Kansas City	MO	64102	816	KWIN Radio	intrigued by announcer
24	Lopez	Luis	1212 City Ave.	Kansas City	MO	64105	816	TV	liked characters
25	Majors	Kendra	1 Spring St	San Luis	CA	94108	510	KWIN Radio	loved ad voice

Excel 2000

Rotating and indenting to improve label appearance

The column label you added in cell J1 is considerably wider than the data in the column. In cases like this, you can adjust the format of any label or value: Select the cell, click Format on the menu bar, click Cells, and on the Alignment tab drag the red diamond under Orientation to 90 degrees. You can also add space to the left of any label or value by selecting the cells(s) and clicking the Increase Indent button on the Formatting toolbar.

Excel 2000

Sorting a List by Multiple Fields

You can sort lists by as many as three fields by specifying **sort keys**, the criteria on which the sort is based. To perform sorts on multiple fields, you must use the Sort dialog box, which you access through the Sort command on the Data menu. Jim wants to sort the records alphabetically by state first, then within the state by Zip code.

Steps

QuickTip

You can specify a capitalization sort by clicking Options in the Sort dialog box, then clicking the Case sensitive box. When you choose this option, lowercase entries precede uppercase entries.

1. Click the **name box list arrow**, then click **Database**
   The list is selected. To sort the list by more than one field, you will need to use the Sort command on the Data menu.
2. Click **Data** on the menu bar, then click **Sort**
   The Sort dialog box opens, as shown in Figure H-14. You want to sort the list by state and then by Zip code.
3. Click the **Sort by** list arrow, click **State**, then click the **Ascending option button** to select it, if necessary
   The list will be sorted alphabetically in ascending order (A-Z) by the State field. A second sort criterion will sort the entries within each state grouping.
4. Click the top **Then by list arrow**, click **Zip**, then click the **Descending option button**
   You also could sort by a third key by selecting a field in the bottom Then by list box.
5. Click **OK** to execute the sort, press **[Ctrl][Home]**, then scroll through the list to see the result of the sort
   The list is sorted alphabetically by state in ascending order, then within each state by Zip code in descending order. Compare your results with Figure H-15.
6. Return to cell A1, then save the workbook

FIGURE H-14: Sort dialog box

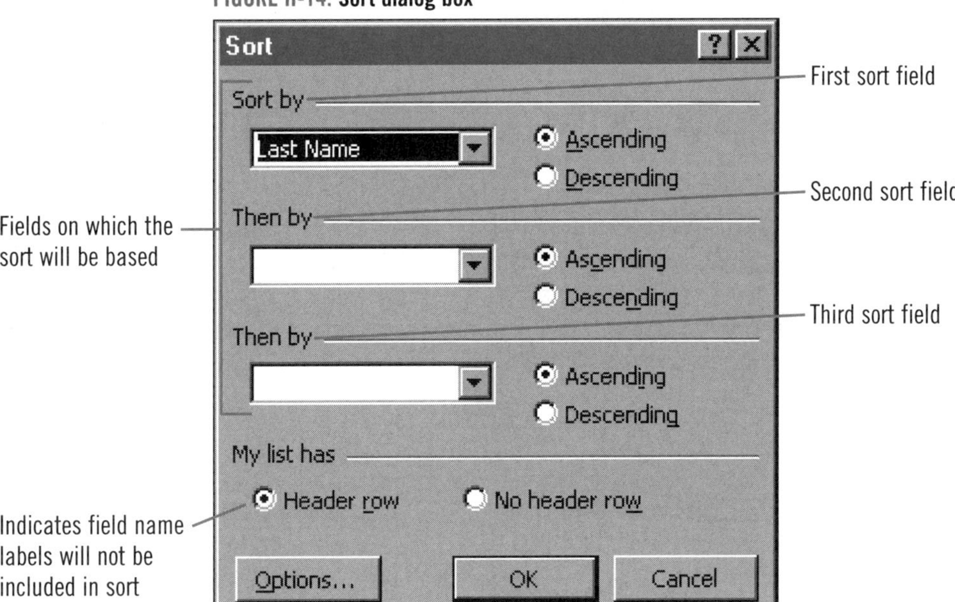

FIGURE H-15: List sorted by multiple fields

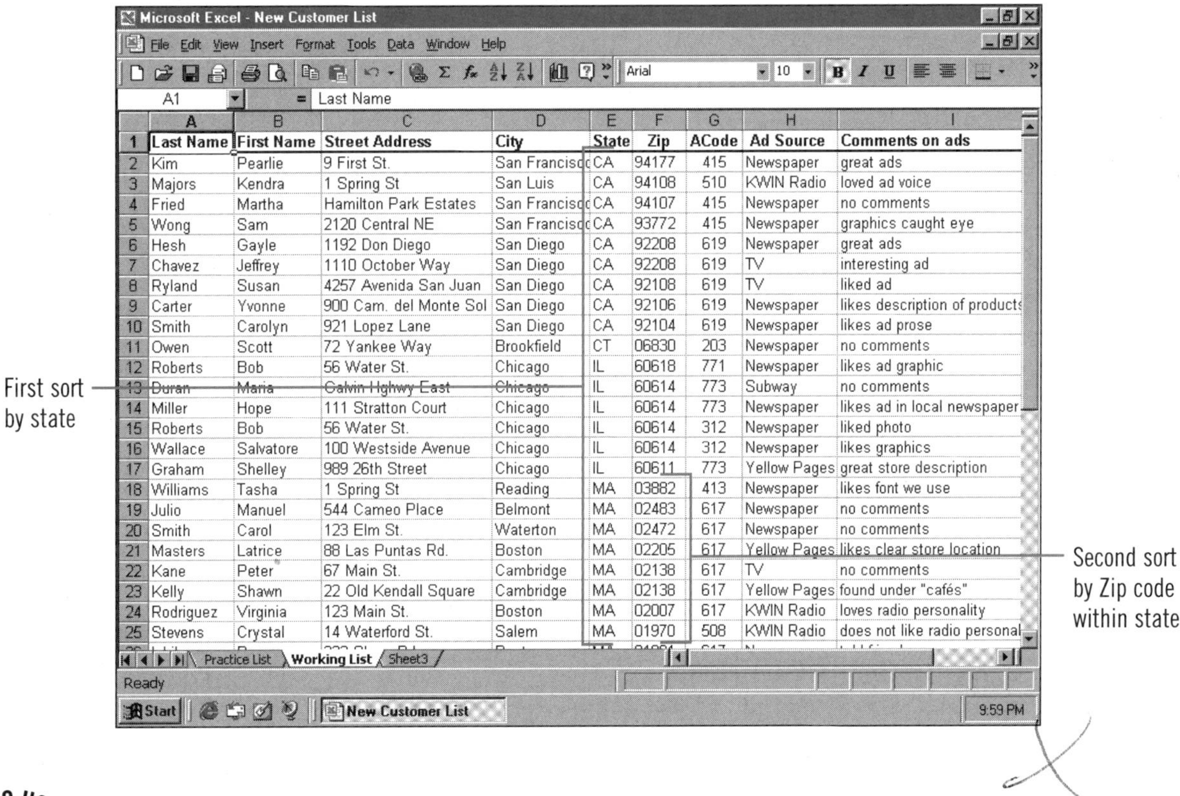

Specifying a custom sort order

CLUES TO USE

You can identify a custom sort order for the field selected in the Sort by box. To do this, click Options in the Sort dialog box, click the First key sort order list arrow, then click the desired custom order. Commonly used custom sort orders are days of the week (Mon, Tues, Wed, etc.) and months (Jan, Feb, Mar, etc.); alphabetic sorts do not sort these items properly.

Excel 2000

Printing a List

If a list is small enough to fit on one page, you can print it as you would any other Excel worksheet. If you have more columns than can fit on a portrait-oriented page, try setting the page orientation to landscape. Because lists often have more rows than can fit on a page, you can define the first row of the list (containing the field names) as the **print title**, which prints at the top of every page. Most lists do not have any descriptive information above the field names on the worksheet. To augment the information contained in the field names, you can use headers and footers to add identifying text, such as the list title or report date. If you want to exclude any fields from your list report, you can hide the desired columns from view so that they do not print. Jim has finished updating his list and is ready to print it. He begins by previewing the list.

1. Click the **Print Preview button** on the Standard toolbar
   Notice that the status bar reads Page 1 of 2. You want all the fields in the list to fit on a single page, but you'll need two pages to fit all the data. The landscape page orientation and the Fit to options will help you do this.

QuickTip

You can print multiple ranges at the same time by clicking the Print area box in the Sheet tab. Then drag to the select areas you wish to print.

2. From the Print Preview window, click **Setup**, click the **Page tab**, click the **Landscape option button** under Orientation, click the **Fit to option button** under Scaling, double-click the **tall box** and type **2**, click **OK**, then click **Next**
   The list still does not fit on a single page. Because the records on page 2 appear without column headings, you want to set up the first row of the list, containing the field names, as a repeating print title.

QuickTip

You can also use the sheet tab to specify whether you want gridlines, high or low print quality, and row and column headings.

3. Click **Close** to exit the Print Preview window, click **File** on the menu bar, click **Page Setup**, click the **Sheet tab**, click the **Rows to repeat at top box** under Print titles, click any cell in row 1, then click OK
   When you select row 1 as a print title, Excel automatically inserts an absolute reference to a beginning row to repeat at the top of each page—in this case, the print title to repeat beginning and ending with row 1. See Figure H-16.
4. Click **Print Preview**, click **Next** to view the second page, then click **Zoom**
   Setting up a print title to repeat row 1 causes the field names to appear at the top of each printed page. You can use the worksheet header to provide information about the list.
5. Click **Setup**, click the **Header/Footer tab**, click **Custom Header**, click the **Left section box** and type your name, then click the **Center section box** and type **MediaLoft–New Customer List**
6. Select the header text in the Center section box, click the **Font button**, change the font size to **14** and the style to **Bold**, click **OK**, click **OK** again to return to the Header/Footer tab, then click **OK** to preview the list
   Page 2 of the report appears as shown in Figure H-17.

QuickTip

To print a selected area instead of the entire worksheet, select the area, click File, click Print, and, under Print what, click Selection.

7. Click **Print** to print the worksheet, then save and close the workbook
   To print more than one worksheet, select each sheet tab while holding down the [Shift] or [Ctrl] keys, then click the print button on the standard toolbar.

FIGURE H-16: Sheet tab of the Page Setup dialog box

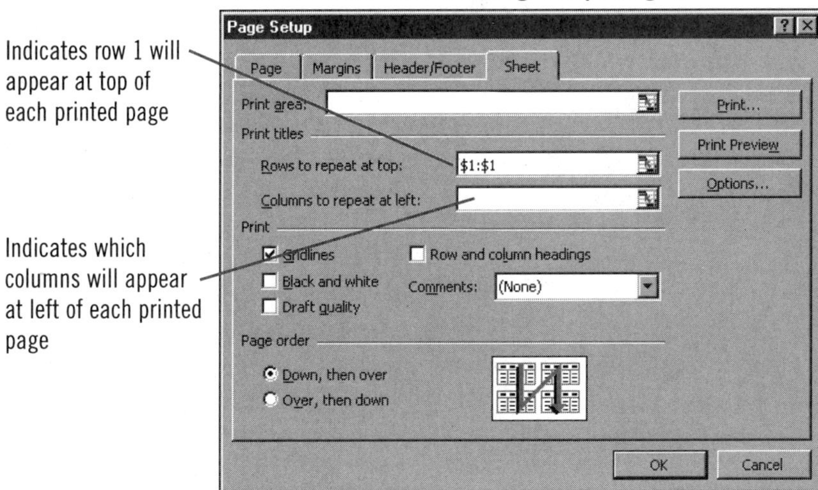

FIGURE H-17: Print Preview window showing page 2 of completed report

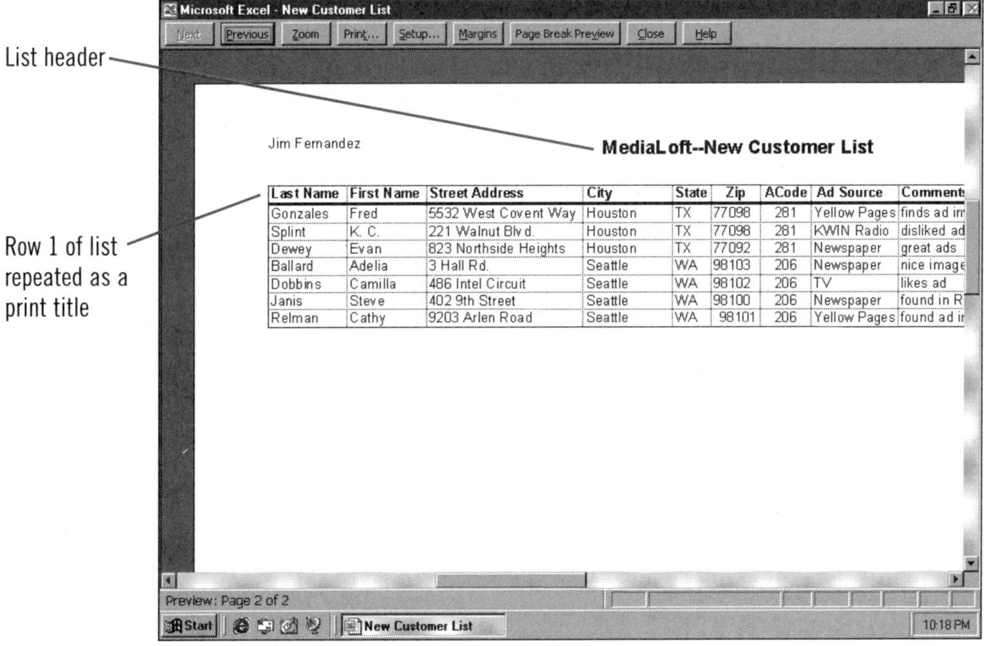

Setting a print area

There are times when you want to print only part of a worksheet. You can do this in the Print dialog box by choosing Selection under Print what. But if you want to print a selected area repeatedly, it's best to define a **print area,** which will print when you click the Print button on the Standard toolbar. To set a print area, click View on the menu bar, then click Page Break Preview. In the preview window, select the area you want to print. Right-click the area, then select Set Print Area. The print area becomes outlined in a blue border. You can drag the border to extend the print area (see Figure H-18) or add nonadjacent cells to it by selecting them, right-clicking them, then selecting Add to Print Area. To clear a print area, click File on the menu bar, point to Print Area, then click Clear Print Area.

FIGURE H-18: Defined print area

Excel 2000

Practice

► Concepts Review

Label each of the elements of the Excel screen shown in Figure H-19.

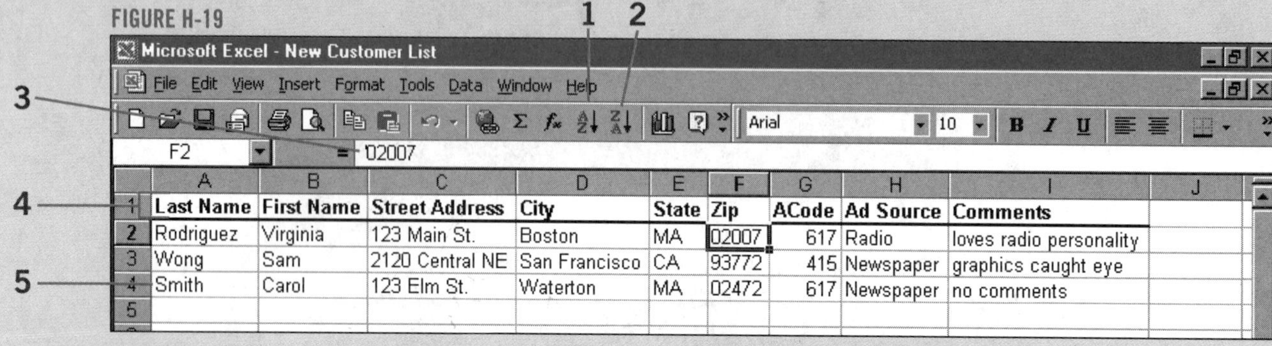

FIGURE H-19

Match each term with the statement that best describes it.

6. **List** b
7. **Record** C
8. **Database** d
9. **Sort** A
10. **Field name** e

a. Arrange records in a particular sequence
b. Organized collection of related information in Excel
c. Row in an Excel list
d. Type of software used for lists containing more than 65,536 records
e. Label positioned at the top of the column identifying data for that field

Select the best answer from the list of choices.

11. Which of the following Excel sorting options do you use to sort a list of employee names in A-to-Z order?

a. Ascending
b. Absolute
c. Alphabetic
d. Descending

12. Which of the following series is in descending order?

a. 4, 5, 6, A, B, C
b. C, B, A, 6, 5, 4
c. 8, 7, 6, 5, 6, 7
d. 8, 6, 4, C, B, A

13. Once the __________ is defined, any new records added to the list using the data form are included in the __________.

a. database, database
b. data form, data form
c. worksheet, worksheet
d. list range, list range

14. When printing a list on multiple pages, you can define a print title containing repeating row(s) to

a. Include appropriate fields in the printout.
b. Include field names at the top of each printed page.
c. Include the header in list reports.
d. Exclude from the printout all rows under the first row.

Skills Review

1. Create a list.

a. Create a new workbook, then save it as "MediaLoft New York Employee List".
b. In cell A1, type the title "MediaLoft New York Employees".
c. Enter the field names and records using the information in Table H-4.
d. Apply bold formatting to the field names.
e. Center the entries in the Years, Full/Part Time, and Training? fields.
f. Adjust the column widths to make the data readable.
g. Save, then print the list.

TABLE H-4

Last Name	First Name	Years	Position	Full/Part Time	Training?
Lustig	Sarah	3	Book Sales	F	Y
Marino	Donato	2	CD Sales	P	N
Khederian	Jay	4	Video Sales	F	Y
Finney	Carol	1	Stock	F	N
Rabinowicz	Miriam	2	Café Sales	P	Y

2. Add records with the data form.
   a. Select all the records in the list, including the field names, then define the range as "Database".
   b. Open the data form and add a new record for David Gitano, a one-year employee in Book Sales. David is full time and has not completed the training.
   c. Add a new record for George Worley, the café manager. George is full time, has worked there two years, and he has completed the training.
   d. Save the list.

3. Find and delete records.
   a. Find the record for Carol Finney.
   b. Delete the record.
   c. Save the list.

4. Sort a list by one field.
   a. Select the Database list range.
   b. Sort the list alphabetically in ascending order by last name.
   c. Save the list.

5. Sort a list by multiple fields.
   a. Select the Database list range.
   b. Sort the list alphabetically in ascending order, first by whether or not the employees have completed training and then by last name.
   c. Save the list.

6. Print a list.
   a. Add a header that reads "Employee Information" in the center and that includes your name on the right; format both header items in bold.
   b. Set the print area to include the range A1:F9.
   c. Delete the database range.
   d. Print the list, then save and close the workbook.
   e. Exit Excel.

► Independent Challenges

1. Your advertising firm, Personalize IT, sells specialty items imprinted with the customer's name and/or logo such as hats, pens, and T-shirts. Plan and build a list of information with a minimum of 10 records using the three items sold. Your list should contain at least five different customers. (Some customers will place more than one order.) Each record should contain the customer's name, item(s) sold, and the individual and extended cost of the item(s). Enter your own data and make sure you include at least the following list fields:

- Item—Describe the item.
- Cost-Ea.—What is the item's individual cost?
- Quantity—How many items did the customer purchase?
- Ext. Cost—What is the total purchase price?
- Customer—Who purchased the item?

To complete this independent challenge:

a. Prepare a list plan that states your goal, outlines the data you'll need, and identifies the list elements.
b. Sketch a sample list on a piece of paper, indicating how the list should be built. What information should go in the columns? In the rows? Which of the data fields will be formatted as labels? As values?
c. Build the list first by entering the field names, then by entering the records. Remember, you will invent your own data. Save the workbook as "Personalize IT".
d. Reformat the list, as needed. For example, you might need to adjust the column widths to make the data more readable. Also, remember to check your spelling.
e. Sort the list in ascending order by item, then by Customer, then by Quantity.
f. Select only the cells with data in the last row. Use the Delete command on the Edit menu to delete those cells, moving the existing cells up to fill the space.
g. Type your name in a blank cell and review the worksheet; adjust any items as needed; then print a copy.
h. Save your work before closing.

2. You are taking a class titled "Television Shows: Past and Present" at a local community college. The instructor has provided you with an Excel list of television programs from the '60s and '70s. She has included fields tracking the following information: the number of years the show was a favorite, favorite character, least favorite character, the show's length in minutes, the show's biggest star, and comments about the show. The instructor has included data for each show in the list. She has asked you to add a field (column label) and two records (shows of your choosing) to the list. Because the list should cover only 30-minute shows, you need to delete any records for shows longer than 30 minutes. Also, your instructor wants you to sort the list by show name and format the list as needed prior to printing. Feel free to change any of the list data to suit your tastes and opinions.

To complete this independent challenge:

a. Open the workbook titled EX H-2, then save it as "Television Shows of the Past".
b. Using your own data, add a field, then use the data form to add two records to the list. Make sure to enter information in every field.
c. Delete any records having show lengths other than 30. (*Hint*: Use the Criteria data form to set the criteria, then find and delete any matching records.)
d. Make any formatting changes to the list as needed and save the list.
e. Sort the list in ascending order by show name.
f. Preview, then print the list. Adjust any items as needed so that the list can be printed on a single page.
g. Sort the list again, this time in descending order by number of years the show was a favorite.
h. Change the header to read "Television Shows of the Past: '60s and '70s".
i. Type your name in a blank cell, then preview and print the list.
j. Save the workbook.

3. You work as a sales clerk at Nite Owl Video. Your roommate and co-worker, Albert Lee, has put together a list of his favorite movie actors and actresses. He has asked you to add several names to the list so he can determine which artists and what kinds of films you enjoy most. He has recorded information in the following fields: artist's first and last name, life span, birthplace, the genre or type of role the artist plays most (for example, dramatic or comedic), the name of a film for which the artist has received or been nominated for an Academy Award, and, finally, two additional films featuring the artist. Using your own data, add at least two artists known for dramatic roles and two artists known for comedic roles.

To complete this independent challenge:

a. Open the workbook titled EX H-3, then add at least four records using the criteria mentioned above. Remember, you are creating and entering your own movie data for all relevant fields.
b. Save the workbook as "Film Star Favorites". Make formatting changes to the list as needed. Remember to check your spelling.
c. Sort the list alphabetically by Genre. Perform a second sort by Last Name.
d. Preview the list, adjust any items as needed, then print a copy of the list sorted by Genre and Last Name.
e. Sort the list again, this time in descending order by the Life Span field, then by Last Name.
f. Enter your name in a blank cell, then print a copy of the list sorted by Life Span and Last Name.
g. Save your work.

4. You work at MediaLoft corporate headquarters, and the Products Department has asked you to create a database to keep track of all CD products that win the People's Choice poll. The poll is new and will be conducted monthly.

To complete this independent challenge:

a. Start Excel, and create a new file with the following list headings: Artist LN, Artist FN, Title, Category, and In Stock, and save the file as "People's Choice". Format the title row with formats of your choice.
b. Connect to the Internet, and go to the MediaLoft intranet site at http://www.course.com/Illustrated/MediaLoft. Click the Products link, and print the page, which contains a table entitled "Results of People's Choice Poll". Disconnect from the Internet.
c. Use the information from the table to create the first six records of your list. For the In Stock column, show the first three products as in stock (Y) and the second three as not in stock (N). AutoFit the columns and save the file.
d. Open the file EX H-4, copy the records, and paste them into your database.
e. Find the CD by Jim Brickman.
f. Find the CD with the title "Mellow".
g. Use the Replace command to find all the records in the Rock category and change the category name to Rock N Roll. Adjust the column widths as necessary.
h. Sort the list by category.
i. Add a new field for Month, indicating the month each recording won the award. Assign a month (January, February, or March) to each winner so that each category has one winner per month.
j. Sort the list by month.
k. Sort the list by category and the artist's last name.
l. Sort by stock status, category, and the artist's last name.
m. Print the list, then save and close the file.

► Visual Workshop

Create the worksheet shown in Figure H-20. Save the workbook as "Famous Jazz Performers". Once you've entered the field names and records, sort the list by Contribution to Jazz and then by Last Name. Change the page setup so that the list is centered on the page horizontally and the header reads "Famous Jazz Performers". Preview and print the list, then save the workbook.

FIGURE H-20

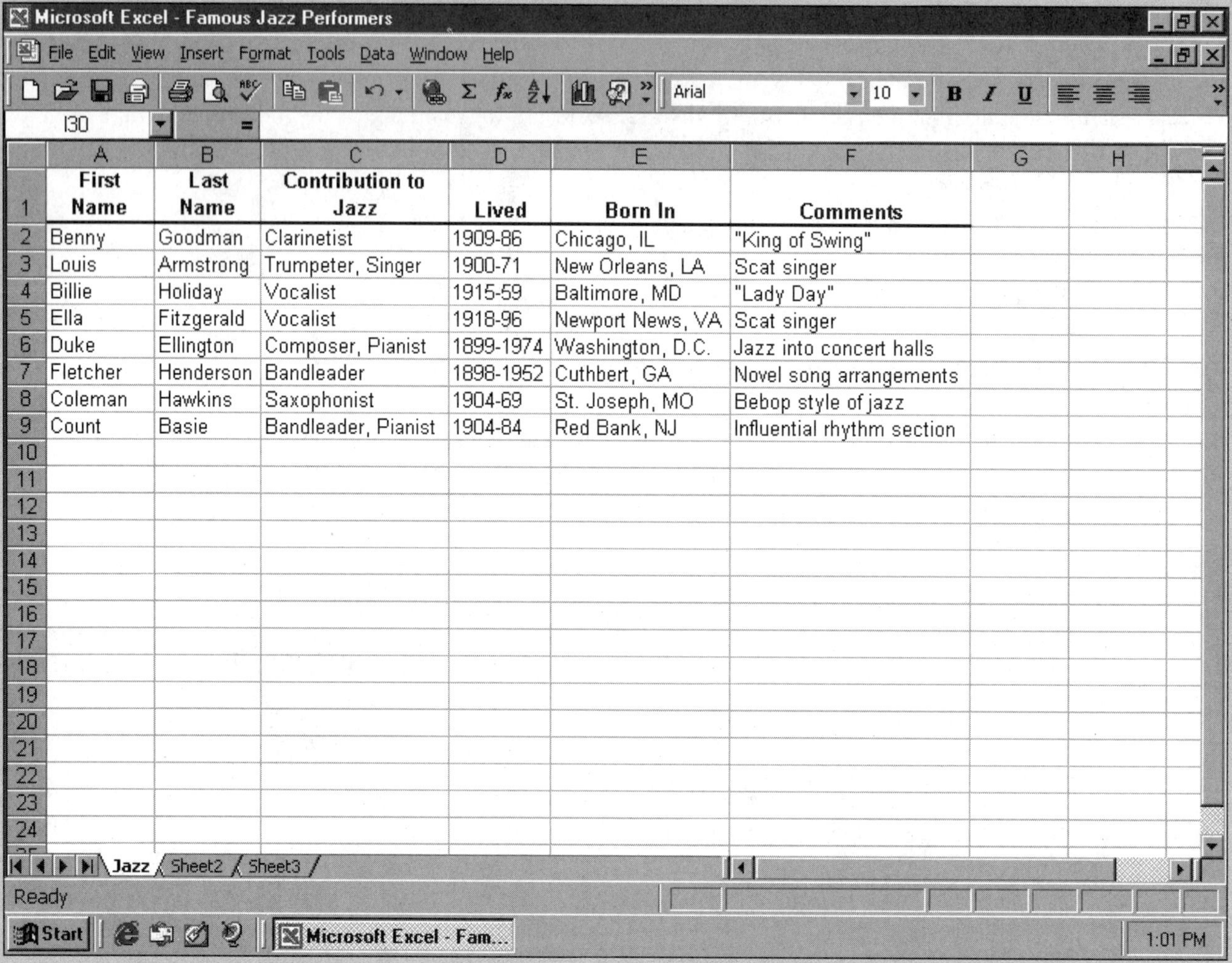

Microsoft Excel - Famous Jazz Performers

	A	B	C	D	E	F
1	**First Name**	**Last Name**	**Contribution to Jazz**	**Lived**	**Born In**	**Comments**
2	Benny	Goodman	Clarinetist	1909-86	Chicago, IL	"King of Swing"
3	Louis	Armstrong	Trumpeter, Singer	1900-71	New Orleans, LA	Scat singer
4	Billie	Holiday	Vocalist	1915-59	Baltimore, MD	"Lady Day"
5	Ella	Fitzgerald	Vocalist	1918-96	Newport News, VA	Scat singer
6	Duke	Ellington	Composer, Pianist	1899-1974	Washington, D.C.	Jazz into concert halls
7	Fletcher	Henderson	Bandleader	1898-1952	Cuthbert, GA	Novel song arrangements
8	Coleman	Hawkins	Saxophonist	1904-69	St. Joseph, MO	Bebop style of jazz
9	Count	Basie	Bandleader, Pianist	1904-84	Red Bank, NJ	Influential rhythm section

Excel 2000

Unit I

Analyzing
List Data

Objectives

- MOUS ▶ Retrieve records with AutoFilter
- MOUS ▶ Create a custom filter
- MOUS ▶ Filter a list with Advanced Filter
- MOUS ▶ Extract list data
- MOUS ▶ Create subtotals using grouping and outlines
- MOUS ▶ Look up values in a list
- MOUS ▶ Summarize list data
- MOUS ▶ Use data validation for list entries

There are many ways to **analyze**, or manipulate, list data with Excel. One way is to filter a list so that only the rows that meet certain criteria are retrieved. In this unit you will retrieve records using AutoFilter, create a custom filter, and filter a list using Excel's Advanced Filter feature. In addition, you will learn to insert automatic subtotals, use lookup functions to locate list entries, and apply database functions to summarize list data that meets specific criteria. You'll also learn how to restrict entries in a column using data validation. Jim Fernandez recently conducted a survey for the MediaLoft Marketing department. He mailed questionnaires to a random selection of customers at all stores. After the questionnaires were returned, he entered all the data into Excel, where he will analyze the data and create reports.

Excel 2000

Retrieving Records with AutoFilter

The Excel AutoFilter feature searches for records that meet criteria the user specifies, and then lists those matching records. One way is to **filter** out, or hide, data that fails to meet certain criteria. You can filter specific values in a column, use the predefined Top 10 option to filter records based on upper or lower values in a column, or create a custom filter. For example, you can filter a customer list to retrieve names of only those customers residing in Canada. You also can filter records based on a specific field and request that Excel retrieve only those records having an entry (or no entry) in that field. Once you create a filtered list, you can print it or copy it to another part of the worksheet to manipulate it further. Jim is now ready to work on his survey information. He begins by retrieving data on only those customers who live in Chicago, Illinois.

Steps

QuickTip

To return personalized toolbars and menus to their default state, click Tools on the menu bar, click Customize, click the Options tab in the Customize dialog box, click Reset my usage data to restore the default settings, click Yes, click Close, then close the Drawing toolbar if it is displayed.

1. Open the workbook titled **EX I-1**, then save it as **Survey Data**
   The AutoFilter feature will enable you to retrieve the records for the report.
2. Click **Data** on the menu bar, point to **Filter**, then click **AutoFilter**
   List arrows appear to the right of each field name.
3. Click the **City** list arrow
   An AutoFilter list containing the different city options appears below the field name, as shown in Figure I-1. Because you want to retrieve data for only those customers who live in Chicago, "Chicago" will be your **search criterion.**
4. In the filter list, click **Chicago**
   Only those records containing Chicago in the City field appear, as shown in Figure I-2. The status bar indicates the number of matching records (in this case, 5 of 35), the color of the row numbers changes for the matching records, and the color of the list arrow for the filtered field changes. Next, you want to retrieve information about those customers who purchased the most merchandise. To do so, you must clear the previous filter.
5. Click **Data** on the menu bar, point to **Filter**, then click **Show All**
   All the records reappear.

Trouble?

If the column label in cell A1 covers the column headers, making it difficult to find the appropriate columns, select A2 before scrolling.

6. Scroll right until columns G through N are visible, click the **Purchases to Date** list arrow, then click **(Top 10 . . .)**
   The Top 10 AutoFilter dialog box opens. The default is to select the ten records with the highest value. You need to display only the top 2.
7. With **10** selected in the middle box, type **2**, then click **OK**
   The records are retrieved for the two customers who purchased the most merchandise, $3,200 and $2,530. See Figure I-3.
8. Click the **Purchases to Date** list arrow, click **(All)**, press **[Ctrl][Home]**, add your name to the right side of the footer, then print the list
   You have cleared the filter and all the records reappear. Because you didn't make any changes to the list, there is no need to save the file.

FIGURE I-1: Worksheet showing AutoFilter options

City field

Click Chicago to filter by this city

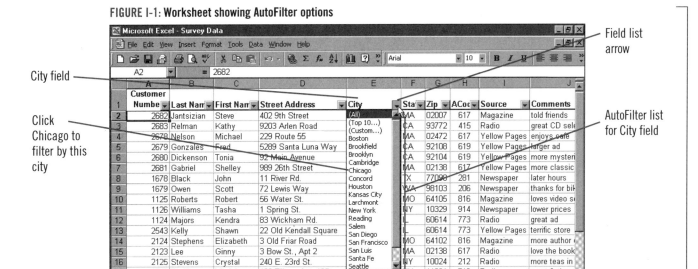

Field list arrow

AutoFilter list for City field

FIGURE I-2: List filtered with AutoFilter

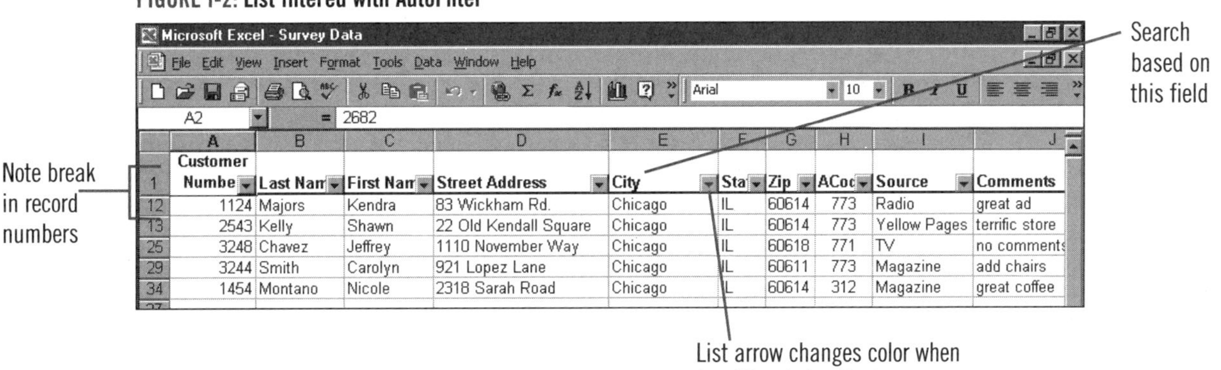

FIGURE I-3: List filtered with Top 2 AutoFilter criteria

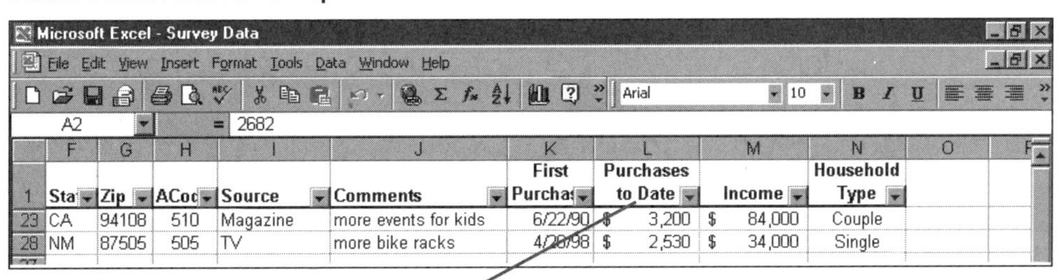

Excel 2000

Creating a Custom Filter

So far, you have used the AutoFilter command to filter rows based on an entry in a single column. You can perform more complex filters using options in the Custom AutoFilter dialog box. For example, you can filter rows based on two entries in a single column or use comparison operators such as "greater than" or "less than" to display only those records with amounts greater than $50,000 in a particular column. Jim's next task is to locate those customers who live west of the Rocky Mountains, who live in a "single" household, and who heard about MediaLoft through a magazine advertisement.

Steps

QuickTip

When specifying criteria in the Custom AutoFilter dialog box, use the ? wildcard to specify any single character and the * wildcard to specify any series of characters.

Trouble?

If no records are displayed in the worksheet, you may have forgotten to type the apostrophe before the number 81000. Repeat Steps 2 and 3, making sure you include the leading apostrophe.

1. Click the **Zip** list arrow, then click **(Custom . . .)**
   The Custom AutoFilter dialog box opens. Because you know that all residents west of the Rockies have a zip code greater than 81000, you specify this criterion here. Because all the zip codes in the list were originally entered as labels with leading apostrophes, you need to include this apostrophe when entering the zip code value.
2. Click the **Zip** list arrow, click **is greater than**, press **[Tab]**, then type **'81000**
   Your completed Custom AutoFilter dialog box should match Figure I-4.
3. Click **OK**
   The dialog box closes, and only those records having a zip code greater than 81000 appear in the worksheet. Now, you'll narrow the list even further by displaying only those customers who live in a single household.
4. Scroll right until columns G through N are visible, click the **Household Type** list arrow, then click **Single**
   The list of records retrieved has narrowed. Finally, you need to filter out all customers except those who heard about MediaLoft through a magazine advertisement.
5. Click the **Source** list arrow, then click **Magazine**
   Your final filtered list now shows only customers in single households west of the Rocky Mountains who heard about MediaLoft through magazine ads. See Figure I-5.
6. Preview, then print the worksheet
   The worksheet prints using the existing print settings—landscape orientation, scaled to fit on a single page.
7. Click **Data** on the menu bar, point to **Filter**, click **AutoFilter** to deselect it, then press **[Ctrl][Home]**
   You have cleared the filter, and all the customer records appear.

FIGURE I-4: Custom AutoFilter dialog box

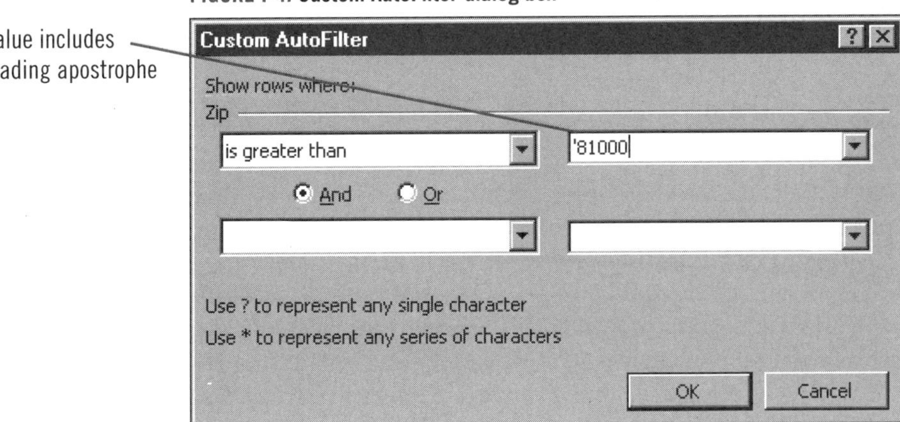

FIGURE I-5: Results of custom filter

	F	G	H	I	J	K	L	M	N	O
1	Sta	Zip	ACod	Source	Comments	First Purchas	Purchases to Date	Income	Household Type	
19	WA	98102	206	Magazine	no comments	6/16/96	$ 895	$ 45,000	Single	
30	WA	98100	206	Magazine	more world music	5/14/93	$ 2,100	$ 63,000	Single	
37										

CLUES TO USE

And and Or logical conditions

You can narrow a search even further by using the And or Or buttons in the Custom AutoFilter dialog box. For example, you can select records for those customers with homes in California *and* Texas as well as select records for customers with homes in California *or* Texas. See Figure I-6. When used in this way, "And" and "Or" are often referred to as logical conditions. When you search for customers with homes in California *and* Texas, you are specifying an And condition. When you search for customers with homes in either California *or* Texas, you are specifying an Or condition.

FIGURE I-6: Using the Custom AutoFilter dialog box

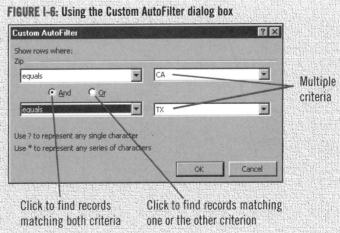

Excel 2000

Filtering a List with Advanced Filter

The Advanced Filter command allows you to search for data that matches complicated criteria in more than one column, using And and Or conditions. To use advanced filtering, you must define a criteria range. A **criteria range** is a cell range containing one row of labels (usually a copy of the column labels) and at least one additional row underneath the row of labels that contains the criteria you want to match. Jim's next task is to identify customers who have been buying at MediaLoft since before May 1, 1999, and whose total purchases are less than or equal to $1,000. He will use the Advanced Filter command to retrieve this data. Jim begins by defining the criteria range.

Steps

1. Select **rows 1 through 6**, click **Insert** on the menu bar, then click **Rows**; click cell **A1**, type **Criteria Range**, click cell **A6**, type **List Range**, then click the **Enter button** on the formula bar
   See Figure I-7. Six blank rows are added above the list. Excel does not require the labels "Criteria Range" and "List Range," but they are useful because they help organize the worksheet. It will be helpful to see the column labels. (In the next step, if the column labels make it difficult for you to drag the pointer to cell N7, try clicking N7 first; then drag the pointer all the way left to cell A7.)

Trouble?

If the Copy button does not appear on your Standard toolbar, click the More Buttons button to view it.

2. Select range **A7:N7**, click the **Copy button** on the Standard toolbar, click cell **A2**, then press **[Enter]**
   Next, you need to specify that you want records for only those customers who have been customers since before May 1 and who have purchased no more than $1,000. In other words, you need records with a date before (less than) May 1, 1999 (<5/1/99) and a Purchases to Date amount that is less than or equal to $1,000 (<=1000).
3. Scroll right until columns H through N are visible, click cell **K3**, type **< 5/1/99**, click cell **L3**, type **<=1000**, then click
   This enters the criteria in the cells directly beneath the Criteria Range labels. See Figure I-8. Placing the criteria in the same row indicates that the records you are searching for must match both criteria; that is, it specifies an And condition.
4. Press **[Ctrl][Home]**, click **Data** on the menu bar, point to **Filter**, then click **Advanced Filter**
   The Advanced Filter dialog box opens, with the list range already entered. (Notice that the default setting under Action is to filter the list in its current location rather than copy it to another location. You will change this setting later.)
5. Click the **Criteria Range box**, select range **A2:N3** in the worksheet (move the dialog box if necessary), then click **OK**
   You have specified the criteria range. The filtered list contains 19 records that match both the criteria—their first purchase was before 5/1/99 and their purchases to date total less than $1,000. You'll filter this list even further in the next lesson.

FIGURE I-7: Using the Advanced Filter command

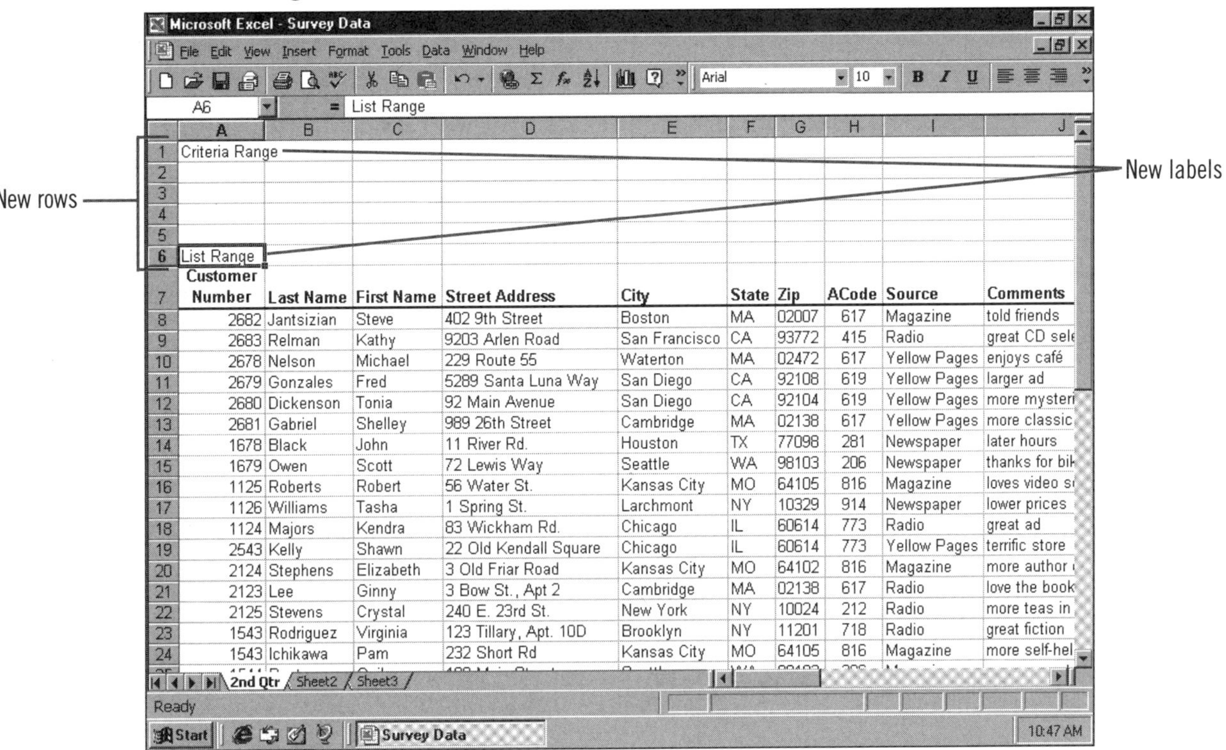

	A	B	C	D	E	F	G	H	I	J
1	Criteria Range									
2										
3										
4										
5										
6	List Range									
7	Customer Number	Last Name	First Name	Street Address	City	State	Zip	ACode	Source	Comments
8	2682	Jantsizian	Steve	402 9th Street	Boston	MA	02007	617	Magazine	told friends
9	2683	Relman	Kathy	9203 Arlen Road	San Francisco	CA	93772	415	Radio	great CD sel
10	2678	Nelson	Michael	229 Route 55	Waterton	MA	02472	617	Yellow Pages	enjoys café
11	2679	Gonzales	Fred	5289 Santa Luna Way	San Diego	CA	92108	619	Yellow Pages	larger ad
12	2680	Dickenson	Tonia	92 Main Avenue	San Diego	CA	92104	619	Yellow Pages	more myster
13	2681	Gabriel	Shelley	989 26th Street	Cambridge	MA	02138	617	Yellow Pages	more classic
14	1678	Black	John	11 River Rd.	Houston	TX	77098	281	Newspaper	later hours
15	1679	Owen	Scott	72 Lewis Way	Seattle	WA	98103	206	Newspaper	thanks for bik
16	1125	Roberts	Robert	56 Water St.	Kansas City	MO	64105	816	Magazine	loves video s
17	1126	Williams	Tasha	1 Spring St.	Larchmont	NY	10329	914	Newspaper	lower prices
18	1124	Majors	Kendra	83 Wickham Rd.	Chicago	IL	60614	773	Radio	great ad
19	2543	Kelly	Shawn	22 Old Kendall Square	Chicago	IL	60614	773	Yellow Pages	terrific store
20	2124	Stephens	Elizabeth	3 Old Friar Road	Kansas City	MO	64102	816	Magazine	more author
21	2123	Lee	Ginny	3 Bow St., Apt 2	Cambridge	MA	02138	617	Radio	love the book
22	2125	Stevens	Crystal	240 E. 23rd St.	New York	NY	10024	212	Radio	more teas in
23	1543	Rodriguez	Virginia	123 Tillary, Apt. 10D	Brooklyn	NY	11201	718	Radio	great fiction
24	1543	Ichikawa	Pam	232 Short Rd	Kansas City	MO	64105	816	Magazine	more self-hel

FIGURE I-8: Criteria in the same row

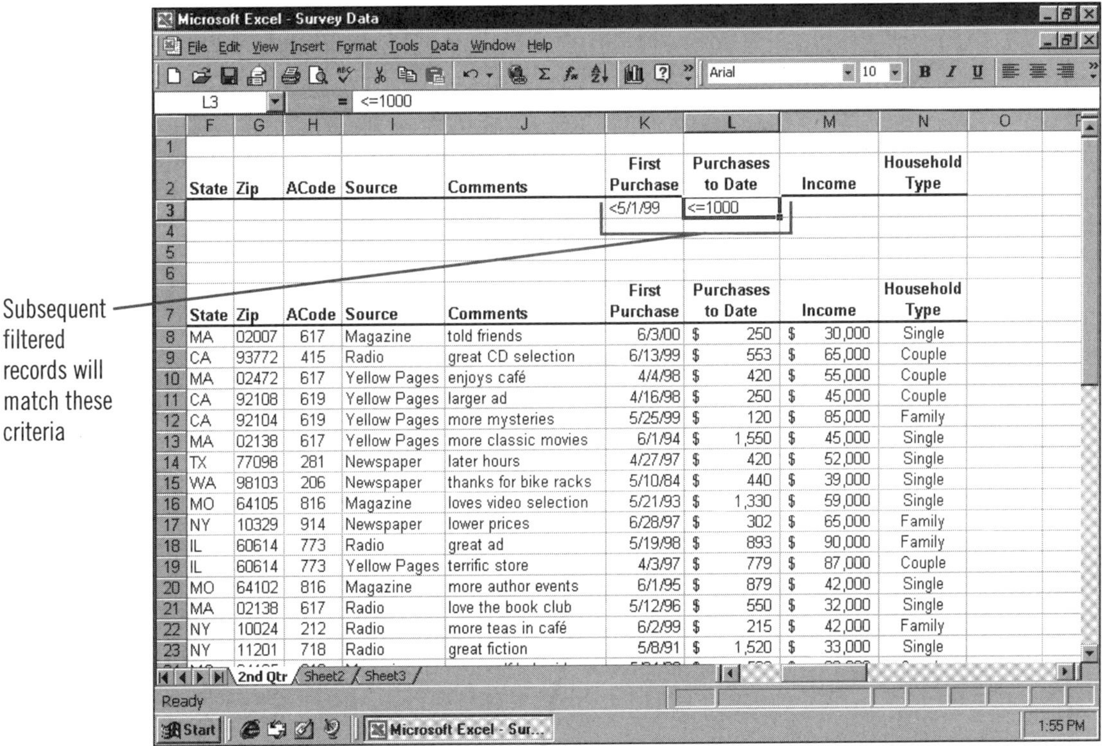

	F	G	H	I	J	K	L	M	N
1									
2	State	Zip	ACode	Source	Comments	First Purchase	Purchases to Date	Income	Household Type
3						<5/1/99	<=1000		
4									
5									
6									
7	State	Zip	ACode	Source	Comments	First Purchase	Purchases to Date	Income	Household Type
8	MA	02007	617	Magazine	told friends	6/3/00	$ 250	$ 30,000	Single
9	CA	93772	415	Radio	great CD selection	6/13/99	$ 553	$ 65,000	Couple
10	MA	02472	617	Yellow Pages	enjoys café	4/4/98	$ 420	$ 55,000	Couple
11	CA	92108	619	Yellow Pages	larger ad	4/16/98	$ 250	$ 45,000	Couple
12	CA	92104	619	Yellow Pages	more mysteries	5/25/99	$ 120	$ 85,000	Family
13	MA	02138	617	Yellow Pages	more classic movies	6/1/94	$ 1,550	$ 45,000	Single
14	TX	77098	281	Newspaper	later hours	4/27/97	$ 420	$ 52,000	Single
15	WA	98103	206	Newspaper	thanks for bike racks	5/10/84	$ 440	$ 39,000	Single
16	MO	64105	816	Magazine	loves video selection	5/21/93	$ 1,330	$ 59,000	Single
17	NY	10329	914	Newspaper	lower prices	6/28/97	$ 302	$ 65,000	Family
18	IL	60614	773	Radio	great ad	5/19/98	$ 893	$ 90,000	Family
19	IL	60614	773	Yellow Pages	terrific store	4/3/97	$ 779	$ 87,000	Couple
20	MO	64102	816	Magazine	more author events	6/1/95	$ 879	$ 42,000	Single
21	MA	02138	617	Radio	love the book club	5/12/96	$ 550	$ 32,000	Single
22	NY	10024	212	Radio	more teas in café	6/2/99	$ 215	$ 42,000	Family
23	NY	11201	718	Radio	great fiction	5/8/91	$ 1,520	$ 33,000	Single

CLUES TO USE

Understanding the criteria range

When you define the criteria range in the Advanced Filter dialog box, Excel automatically creates a name for this range in the worksheet (Criteria). The criteria range includes the field names and any criteria rows underneath the names.

Excel 2000

Extracting List Data

Whenever you take the time to specify a complicated set of search criteria, it's a good idea to extract the matching records. When you **extract** data, you place a copy of a filtered list in a range you specify in the Advanced Filter dialog box. That way, you won't accidentally clear the filter or lose track of the records you spent time compiling. Jim needs to filter the previous list one step further to reflect only those customers in the current filtered list who heard of MediaLoft through TV or a magazine ad. To complete this filter, he will specify an Or condition by entering two sets of criteria in two separate rows. He decides to save the matching records by extracting them to a different location in the worksheet.

Steps

1. Click cell **I3**, type **TV**, then press **[Enter]**; in cell **I4**, type **Magazine**, click the **Enter button** on the formula bar, then copy the criteria in **K3:L3** to **K4:L4**
   See Figure I-9. This time, you'll indicate that you want to copy the filtered list to a range beginning in cell A50.
2. Click **Data** on the menu bar, point to **Filter**, then click **Advanced Filter**; under Action, click the **Copy to another location option button** to select it, click the **Copy to** box, then type **A50**
   The last time you filtered the list, the criteria range included only rows 2 and 3, and now you have criteria in row 4.
3. In the **Criteria Range box**, edit the current formula to read **$A$2:$N$4**, click **OK**; then scroll down until row 50 is visible
   You have changed the criteria range to include row 4. The matching records are copied to the range beginning in cell A50. The original list (starting in cell A7) contains the records filtered in the previous lesson. See Figure I-10.
4. Select range **A50:N61**, click **File** on the menu bar, click **Print**, under Print what, click the **Selection option button**, click **Preview**, then click **Print**
   The selected area prints.
5. Press **[Ctrl][Home]**, click **Data** on the menu bar, point to **Filter**, then click **Show All**
   All the records in the range reappear. You return to the original list, which starts at its new location in cell A7.
6. Save, then close the workbook

Trouble?

Make sure the criteria range in the Advanced Filter dialog box includes the field names and the number of rows underneath the names that contain criteria. If you leave a blank row in the criteria range, Excel filters nothing and shows all records.

FIGURE I-9: Criteria in separate rows

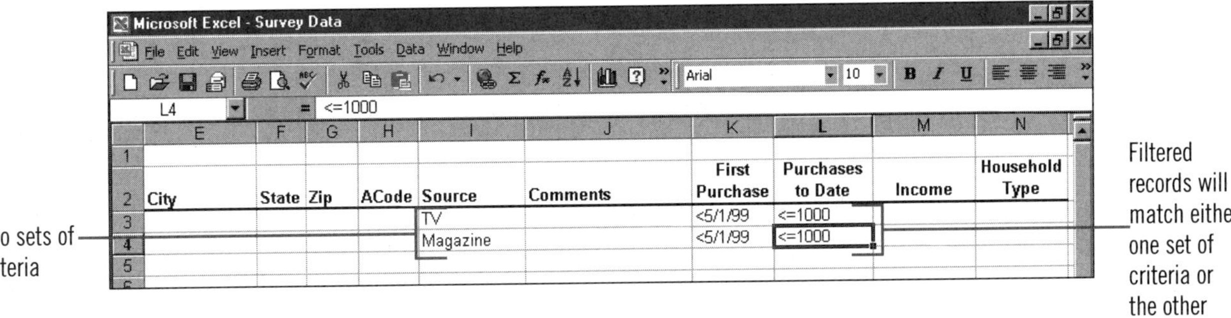

FIGURE I-10: Extracted data records

	Street Address	City	State	Zip	ACode	Source	Comments	First Purchase	Purchases to Date
51	3 Old Friar Road	Kansas City	MO	64102	816	Magazine	more author events	6/1/95	$ 879
52	232 Short Rd	Kansas City	MO	64105	816	Magazine	more self-help videos	5/24/96	$ 530
53	100 Main Street	Seattle	WA	98102	206	Magazine	no comments	6/16/96	$ 895
54	123 Elm St.	Houston	TX	77098	281	Magazine	salespeople helpful	6/28/98	$ 320
55	1110 November Way	Chicago	IL	60618	771	TV	no comments	3/22/99	$ 250
56	42 Silver Street	Reading	MA	03882	413	TV	fun store	4/6/87	$ 420
57	921 Lopez Lane	Chicago	IL	60611	773	Magazine	add chairs	4/9/93	$ 480
58	900 Monument St.	Concord	MA	01742	508	Magazine	love the book club	6/15/97	$ 450
59	486 Intel Circuit	Houston	TX	77092	281	TV	very effective ad	5/26/96	$ 990
60	2318 Sarah Road	Chicago	IL	60614	312	Magazine	great coffee	4/29/97	$ 640
61	2120 Witch Way	Salem	MA	01970	508	Magazine	loves our staff	5/25/97	$ 820

Extracted records copied to the range starting at cell A50

Extracted records for customers with first purchase before 5/1/99 or purchases less than $1,000 and who heard about MediaLoft through TV or magazines

Excel 2000

Understanding the criteria range and the copy-to location

When you define the criteria range and/or copy-to location in the Advanced Filter dialog box, Excel automatically creates names for these ranges in the worksheet (Criteria and Extract). The criteria range includes the field names and any criteria rows underneath them. The extract range includes just the field names above the extracted list. To extract a different list, simply select Extract as the copy-to location. Excel automatically deletes the old list in the extract area and generates a new list under the field names. Make sure the worksheet has enough blank rows underneath the field names for your data.

Excel 2000

Creating Subtotals Using Grouping and Outlines

The Excel subtotals feature provides a quick, easy way to group and summarize data in a list. Usually, you create subtotals with the SUM function. You also can subtotal groups with functions such as COUNT, AVERAGE, MAX, and MIN. Your list must have field names and be sorted before you can issue the Subtotal command. Jim wants to create a list grouped by advertising source, with subtotals for purchases to date and household income. He starts by sorting the list in ascending order—first by advertising source, then by state, and, finally, by city.

Steps

1. Open the workbook titled **EX I-1**, then save it as **Survey Data 2**
2. Click the **Name Box** list arrow, click **Database**, click **Data** on the menu bar, then click **Sort**; click the **Sort by** list arrow, click **Source**, click the first **Then by** list arrow, click **State**, click the **Ascending option button** to set the Then by sort order; click the second **Then by** list arrow, click **City**, then click **OK**
   You have sorted the list in ascending order, first by advertising source, then by state, and, finally, by city.
3. Press **[Ctrl][Home]**, click **Data** on the menu bar, then click **Subtotals**
   Before you use the Subtotals command, you must position the cell pointer within the list range (in this case, range A1:N36). The Subtotal dialog box opens. Here, you specify the items you want subtotaled, the function you want to apply to the values, and the fields you want to summarize.
4. Click the **At each change in** list arrow, click **Source**, click the **Use function** list arrow, click **Sum**; in the Add subtotal to list, click the **Purchases to Date** and **Income** check boxes to select them; if necessary, click the **Household□Type** check box to deselect it; then, if necessary, click the **Replace current subtotals** and **Summary below data** check boxes to select them
   Your completed Subtotal dialog box should match Figure I-11.
5. Click **OK**, then scroll to and click cell **L41**
   The subtotaled list appears, showing the calculated subtotals and grand total in columns L and M. See Figure I-12. Notice that Excel displays an outline to the left of the worksheet showing the structure of the subtotaled lists.
6. Preview the worksheet, click **Setup** and place your name on the right side of the footer, then print the worksheet using the current settings
7. Press **[Ctrl][Home]**, click **Data** on the menu bar, click **Subtotals**, then click **Remove All**
   You have turned off the Subtotaling feature. The subtotals are removed, and the Outline feature is turned off automatically. Because you did not alter the worksheet data, there's no need to save the file.

Trouble?

You may receive the following message: "No list found. Select a single cell within your list and Microsoft Excel will select the list for you." If you do, this means that you did not select the list before issuing the Subtotals command. Click OK, then repeat Steps 2 and 3.

FIGURE I-11: Completed Subtotal dialog box

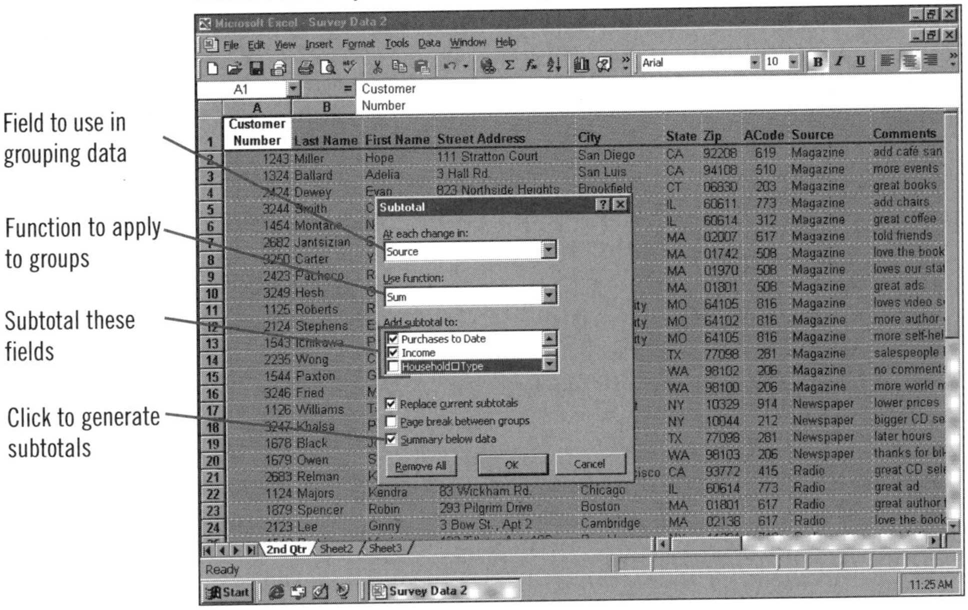

Field to use in grouping data

Function to apply to groups

Subtotal these fields

Click to generate subtotals

FIGURE I-12: Portion of subtotaled list

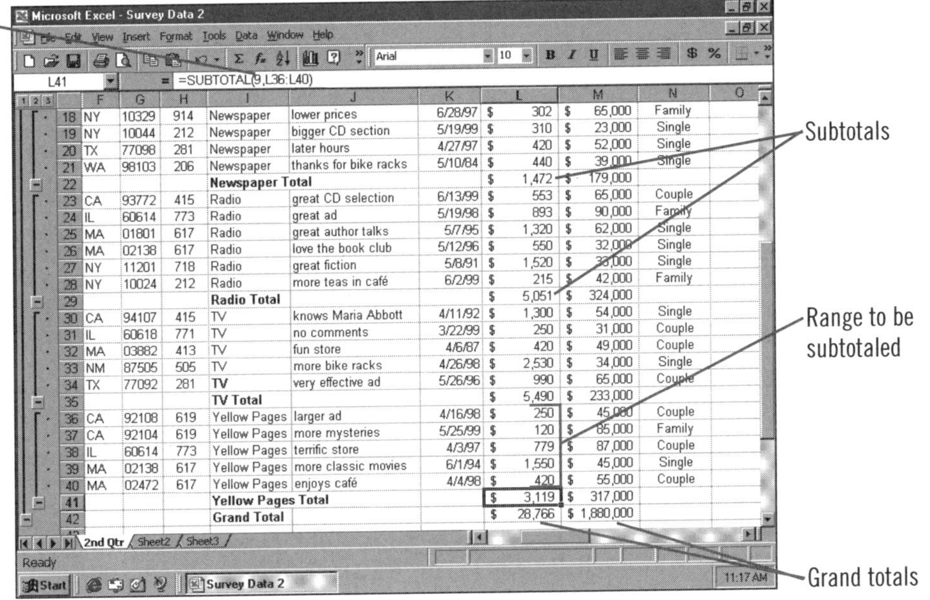

Show or hide details in an Excel outline

Clues to Use

Once subtotals have been generated, all detail records are displayed in an outline. See Figure I-13. You can then click the Hide Details button [−] of your choice to hide that group of records, creating a summary report. You can also create a chart that shows the summary data. Any chart you create will be automatically updated as you show or hide data. You can also click the Show Details button [+] for the group of data you want to display. To show a specific level of detail, click the row or column level button for the lowest level you want to display. For example, to display levels 1 through 3, click [3].

FIGURE I-13: Subtotaled list with level 2 details hidden

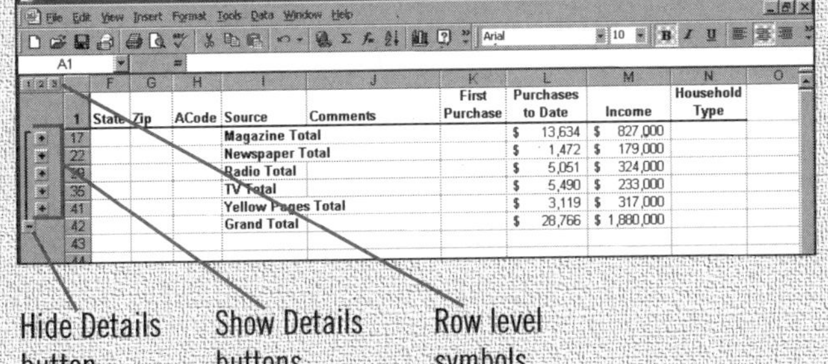

Excel 2000

Excel 2000

Looking Up Values in a List

The Excel VLOOKUP function helps you locate specific values in a list. The VLOOKUP searches vertically (V) down the leftmost column of a list and then reads across the row to find the value in the column you specify. The process of looking up a number in a phone book uses the same logic as the Excel VLOOKUP function: You locate a person's name and then read across the row to find the phone number you are looking for. At times, Jim wants to be able to find out what type of household a particular customer lives in simply by entering his or her specific customer number. To do this, he uses the VLOOKUP function. He begins by creating a special list, or table, containing the customer numbers he wants to look up. Then he copies names to a separate location.

Steps

QuickTip

Excel also has a Lookup Wizard to help you perform lookups. It is an Excel add-in (or extra) program. Open the Tools menu, point to Wizards, then click Lookup. If you don't see Wizards on the Tools menu, install the add-in from the Microsoft Office CD.

Trouble?

If the Office Assistant activates for this task, select the "No" option to indicate you don't want to learn more about this function at the present time. Continue with Step 5.

Trouble?

If an exact match is not returned, make sure the Range_lookup is set to FALSE.

1. Click cell **C2**, click **Window** on the menu bar, then click **Freeze Panes**; scroll right until columns N through T and rows 1 through 15 are visible
2. Click cell **P1**, type **VLOOKUP Function**, click the **Enter button** on the formula bar; copy the contents of cell **A1** to cell **R1**, copy the contents of cell **N1** to cell **S1**, widen the columns as necessary to display the text, then click any blank cell
   See Figure I-14. Jim wants to know the household type for customer number 3247.
3. Click cell **R2**, type **3247**, then press **[→]**
   The VLOOKUP function in the Paste Function dialog box will let Jim find the household type for customer number 3247.
4. Make sure cell S2 is still selected, click the **Paste Function button** on the Standard toolbar, under Function category click **Lookup & Reference**, under Function name click **VLOOKUP**, then click **OK**
   The VLOOKUP dialog box opens. Because the value you want to find is in cell R2, that will be the Lookup_value. The list you want to search is the customer list, so its name ("Database") will be the Table_array.
5. Drag the **VLOOKUP dialog box** down so that at least rows 1 and 2 of the worksheet are visible; with the insertion point in the Lookup_value box, click cell **R2**, click the **Table_array box**, then type **DATABASE**
   The column you want to search (Household Type) is the fourteenth column from the left, so the Col_index_num will be 14. Because you want to find an exact match for the value in cell R2, the Range_lookup argument will be FALSE. (If you want to find only the closest match for a value, you enter TRUE in the Range_lookup box, as indicated in the bottom of the VLOOKUP dialog box.)
6. Click the **Col_index_num box**, type **14**, click the **Range_lookup box**, then type **FALSE**
   Your completed VLOOKUP dialog box should match Figure I-15.
7. Click **OK**
   Excel searches down the leftmost column of the customer list until it finds a value matching the one in cell R2. Then it finds the household type for that record ("Single") and displays it in cell S2. Now, you'll use this function to determine the household type for one other customer.
8. Click cell **R2**, type **2125**, then click
   The VLOOKUP function returns the value Family in cell S2.
9. Press **[Ctrl][Home]**, then save the workbook.

FIGURE I-14: Worksheet with headings for VLOOKUP

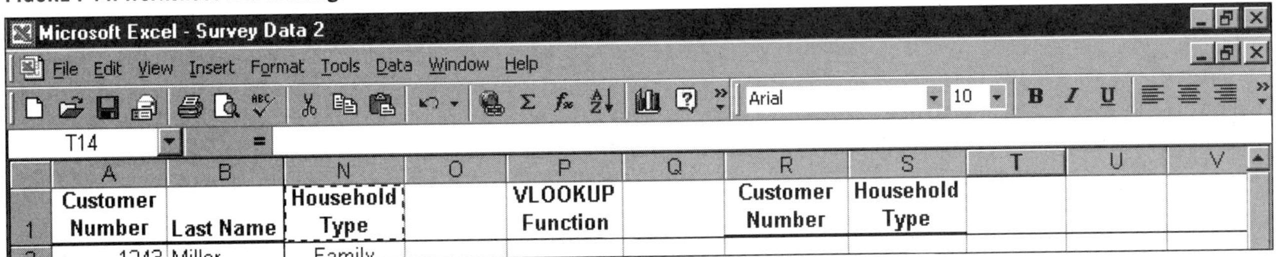

FIGURE I-15: Completed VLOOKUP dialog box

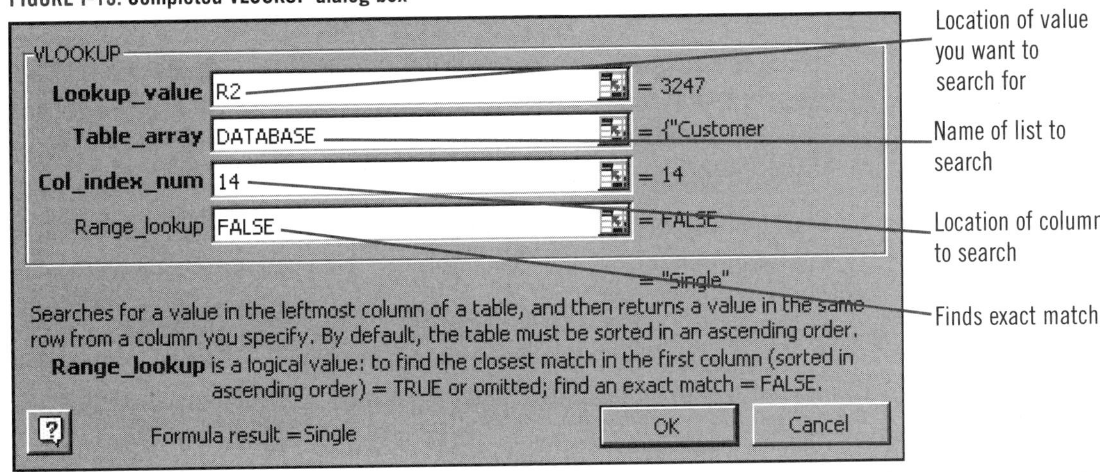

Excel 2000

CLUES TO USE

Using the HLOOKUP function

The VLOOKUP (Vertical Lookup) function is useful when your data is arranged vertically in columns. The HLOOKUP (Horizontal Lookup) function is useful when your data is arranged horizontally in rows. HLOOKUP searches horizontally across the topmost row of a list until the matching value is found, then looks down the number of rows you specify. The arguments for this function are identical to those for the VLOOKUP function, with one exception. Instead of a Col_index_number, HLOOKUP uses a Row_index_number, which indicates the location of the row you want to search. For example, if you want to search the fourth row from the top, the Row_index_number should be 4.

Excel 2000

Summarizing List Data

Database functions allow you to summarize list data in a variety of ways. For example, you can use them to count, average, or total values in a field for only those records that meet specified criteria. When working with a sales activity list, for instance, you can use Excel to count the number of client contacts by sales representative or to total the amount sold to specific accounts by month. The format for database functions is explained in Figure I-16. Jim wants to summarize the information in his list in two ways. First, he wants to find the total purchases to date for each advertising source. He also wants to count the number of records for each advertising source. Jim begins by creating a criteria range that includes a copy of the column label for the column he wants to summarize, as well as the criterion itself.

Steps

1. With the panes still frozen, scroll down until row 31 is the top row underneath the frozen headings, then enter and format the five labels shown in Figure I-17 in the range: **I39:K41**
   The criteria range in I40:I41 tells Excel to summarize records with the entry "Yellow Pages" in the Source column. The functions will be in cells L39 and L41.
2. Click cell **L39**, type **=DSUM(DATABASE,12,I40:I41)**, then click the **Enter button** on the formula bar
   The result in cell L39 is 3119. For the range named Database, Excel totaled the information in column 12 (Purchases to Date) for those records that meet the criteria of Source = Yellow Pages. The DCOUNTA function will help you determine the number of nonblank records meeting the criteria Source = Yellow Pages.
3. Click cell **L41**, type **=DCOUNTA(DATABASE,1,I40:I41)**, then click
   The result in cell L41 is 5, meaning that there are five customers who heard about MediaLoft through the Yellow Pages. This function uses the first field in the list, Customer Number, to check for nonblank cells within the criteria range Source = Yellow Pages. Jim also wants to see total purchases and a count for the magazine ads.
4. Click cell **I41**, type **Magazine**, then click
   With total purchases of $13,634, it's clear that magazine advertising is the most effective way of attracting MediaLoft customers. Compare your results with Figure I-18.
5. Press **[Ctrl][Home]**, then save and close the workbook

QuickTip

You can use a column label, such as "City", in place of a column number. Type the text exactly as it is entered in the list and enclose it in double quotation marks.

Trouble?

If the result you receive is incorrect, make sure you entered the formula correctly, using the letter "I" in the criteria range address, and the number one (1) for the column number.

FIGURE I-16: Format of database function

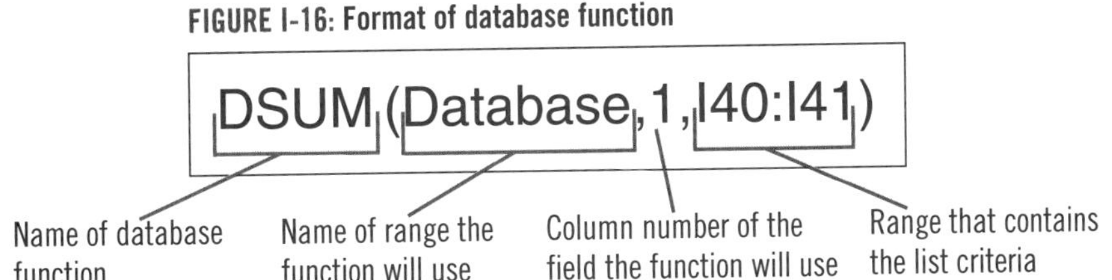

FIGURE I-17: Portion of worksheet showing summary area

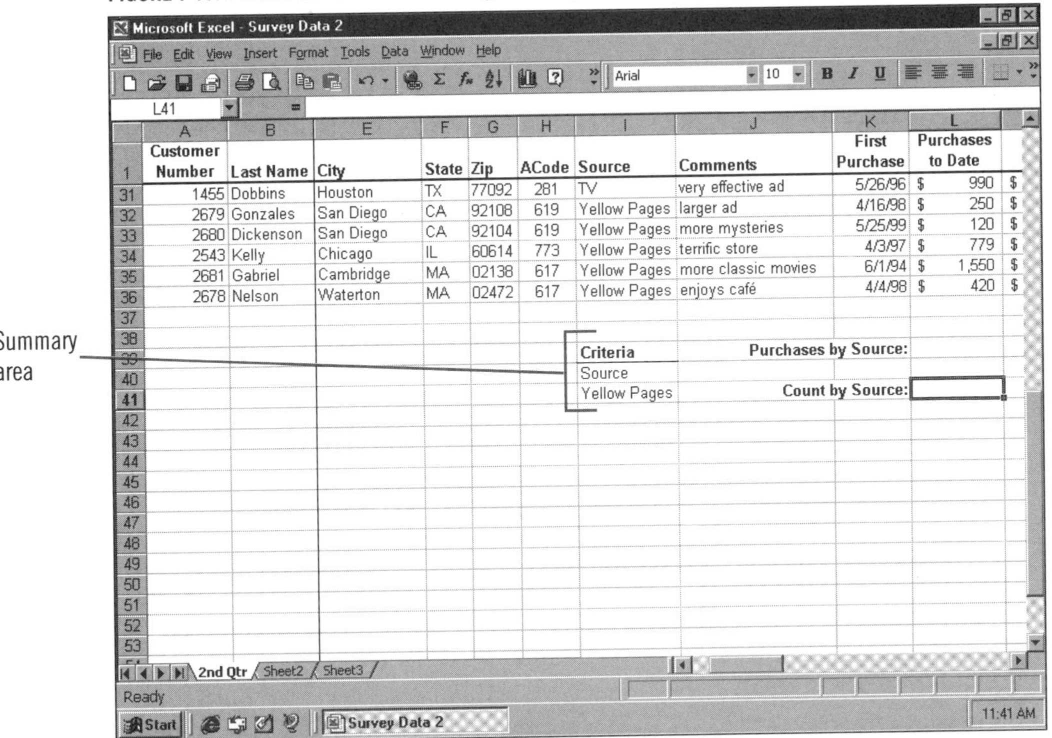

	Customer Number	Last Name	City	State	Zip	ACode	Source	Comments	First Purchase	Purchases to Date
31	1455	Dobbins	Houston	TX	77092	281	TV	very effective ad	5/26/96	$ 990
32	2679	Gonzales	San Diego	CA	92108	619	Yellow Pages	larger ad	4/16/98	$ 250
33	2680	Dickenson	San Diego	CA	92104	619	Yellow Pages	more mysteries	5/25/99	$ 120
34	2543	Kelly	Chicago	IL	60614	773	Yellow Pages	terrific store	4/3/97	$ 779
35	2681	Gabriel	Cambridge	MA	02138	617	Yellow Pages	more classic movies	6/1/94	$ 1,550
36	2678	Nelson	Waterton	MA	02472	617	Yellow Pages	enjoys café	4/4/98	$ 420

FIGURE I-18: Result generated by database function

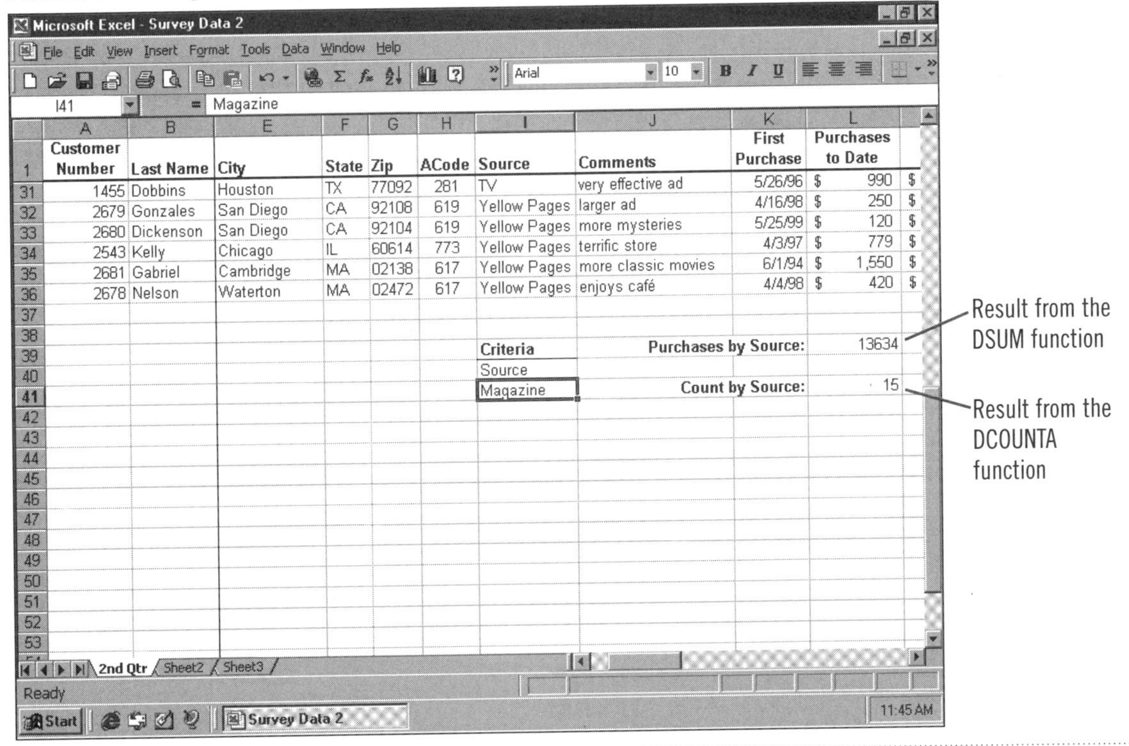

	Customer Number	Last Name	City	State	Zip	ACode	Source	Comments	First Purchase	Purchases to Date
31	1455	Dobbins	Houston	TX	77092	281	TV	very effective ad	5/26/96	$ 990
32	2679	Gonzales	San Diego	CA	92108	619	Yellow Pages	larger ad	4/16/98	$ 250
33	2680	Dickenson	San Diego	CA	92104	619	Yellow Pages	more mysteries	5/25/99	$ 120
34	2543	Kelly	Chicago	IL	60614	773	Yellow Pages	terrific store	4/3/97	$ 779
35	2681	Gabriel	Cambridge	MA	02138	617	Yellow Pages	more classic movies	6/1/94	$ 1,550
36	2678	Nelson	Waterton	MA	02472	617	Yellow Pages	enjoys café	4/4/98	$ 420

Excel 2000

Using Data Validation for List Entries

The Excel Data Validation feature allows you to specify what data is valid for a range of cells. You can restrict data to whole numbers, decimal numbers, or text, or you can set limits on entries. You can also specify a list of acceptable entries. Once you've specified what data is considered valid, Excel prevents users from entering any other data (considered invalid) except your specified choices. Jim wants to make sure that information in the Household Type column is entered consistently in the future. He decides to restrict the entries in that column to three options: Couple, Single, and Family. First, he selects the column he wants to restrict.

Steps

1. Open the workbook titled **EX I-1**, then save it as **Survey Data 3**
2. Scroll right until column N is displayed, then click the **Column N** column header
   The entire column is selected.
3. Click **Data** on the menu bar, click **Validation**, click the **Settings tab** if necessary, click the **Allow** list arrow, then click **List**
   Selecting the List option enables you to type a list of specific options.
4. Click the **Source** box, then type **Couple, Single, Family**
   You have entered the list of acceptable entries, separated by commas. See Figure I-19. Jim wants the data entry person to be able to select a valid entry from a drop-down list.
5. Click the **In-cell Drop-down check box** to select it if necessary, then click **OK**
   The dialog box closes, and you return to the worksheet. The new data restrictions will apply only to new entries in the Household Type column.
6. Click cell **N37**, then click the **list arrow** to display the list of valid entries
   See Figure I-20. You could click an item in the list to have it entered in the cell, but Jim first wants to know what happens if you enter an invalid entry.
7. Click the **list arrow** to close the list, type **Individual**, then press **[Enter]**
   A warning dialog box appears to prevent you from entering the invalid data. See Figure I-21.
8. Click **Cancel**, click the **list arrow**, then click **Single**
   The cell accepts the valid entry. The data restriction ensures that new records will contain only one of the three correct entries in the Household Type column. The customer list is finished and ready for future data entry.
9. Save and close the workbook

QuickTip

To restrict entries to decimal or whole numbers, dates, or times, select the appropriate option in the Allow list. To specify a long list of valid entries, type the list in a column elsewhere in the worksheet, then type the address of the list in the Source box.

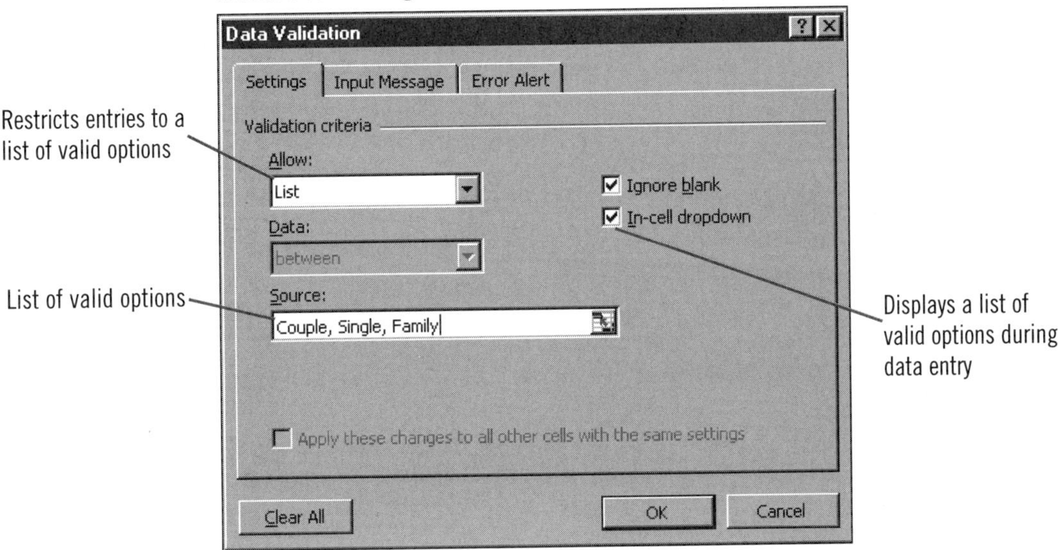

FIGURE I-19: Creating data restrictions

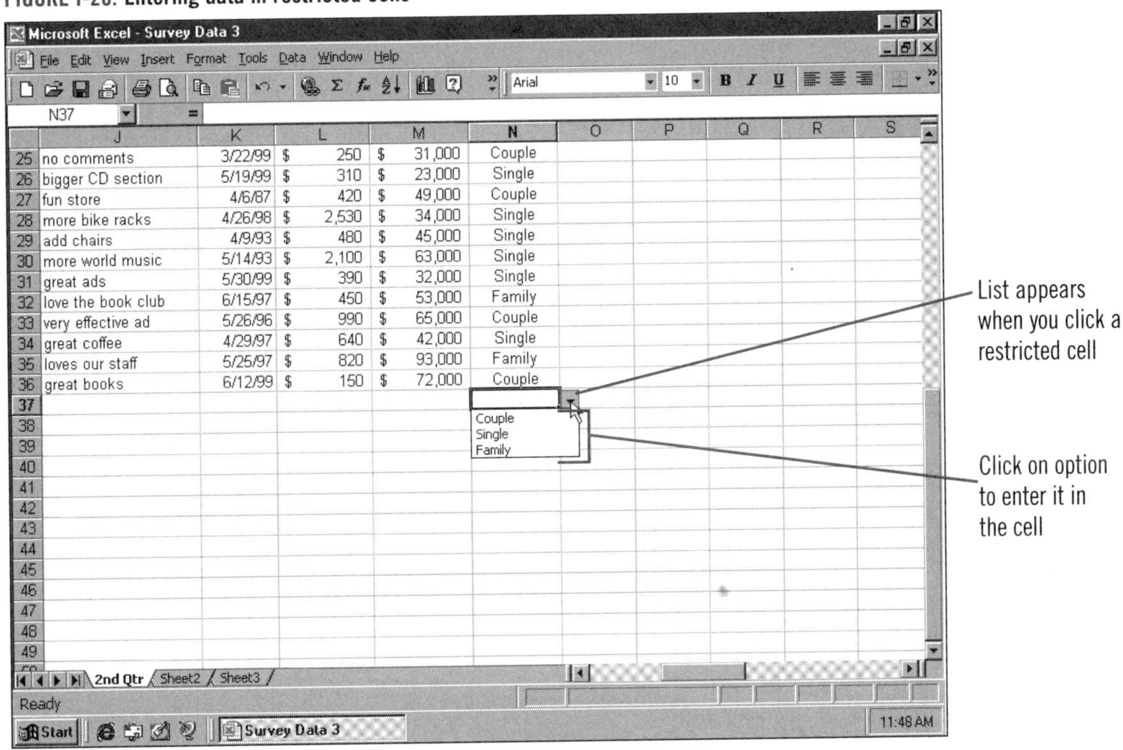

FIGURE I-20: Entering data in restricted cells

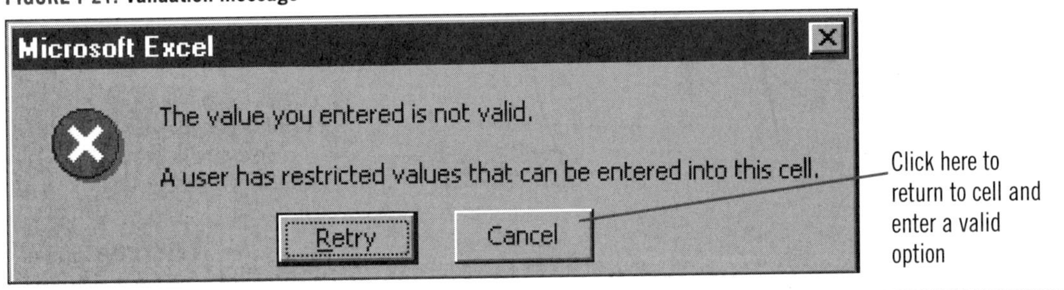

FIGURE I-21: Validation message

Excel 2000

Practice

► Concepts Review

Explain the function of each element of the Excel screen labeled in Figure I-22.

FIGURE I-22

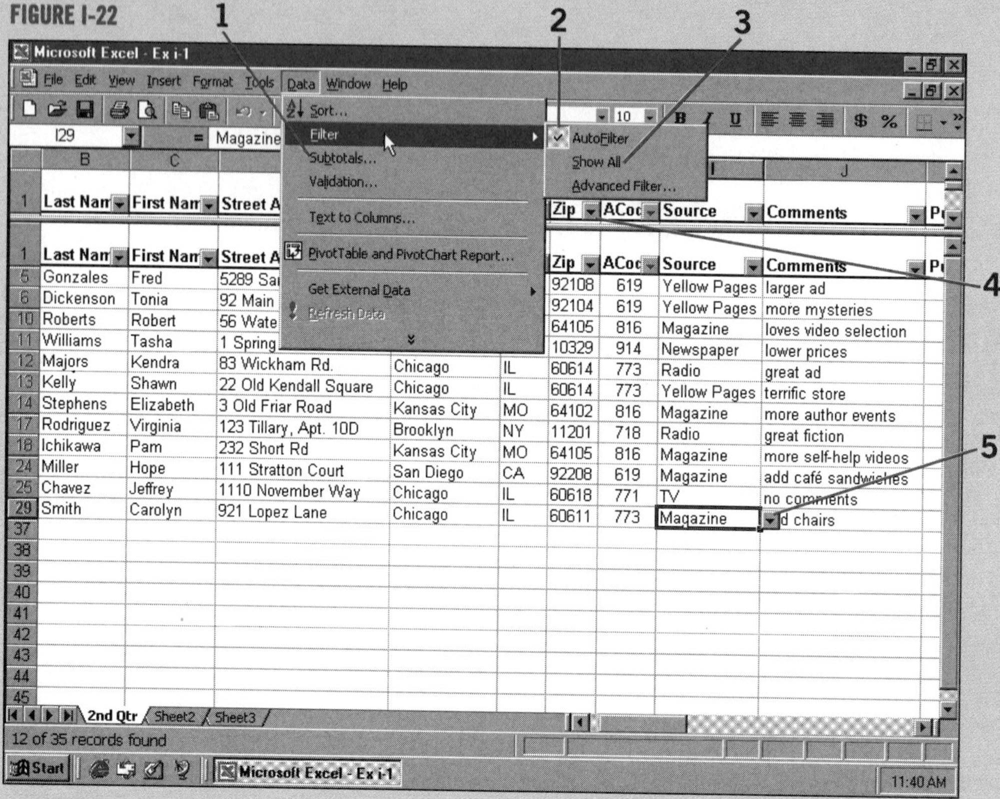

Match each term with the statement that describes it.

6. **HLOOKUP**
7. **Extracted list**
8. **Data validation**
9. **Criteria range**
10. **List range**

a. Cell range when advanced filter results are copied to another location
b. Range in which search conditions are set
c. Restricts list entries to specified options
d. Range used to specify a database in database functions
e. Function to use when data is arranged horizontally in rows

Select the best answer from the list of choices.

11. You might perform an AutoFilter and search for nonblank entries in order to

a. Identify missing data.
b. Find records with data in a particular field.
c. Sum records with data in a particular field.
d. b and c.

12. What does it mean when you select the Or option when creating a custom filter?

- **a.** Neither criterion has to be 100% true.
- **b.** Either criterion can be true to find a match.
- **c.** Both criteria must be true to find a match.
- **d.** Custom filter requires a criteria range.

13. What must a list have before automatic subtotals can be inserted?

- **a.** Enough records to show multiple subtotals
- **b.** Grand totals
- **c.** Column or field headings
- **d.** Formatted cells

► Skills Review

1. Retrieve records with AutoFilter.

- **a.** Open the workbook titled EX I-2, then save it as "Compensation Summary".
- **b.** Use AutoFilter to list records for employees in the Accounting department.
- **c.** Redisplay all employees, then use AutoFilter to show the three employees with the highest annual salary.
- **d.** Redisplay all the records.

2. Create a custom filter.

- **a.** Create a custom filter showing employees hired prior to 1/1/90 or after 1/1/94.
- **b.** Preview, then print the list in A1:J11.
- **c.** Redisplay all records.
- **d.** Turn off AutoFilter.

3. Filter and extract a list with Advanced Filter.

- **a.** You will retrieve a list of employees who were hired prior to 1/1/90 and earn more than $60,000 a year. Define a criteria range by copying the field names in range A1:J1 to cell A14.
- **b.** In cell D15, enter the criterion < 1/1/90, then in cell G15 enter >60000.
- **c.** Return to cell A1.
- **d.** Open the Advanced Filter dialog box.
- **e.** Indicate that you want to copy to another location, enter the criteria range A14:J15, then indicate that you want to copy to cell A18.
- **f.** If necessary, scroll so that rows 18 through 20 are visible to confirm that the retrieved list meets the criteria.
- **g.** Change the page setup to landscape orientation, then select and print only the extracted list in range A18:J20.
- **h.** Use the Edit menu to clear data and formats from the range A14:J20.

4. Creating subtotals using grouping and outlines.

- **a.** Move to cell A1. Sort the list in ascending order by department, then in descending order by monthly salary.
- **b.** Group and create subtotals by department, using the Sum function; select Monthly Salary in the Add Subtotal to list box, deselect Annual Comp., then click OK.
- **c.** AutoFit column E.
- **d.** Use the outline to display only the subtotals, preview, then print only the subtotaled list in landscape orientation fitting the data to one page.
- **e.** Remove the subtotals.

5. **Look up values in a list.**
   a. You will locate annual compensation information by entering a social security number. Scroll so that columns I through Q are visible.
   b. In cell N2, enter 556-53-7589.
   c. In cell O2, enter the following function: =VLOOKUP(N2,A2:J11,10,FALSE), then view the results.
   d. Enter another social security number, 356-93-2123, in cell N2 and view the annual compensation for that employee.
   e. Save your worksheet.

6. **Summarize list data.**
   a. You'll enter a database function to average the annual salaries by department, using the Marketing department as the initial criterion.
   b. Define the criteria area: In cell C14, enter "Criteria"; in cell C15, enter "Dept." (make sure you type the period); then in cell C16, enter "Marketing".
   c. In cell E14, enter "Average Annual Salary by Department:".
   d. In cell H14, enter the following database function: =DAVERAGE(Database,7,C15:C16).
   e. Test the function further by entering the text "Accounting" in cell C16. When the criterion is entered, cell H14 should display 58650 as the result.
   f. Save the workbook, then close it.

7. **Use data validation for list entries.**
   a. Open the workbook titled EX I-2 again, then save it as "Compensation Summary 2".
   b. Select column E.
   c. For the validation criteria, specify that you want to allow a list of valid options.
   d. Enter a list of valid options that restricts the entries to "Accounting", "Information Systems", and "Marketing". Remember to use a comma between each item in the list.
   e. Indicate that you want the options to appear in an in-cell dropdown list, then close the dialog box.
   f. Go to cell E12, then select "Accounting" in the dropdown list.
   g. Select column F.
   h. Indicate that you want to restrict the data entered to be only whole numbers.
   i. In the minimum box, enter 1000. In the Maximum box, enter 20000. Close the dialog box.
   j. Click cell F12, enter 25000, then press [Enter].
   k. Click Cancel, then enter 19000.50.
   l. Click Cancel, then enter 19000.
   m. Save, then close the workbook and exit Excel.

▶ Independent Challenges

1. Your neighbor, Phillipe, brought over his wine cellar inventory workbook file on disk and asked you to help him manipulate the data in Excel. Phillipe would like to filter the list to show two subsets: all wines with a 1985 vintage and Chardonnay wines with a vintage prior to 1985. He would also like to subtotal the list and show the total dollar value by type of wine as well as restrict entries in the Type of Wine column to eight possibilities.

To complete this independent challenge:

a. Open the workbook titled EX I-3, then save it as "Wine Cellar Inventory".
b. Use AutoFilter to generate a list of wines with a 1985 vintage. Preview, then print the list.
c. Use Advanced Filter to extract a list of Chardonnay wines with a vintage in or prior to 1985. Preview, then print the list.
d. Clear the filter, and insert subtotals for Total $ according to type of wine. (*Hint:* Make sure to sort the list by type of wine prior to creating the subtotals.) Print the subtotaled list. Turn off subtotaling.
e. Beginning in cell H1, type the list of eight wine types in column H. The list should include Cabernet, Champagne, Chardonnay, Muscat, Pinot Noir, Riesling, Sauvignon Blanc, and Zinfandel.
f. Select column B. Open the Data Validation dialog box, then click List in the Allow box. Enter the range address for the list of wine types in the Source box. Make sure the In-cell dropdown check box is selected. Close the dialog box.
g. Test the data validation by entering valid and invalid data in cell B31.
h. Type your name in the worksheet footer, then save, print, and close the workbook.

2. Your neighbor, Phillipe, was pleased when you delivered his filtered and subtotaled wine inventory list. After viewing your printouts, he asks you to help him with a few more tasks. He wants the list to be sorted by wine label. In addition, he wants to be able to type in the vintage year (starting with 1985) and get a total bottle count and average cost per bottle for that vintage. (*Hint:* You need to define a criteria area outside the list to contain the two database functions.) Finally, Phillipe wants you to provide him with some form of documentation on how to accomplish the summaries.

To complete this independent challenge:

a. Open the workbook titled EX I-3, then save it as "Wine Cellar Inventory 2".
b. Sort the list alphabetically by wine label.
c. Define an area either above or below the list with the label "Criteria". Add appropriate column labels and criteria. Use 1985 as the vintage year for the criterion.
d. Near the criteria area, type labels for the two database functions.
e. Enter the database functions to find total bottle count and average price per bottle for a particular vintage.
f. Save your work. Preview and then print the list. Display the worksheet formulas, add your name to the worksheet footer, then preview and print the criteria area. Hide the formulas again.
g. Create a separate worksheet that documents the functions you used: Format the two cells containing the database functions as text by adding leading apostrophes. Widen any columns as necessary. Print a second copy of the list with the two database functions. Change the page setup so that the gridlines and row and column headings are printed. Leave a valid entry in the cell.
h. Save, then close the workbook.

3. A few months ago, you started your own business, called Books 4 You. You create and sell personalized books for special occasions. You bought a distributorship from an established book company and the rights to use several of the company's titles. Using your personal computer, specialized software, and preprinted book pages, you create personalized books on your laser printer. All you need from a customer is the name of the book's "star," his or her special date if appropriate (usually a birth or anniversary date), and the desired book title. Using the software, you enter the data and generate book pages, which you later bind together. After several months of struggle, you are starting to make a profit. You decided to put together an invoice list to track sales, starting in October. Now that you have this list, you would like to manipulate it in several ways. First, you want to filter the list to retrieve only children's books ordered during the first half of the month (prior to 10/16). Next, you want to subtotal the unit price, sales tax, and total cost columns by book title. Finally, you want to restrict entries in the Order Date column.

To complete this independent challenge:

a. Open the workbook titled EX I-4, then save it as "Books 4 You, Invoice Database".
b. Filter the list to show children's books ordered prior to 10/16/00. Print the filtered list on a single page with gridlines and row and column headings. Clear the filter, then save your work.
c. Create subtotals in the Unit Price, Sales Tax, and Total Cost columns by book title. Print the subtotaled list on a single page without gridlines, row, or column headings. Clear the subtotals.
d. Use the Data Validation dialog box to restrict entries to those with order dates between 12/31/99 and 1/1/01. Select "Date" In the Allow list, then enter the appropriate dates in the Start date and End date boxes. Test the data restrictions by attempting to enter an invalid date.
e. Add your name to the worksheet footer, then save, print, and close the workbook.
f. Open the workbook titled EX I-4, then save it as "Books 4 You, Lookup".
g. Enter a VLOOKUP function to retrieve a customer's book title based on its invoice number. Enter a second VLOOKUP function to look up the order date. Format the cell displaying the date in a date format, then save your work.
h. Below the VLOOKUP area, and to the right of the invoice list, define an area in which to count the number of birthday books ordered on any given date. Save your work.
i. Add your name to the worksheet footer, then print the list on a single page, if possible.
j. Provide documentation for any functions used, then add your name to the range and print the worksheet functions with gridlines and row and column headings on a single page, if possible.
k. Save, then close the workbook.

4. Each month, the MediaLoft Product department lists the top-selling book, video, and CD products on the MediaLoft intranet site. The department also keeps track of these products in an Excel list. As a new employee of the MediaLoft Corporate Headquarters, you have been asked to update the Excel list with the latest information on the intranet site and to then analyze the information using Excel.

To complete this independent challenge:

a. Connect to the Internet, then go to the MediaLoft intranet site at http://www.course.com/Illustrated/MediaLoft. Click the Products link, then click the Bestsellers of the month link. Print the page and disconnect from the Internet.
b. Open the file EX I-5 on your Project Disk, save it as "Bestsellers", and, referring to your printout, add the three top-selling items. (If there is more than one author/performer, choose only the first one.) Enter the date as 12/30/00.
c. Use AutoFilter to display only books.
d. Further filter the list to display only books that were on the bestseller list before 7/30/00.
e. Enter your name in the worksheet footer, then print the filtered list.
f. Clear the filter.
g. Create an advanced filter that retrieves, to its current location, records whose dates were before 9/1/2000 and whose dollar sales were greater than $2,000. Print only the cells containing the filtered list, then clear the filter and redisplay all the records.
h. Create another advanced filter that extracts products whose sales were $3,000 or more and places them in another area of the worksheet.
i. Print the range containing only the extracted list, centered horizontally on the page, with row and column headings.
j. Save and close the Bestsellers workbook.
k. Open the file EX I-5 and save it as "Bestsellers 2".
l. Subtotal the sales by category.
m. Use the outline to display only category names and totals. Enter your name in the worksheet footer and print the worksheet.
n. Redisplay the records and remove the subtotals.
o. Freeze the column headings and scroll to display several blank lines below the last line.
p. Use the DSUM function to let worksheet users find the total sales by category. Format the cell containing the function appropriately.
q. Use data validation to restrict category entries to CD, Book, or Video, then test an entry with valid and invalid entries.
r. Print, save, and close the worksheet.

 Visual Workshop

Create the worksheet shown in Figure I-23. Save the workbook as "Commission Lookup" on your Project disk. (*Hints:* The formula in cell D5 accesses the commission from the table. Calculate the commission by multiplying the Amount of Sale by the Commission Rate. If an exact amount for the Amount of Sale does not exist, the next highest or lowest dollar value is used.) Add your name to the worksheet footer, then preview and print the worksheet.

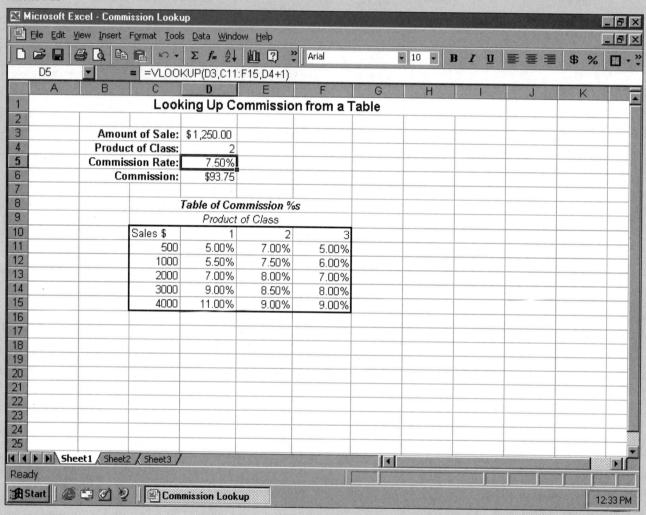

FIGURE I-23

Microsoft Excel - Commission Lookup

D5 = =VLOOKUP(D3,C11:F15,D4+1)

Looking Up Commission from a Table

Amount of Sale:	$1,250.00
Product of Class:	2
Commission Rate:	7.50%
Commission:	$93.75

Table of Commission %s

Product of Class

Sales $	1	2	3
500	5.00%	7.00%	5.00%
1000	5.50%	7.50%	6.00%
2000	7.00%	8.00%	7.00%
3000	9.00%	8.50%	8.00%
4000	11.00%	9.00%	9.00%

Sheet1 / Sheet2 / Sheet3

Ready

Start | Commission Lookup | 12:33 PM

Enhancing

Charts and Worksheets

Objectives

- Select a custom chart type
- Customize a data series
- Format a chart axis
- Add a data table to a chart
- Rotate a chart
- Enhance a chart with WordArt
- Rotate text
- Map data

There are many ways to revise a chart or a worksheet to present its data with greater impact. In this unit, you enhance both charts and worksheets by selecting a custom chart type, customizing a data series, formatting axes, adding a data table, and rotating a chart. You also add special text effects and rotate text. Finally, you increase the impact of geographical data by plotting it on a map. Keep in mind that your goal in enhancing charts or worksheets is to communicate your data more clearly. Avoid excessive customization, which can be visually distracting. MediaLoft's director of café operations, Jeff Shimada, has asked Jim Fernandez to produce two charts showing the sales of café pastry products in the first two quarters. He encourages Jim to enhance the charts and the worksheet data to improve their appearance and make the data more accessible. Finally, he asks Jim to create a map illustrating pastry sales by state.

Excel 2000

Selecting a Custom Chart Type

The Excel Chart Wizard offers a choice between standard and custom chart types. A **standard chart type** is a commonly used column, bar, pie, or area chart with several variations. For each standard chart type, you can choose from several subtypes, such as clustered column or stacked column. You can use the Wizard to add display options, and can later modify the formatting of any chart element. Excel supplies 20 built-in **custom chart types**, with special formatting already applied. You can also define your own custom chart type by modifying any of the existing Excel chart types. For example, you could define a company chart type that has the same title and then distribute it to other users in your office. Jim's first task is to create a chart showing the amount of each pastry type sold for the first quarter. To save time, he decides to use an Excel built-in custom chart.

Steps 1 2 3 4

QuickTip

To return personalized toolbars and menus to their default state, click Tools on the menu bar, click Customize, click the Options tab in the Customize dialog box, click Reset my usage data to restore the default settings, click Yes, click Close, then close the Drawing toolbar if it is displayed.

1. Open the workbook titled **EX J-1**, then save it as **Pastry Sales**
   The first step is to select the data you want to appear in the chart. In this case, you want the row labels in cells A6:A10 and the data for January and February in cells B5:C10.
2. Select the range **A5:C10**
3. Click the **Chart Wizard button** on the Standard toolbar, click the **Custom Types tab** in the Step 1 Chart Wizard dialog box, then under Select from, click the **Built-in option button** to select it if necessary
   See Figure J-1. When the built-in option button in the Custom Types tab is selected, all of the Excel custom chart types are displayed in the Chart type box, and a sample of the default chart appears in the Sample box. Once you make a selection in the Chart type box, the default chart disappears and a preview of the selected chart type appears in the Sample box. If the Chart Wizard button does not appear on your Standard toolbar, click the More Buttons button to view it.
4. Click **Columns with Depth** in the Chart type box
   A preview of the chart appears in the Sample box. Notice that this custom chart type, with its 3-D bars and white background, has a more elegant appearance than the default chart shown in Figure J-1. Unlike the previous default chart, this chart doesn't have gridlines.
5. Click **Next**
6. Make sure = 'TotalSales'!A$5:$C$10 appears as the data range in the Data range box in the Step 2 Chart Wizard dialog box, then click **Next**

Trouble?

If the Chart toolbar does not open, right-click any toolbar and click Chart.

7. In the Step 3 Chart Wizard dialog box, click **Next**; if necessary, click the **As object in option button** in the Step 4 Chart Wizard dialog box to select it; then click **Finish**
   The completed chart appears, covering part of the worksheet data, along with the Chart toolbar. The Chart toolbar can appear anywhere within the worksheet window. As you complete the following steps, you may need to drag the toolbar to a new location.

Trouble?

Remember to drag the Chart toolbar out of the way if it blocks your view of the chart.

8. Scroll down the worksheet until **rows 13** through **28** are visible, click the **chart border** and drag the chart left and down until its upper-left corner is in cell **A13**, drag the **middle right sizing handle** right to the border between **column H** and **column I**, then check that its bottom border is between **rows 25** and **26**
   The new chart fills the range A13:H25, as shown in Figure J-2.
9. Save the workbook

FIGURE J-1: Custom Types tab settings

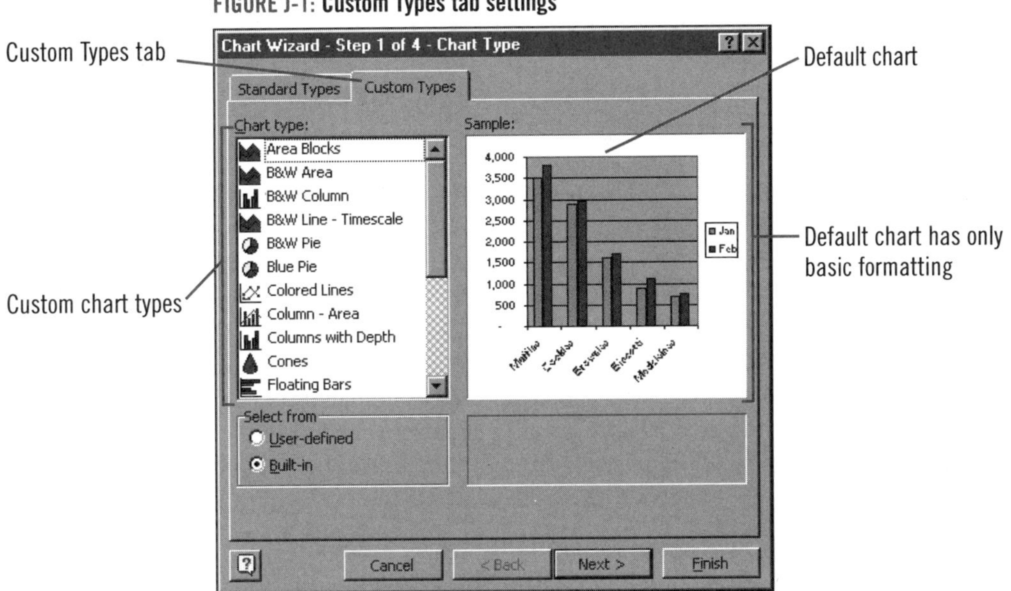

FIGURE J-2: New chart

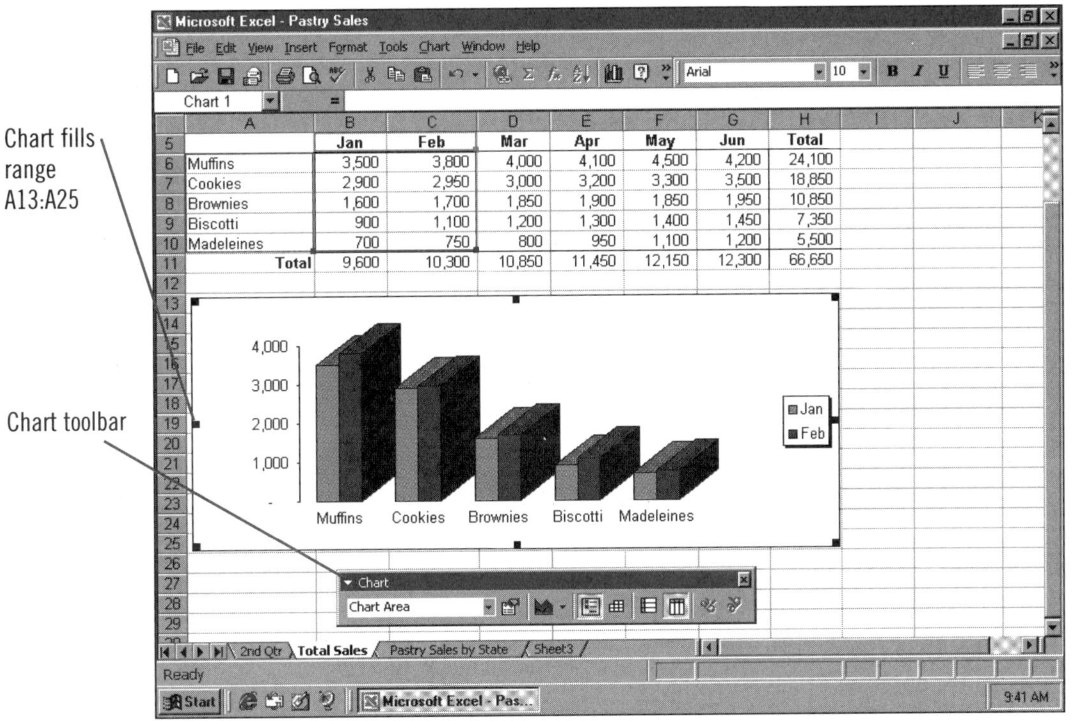

Creating a custom chart type

You can create your own custom chart type by starting with a standard chart and then adding elements (such as a legend, color, or gridlines) that suit your needs. After you've finished creating the chart, click it to activate the Chart menu on the menu bar, click Chart, click Chart type, click the Custom Types tab, then click User-defined. Click Add, then type a name for your chart type in the Name box. To use your custom chart type when creating additional charts, open the Chart Wizard dialog box, then click the User-defined button in the Custom Types tab.

Excel 2000

Customizing a Data Series

A **data series** is the information, usually numbers or values, that Excel plots on a chart. You can customize the data series in a chart easily by altering the spreadsheet range that contains the chart data *or* by entering descriptive text, called a **data label**, that appears above a data marker in a chart. As with other Excel elements, you can change the borders, patterns, or colors of a data series. Jim notices that he omitted the data for March when he created his first-quarter sales chart. He needs to add this information to make the chart accurately reflect the entire first-quarter sales. Also, he wants to customize the updated chart by adding data labels to one of the data series to make it more specific. Then he'll change the color of another data series so its respective column figures will stand out more. He starts by adding the March data.

Steps

1. If necessary, click the **chart** to select it, scroll up until **row 5** is the top row in the worksheet area, select the range **D5:D10**, position the pointer over the lower border of cell D10 until it changes to ↖, then drag the selected range anywhere within the chart area
   The chart now includes data for the entire first quarter: January, February, and March. Next, you will add data labels to the March data series.
2. Click the **Chart Objects list arrow** in the Chart toolbar, then click **Series "Mar"**
   See Figure J-3. Selection handles appear on each of the columns representing the data for March. Now that the data series is selected, you can format it by adding labels.
3. Click the **Format Object button** on the Chart toolbar, then click the **Data Labels tab** in the Format Data Series dialog box
   The Data Labels tab opens. You want the value to appear on top of each selected data marker.
4. Under Data labels, click the **Show value option button** to select it, then click **OK**
   The data labels appear on the data markers, as shown in Figure J-4. The February data series could stand out more.
5. Click the **Chart Objects list arrow** on the Chart toolbar, click **Series "Feb"**, click , then click the **Patterns tab** in the Format Data Series dialog box
   The Patterns tab opens. See Figure J-5. The maroon color in the Sample box matches the current color displayed in the chart for the February data series. You decide that the series would show up better in a brighter shade of red.
6. Under Area, click the **red box** (third row, first color from the left), click **OK**, press **[Esc]** to deselect the data series, press **[Esc]** again to deselect the entire chart, then save the workbook
   The February data series now appears in a brighter shade of red.

QuickTip

If you have difficulty identifying the Chart Objects list arrow, rest your pointer on the first list arrow to the left on the Chart toolbar until the name "Chart Objects" appears.

QuickTip

The ToolTip name for the Format Data Series button changes, depending on what is selected. In this book it is called the Format Object button.

QuickTip

You also can click outside the chart to deselect it.

FIGURE J-3: Selected data series

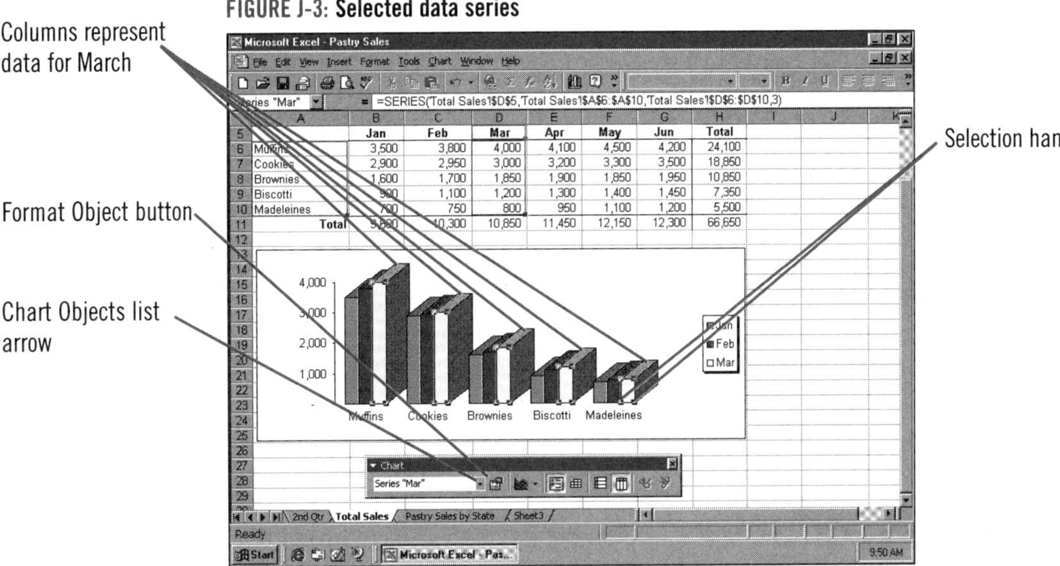

FIGURE J-4: Chart with data labels

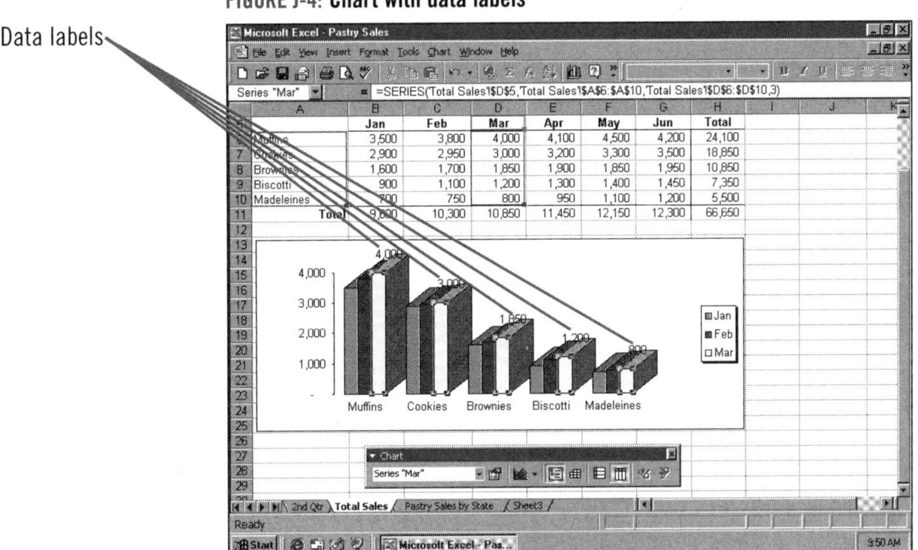

FIGURE J-5: Patterns tab settings

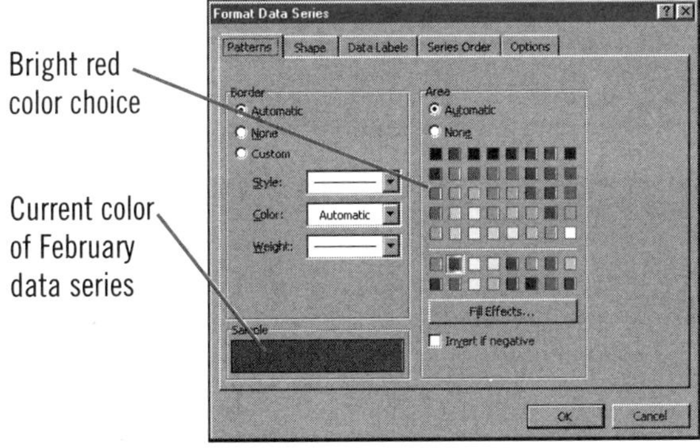

Removing, inserting, and formatting legends

To insert or remove a legend, click the Legend button on the Chart toolbar to toggle the legend on or off. To format legend text, click Legend in the Chart Objects list box of the Chart toolbar. Then click the Format Object button on the Chart toolbar and choose the options you want in the Font tab.

Excel 2000

Formatting a Chart Axis

Excel automatically plots and formats all chart data and places chart axes within the chart's **plot area**. Data values in two-dimensional charts are plotted on the value (*y*) axis and categories are plotted on the category (*x*) axis. Excel creates a scale for the value (*y*) axis that is based on the highest and lowest values in the data series. Then Excel determines the intervals in which the values occur along the scale. In three-dimensional charts, like the one in Figure J-6, Excel generates three axes, where *x* remains the category axis but *z* becomes the value axis and *y* becomes the measure for the third dimension on the chart, depth. In 3-D charts, the value (*z*) axis usually contains the scale. For a list of the axes Excel uses to plot data, see Table J-1. You can override the Excel default formats for chart axes at any time by using the Format Axis dialog box. Because the highest column is so close to the top of the chart, Jim wants to increase the maximum number on the value axis, which in this case is the *y*-axis, and change its number format. To begin, he selects the object he wants to format.

Steps

1. Click the **chart**, click the **Chart Objects list arrow** on the Chart toolbar, then click **Value Axis**
   The vertical axis becomes selected.
2. Click the **Format Object button** on the Chart toolbar, then click the **Scale tab**
   The Scale tab of the Format Axis dialog box opens. The check marks under Auto indicate the default scale settings. You can override any of these settings by entering a new value.
3. In the Maximum box select **4000**, type **5000**, then click **OK**
   The chart adjusts so that 5000 appears as the maximum value on the value axis. Next, you want the minimum value to appear as a zero (0) and not as a hyphen (-).
4. With the Value Axis still selected, click on the Chart toolbar, then click the **Number tab**
   The Number tab of the Format Axis dialog box opens. Currently, a custom format is selected under Category, which instructs Excel to use a hyphen instead of 0 as the lowest value.
5. Under Category click **General**, click **OK**, press **[Esc]** twice, then save the workbook
   The chart now shows 0 as the minimum value, as shown in Figure J-7.

FIGURE J-6: Chart elements in a 3-D chart

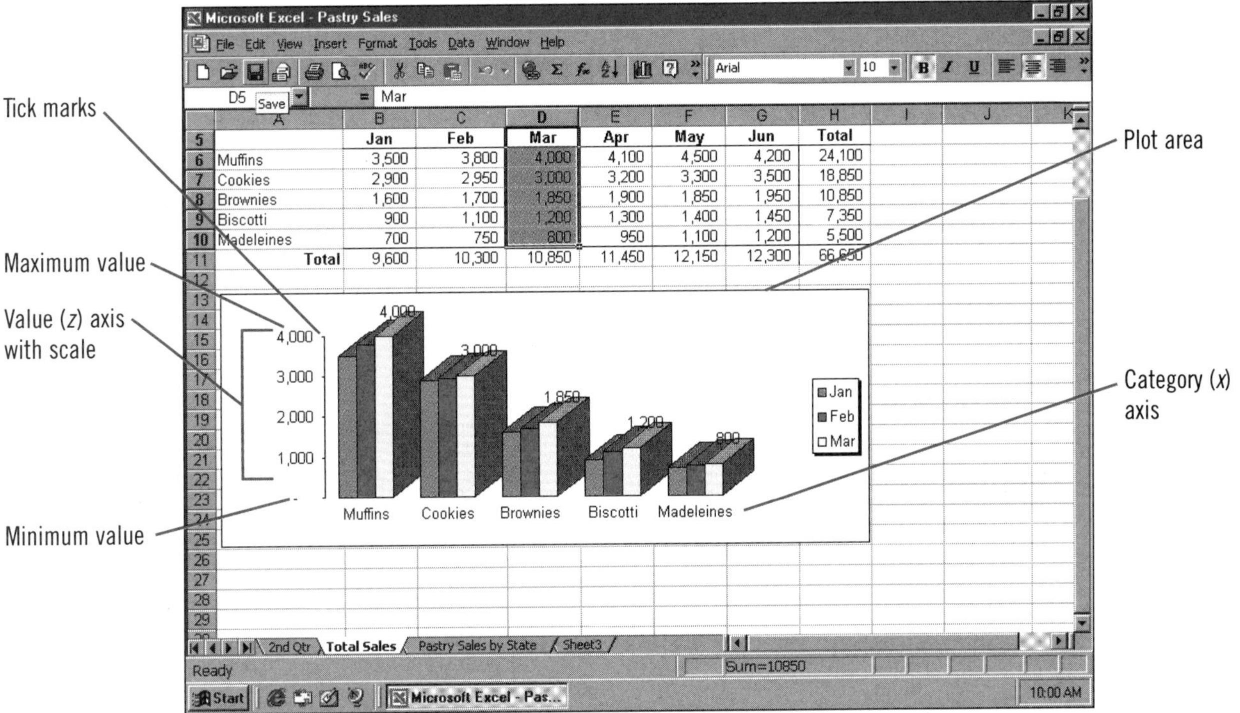

FIGURE J-7: Chart with formatted axis

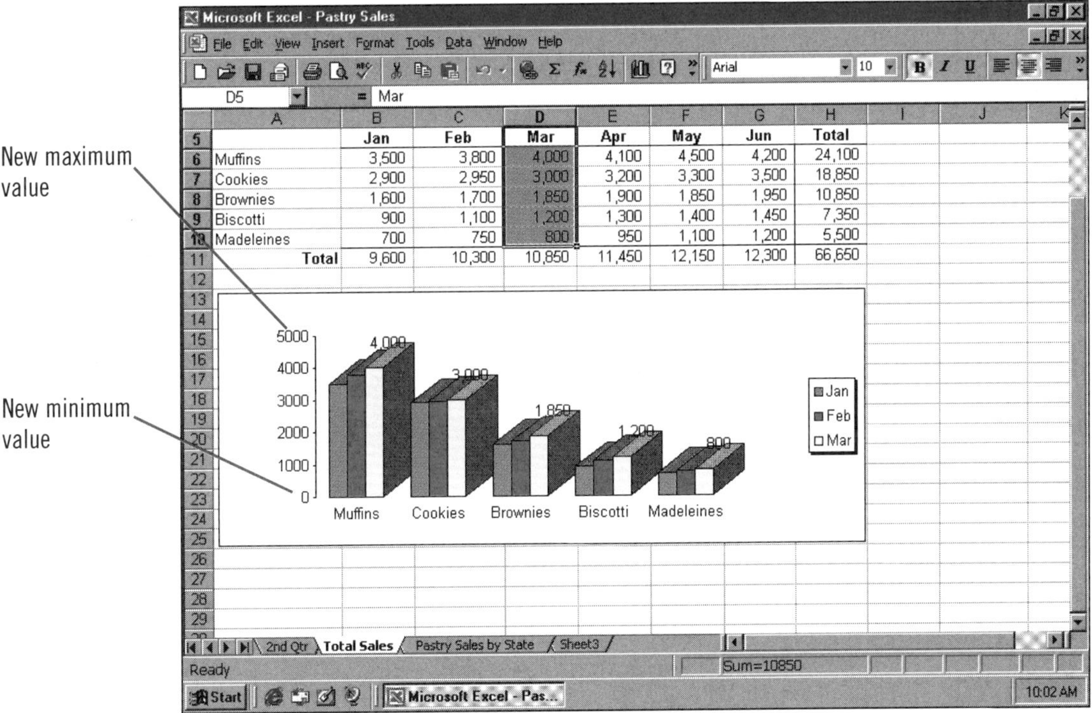

TABLE J-1: Axes used by Excel for chart formatting

axes in a two-dimensional chart	axes in a three-dimensional chart
Category (*x*) axis (horizontal)	Category (*x*) axis (horizontal)
Value (*y*) axis (vertical)	Series (*y*) axis (depth)
	Value (*z*) axis (vertical)

Excel 2000

Adding a Data Table to a Chart

A **data table**, attached to the bottom of a chart, is a grid containing the chart data. Data tables are useful because they highlight the data used to generate a chart, which might otherwise be difficult to find. Data tables can be displayed in line, area, column, and bar charts, and print automatically along with a chart. It's good practice to add data tables to charts stored separately from worksheet data. Jim wants to emphasize the first-quarter data used to generate his chart. He decides to add a data table.

Steps

QuickTip

You also do this when creating a chart in the Step 3 Chart Wizard dialog box.

QuickTip

To hide a data table, open the Data Table tab in the Chart Options dialog box, then clear the Show data table check box.

1. Click the **chart** to select it, click **Chart** on the menu bar, click **Chart Options**, then click the **Data Table tab**
   The Data Table tab in the Chart Options dialog box opens, as shown in Figure J-8. The preview window displays the selected chart.
2. Click the **Show data table check box** to select it
   The chart in the preview window changes to show what the chart will look like with a data table added to the bottom. See Figure J-9. The data table crowds the chart labels, making them hard to read. (Your chart may look slightly different.) You'll fix this problem after you close the Chart Options dialog box.
3. Click **OK**, then, if necessary, scroll down to display the chart
   The chart and the newly added data table look too crowded inside the current chart area. If you were to drag the chart borders to enlarge the chart, you wouldn't be able to see the entire chart displayed on the screen. It's more convenient to move the chart to its own sheet.
4. If necessary, click the **chart** to select it, click **Chart** on the menu bar, click **Location**, click the **As new sheet option button** under Place chart, click **OK**
   The chart is now located on a new sheet, where it is fully displayed in the worksheet window. See Figure J-10.
5. Put your name in the sheet footer, save the workbook, then print the chart sheet

FIGURE J-8: Data Table tab settings

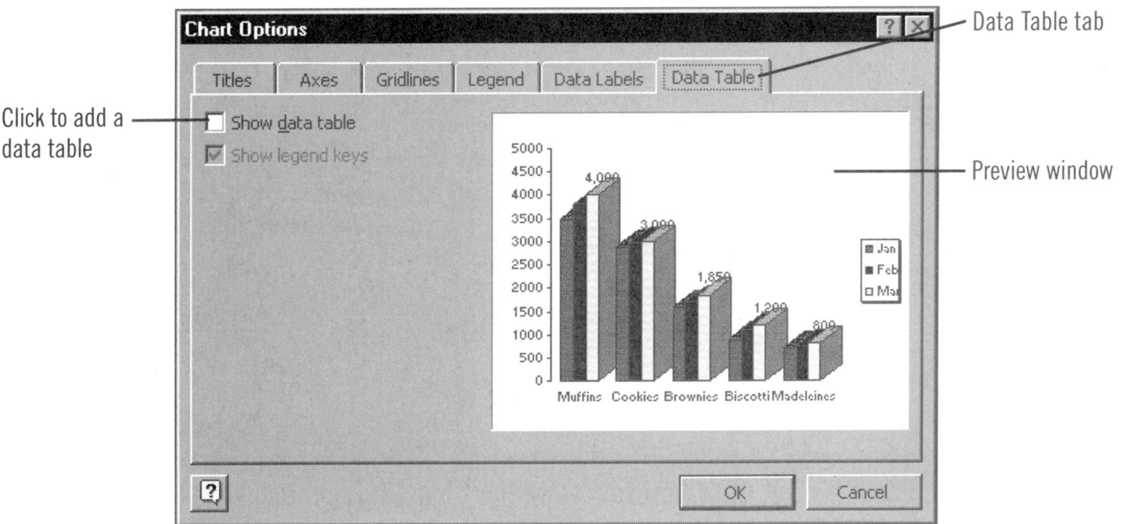

FIGURE J-9: Show Data Table box selected

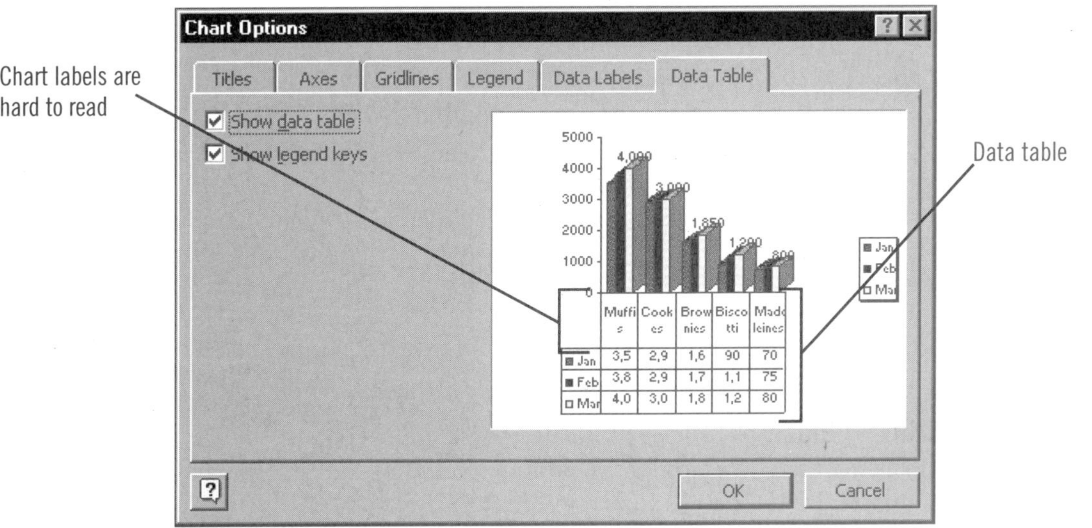

FIGURE J-10: Chart moved to chart sheet

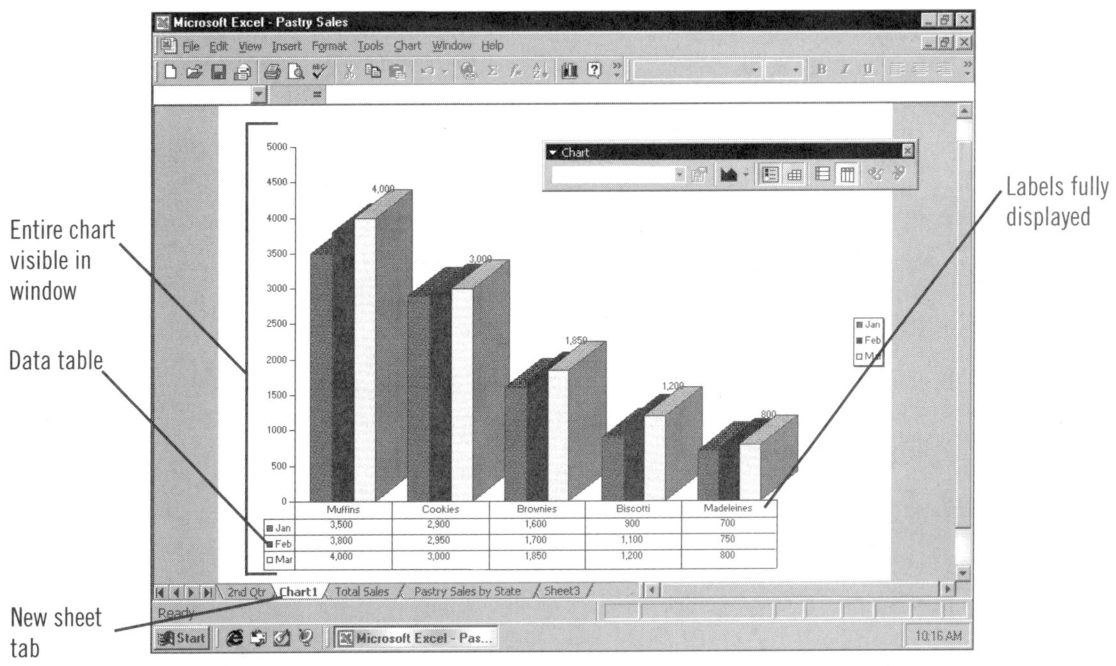

Excel 2000

Excel 2000

Rotating a Chart

Three-dimensional (3-D) charts do not always display data in the most effective way. In many cases, data in these charts can be obscured by one or more of the chart's data markers. By rotating and/or elevating the axes, you can improve the visibility of the chart's data. With Excel, you can adjust the rotation and elevation of a 3-D chart by dragging it with the mouse or using the 3-D View command on the Chart menu. Jim's workbook already contains a 3-D chart illustrating the sales data for the second quarter. He will display that chart, then rotate it so that the June columns are easier to see.

Steps

1. Click the **2nd Qtr sheet tab**, click the **Chart Objects list arrow** on the Chart toolbar, then click **Corners**
   Selection handles appear on the corners of the chart, as shown in Figure J-11.
2. Click the **lower-right corner handle** of the chart, press and hold the left mouse button, then drag the chart left approximately 2" until it looks like the object shown in Figure J-12, then release the mouse button
   The June columns are still not clearly visible. When using the dragging method to rotate a three-dimensional chart, you might need to make several attempts before you're satisfied with the view. It's usually more efficient to use the 3-D View option on the Chart menu.
3. Click **Chart** on the menu bar, click **3-D View**, then drag the **3-D View dialog box** to the upper-right corner of the screen
   See Figure J-13. The preview box in the 3-D View dialog box allows you to preview changes to the chart's orientation in the worksheet.
4. Click **Default**
   The chart returns to its original position. Next, Jim decreases the chart's elevation, the height from which the chart is viewed.
5. To the left of the preview box, click the **Decrease Elevation button**
   Notice how the preview image of the chart changes when you change the elevation.
6. Click **Apply**
   As the number in the Elevation box decreases, the viewpoint shifts downward. Note that the chart gains some vertical tick marks. Next, you'll change the rotation and **perspective**, or depth, of the chart.
7. In the Rotation box, select the current value, then type **55**; in the Perspective box, select the current value, type **0**, then click **Apply**
   The chart is reformatted. You notice, however, that the columns appear crowded. To correct this problem, you change the height as a percent of the chart base.
8. In the Height box, select the current value, type **70**, click **Apply**, then click **OK**
   The 3-D View dialog box closes. The chart columns now appear less crowded, making the chart easier to read.
9. Save your work

Trouble?

Don't worry if your 3-D View dialog box settings are different from the ones shown in Figure J-13.

Trouble?

If you have difficulty locating the Decrease Elevation button, refer to Figure J-13.

FIGURE J-11: Chart corners selected

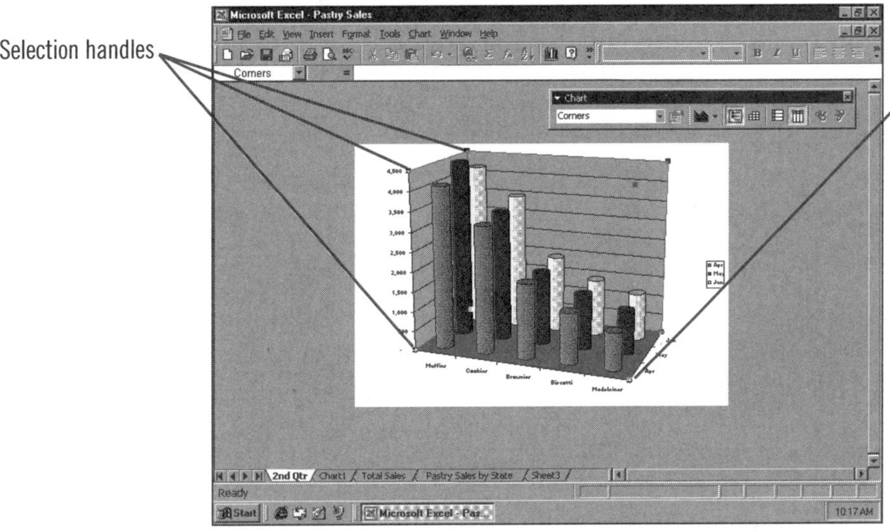

FIGURE J-12: Chart rotation in progress

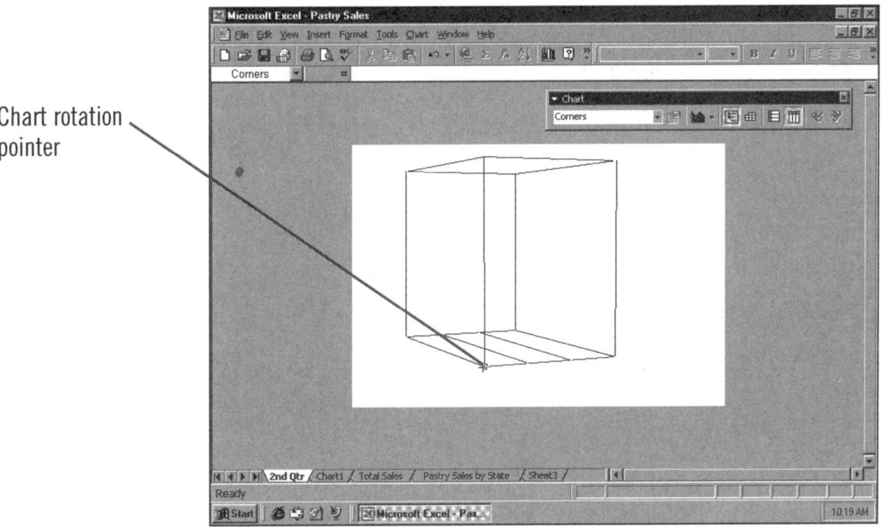

FIGURE J-13: Screen with chart and 3-D View dialog box

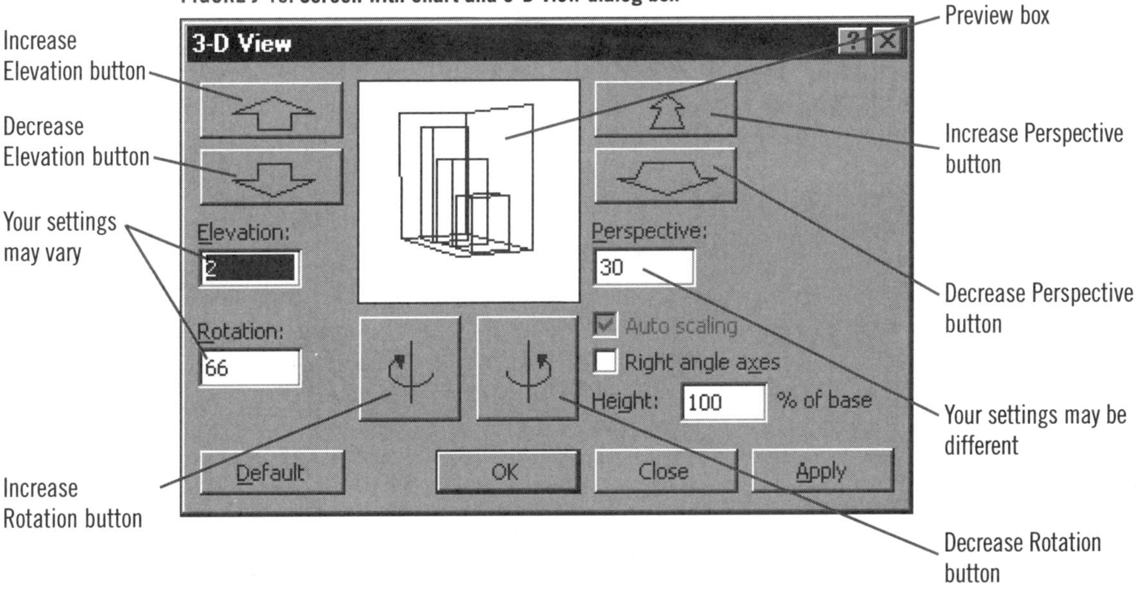

Increase Elevation button
Decrease Elevation button
Your settings may vary
Increase Rotation button
Preview box
Increase Perspective button
Decrease Perspective button
Your settings may be different
Decrease Rotation button

3-D View
Elevation: 2
Rotation: 66
Perspective: 30
Auto scaling
Right angle axes
Height: 100 % of base
Default
OK
Close
Apply

Excel 2000

Excel 2000

Enhancing a Chart with WordArt

You can enhance your chart or worksheet by adding specially formatted text using the WordArt tool on the Drawing toolbar. Once you've added a piece of WordArt to your workbook, you can edit or format it using the tools on the WordArt toolbar. Text formatted as WordArt is considered a drawing object rather than text. This means that WordArt objects cannot be treated as if they were labels entered in a cell; that is, you cannot sort, spell check, or use their cell references in formulas. Jim decides to add a WordArt title to the second-quarter chart. He begins by displaying the Drawing toolbar.

Steps

1. Click the **Drawing button** on the Standard toolbar
   The Drawing toolbar appears at the bottom of the Excel window. The WordArt text will be your chart title.
2. Click the **Insert WordArt button** on the Drawing toolbar
   The WordArt Gallery dialog box opens. This is where you select the style for your text.
3. In the second row, click the **second style from the left**, as shown in Figure J-14; then click **OK**
   The Edit WordArt Text dialog box opens, as shown in Figure J-15. This is where you enter the text you want to format as WordArt. You also can adjust the point size or font of the text or select bold or italic styles.
4. Type **2nd Quarter Sales**, click the **Bold button**, if necessary select **Times New Roman** in the Font list box and **36** in the Size list box, then click **OK**
   The Edit WordArt Text dialog box closes, and the chart reappears with the new title in the middle of the chart.
5. Place the pointer over 2nd Quarter Sales (the WordArt title) until the pointer changes to, then drag **2nd Quarter Sales** up until it appears in the upper-right corner of the chart
   The title is repositioned as shown in Figure J-16. Next, you decide to edit the WordArt to change "2nd" to the word "Second."
6. Click **Edit Text** on the WordArt toolbar, double-click **2nd** in the Edit WordArt Text box, type **Second**, then click **OK**
   The Edit WordArt Text dialog box closes, and the edited title appears over the chart.
7. Press **[Esc]** to deselect the WordArt, click, put your name in the chart sheet footer, save the workbook, then print the sheet

QuickTip

To delete a piece of WordArt, click it to make sure it is selected, then press [Delete].

QuickTip

To change the style of a piece of WordArt, click the WordArt Gallery button on the WordArt toolbar and select a new style.

FIGURE J-14: Selecting a WordArt style

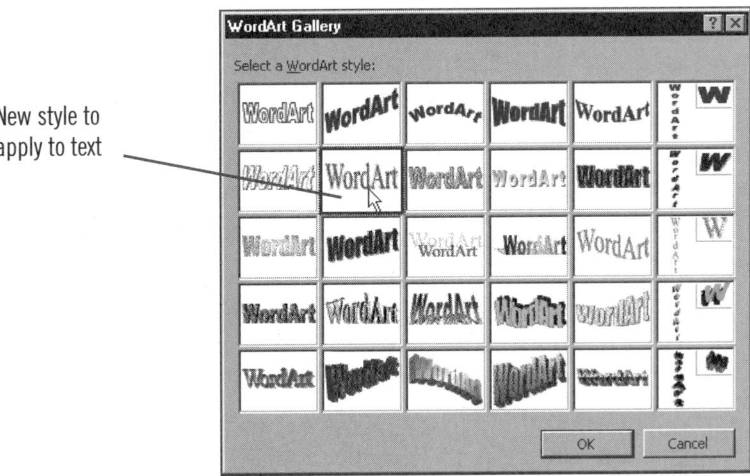

FIGURE J-15: Entering the WordArt text

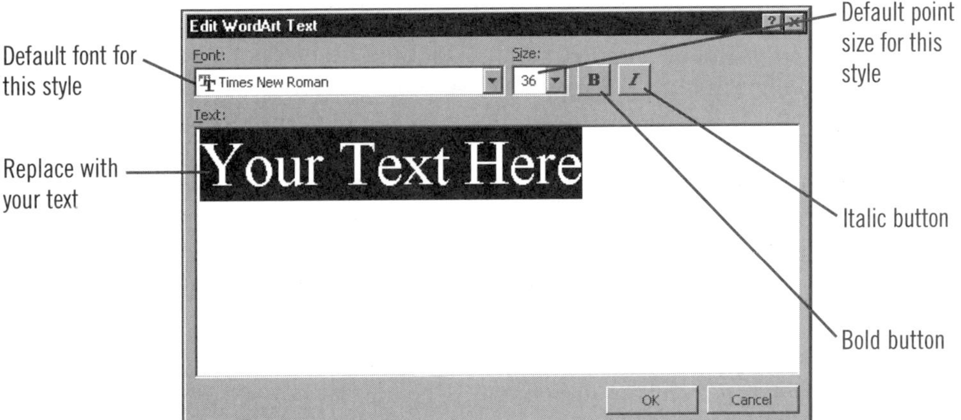

FIGURE J-16: Positioning the WordArt

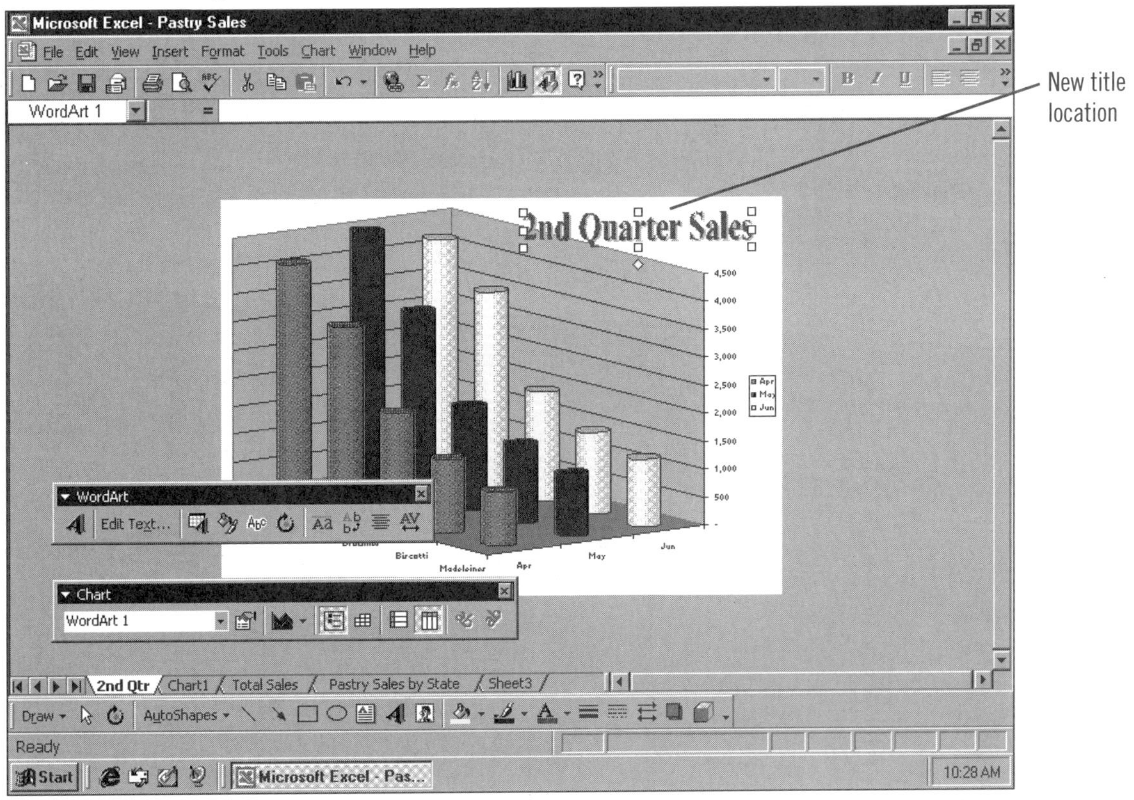

Excel 2000

Excel 2000

Rotating Text

By rotating text within a worksheet cell, you can draw attention to column labels or titles without turning the text into a drawing object (as in WordArt). Unlike WordArt, rotated text retains its usefulness as a worksheet entry, which means you can still sort it, spell check it, and use its cell reference in formulas. Now that he's finished enhancing the two charts in his workbook, Jim wants to improve the worksheet's appearance. He decides to rotate the column labels in cells B5 through G5.

Steps

1. Click the **Total Sales sheet tab**, make sure row 5 is the top row in the worksheet area, then select cells **B5:G5**
2. Click **Format** on the menu bar, click **Cells**, then click the **Alignment tab**
   The Alignment tab of the Format Cells dialog box opens. See Figure J-17. The settings under Orientation enable you to change the rotation of cell entries. Clicking the Vertical Text box on the left (the narrow one) allows you to display text vertically in the cell. To rotate the text to another angle, drag the rotation indicator in the Right Text box to the angle you want, or type the degree of angle you want in the Degrees box. You'll use the Degrees box to rotate the text entries.
3. Double-click the **Degrees box**, type **45**, then click **OK**
   The Format Cells dialog box closes.
4. If necessary, scroll up until row 1 is the top row in the worksheet area, then click cell **A1**
   The column labels for January through June now appear at a 45-degree angle in their cells, as shown in Figure J-18. The worksheet is now finished.
5. Put your name in the sheet footer, then save and print the worksheet

FIGURE J-17: Alignment tab settings

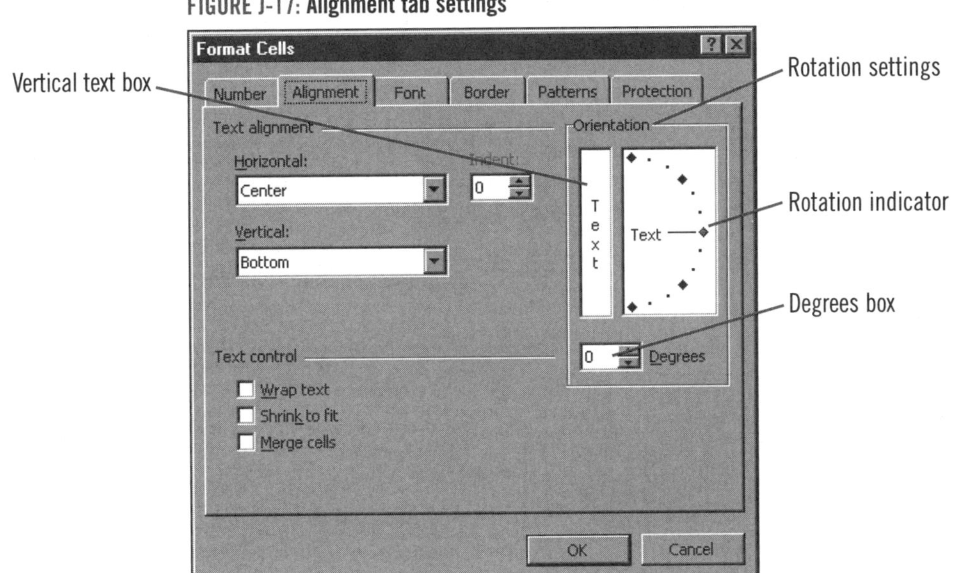

FIGURE J-18: Rotated column labels

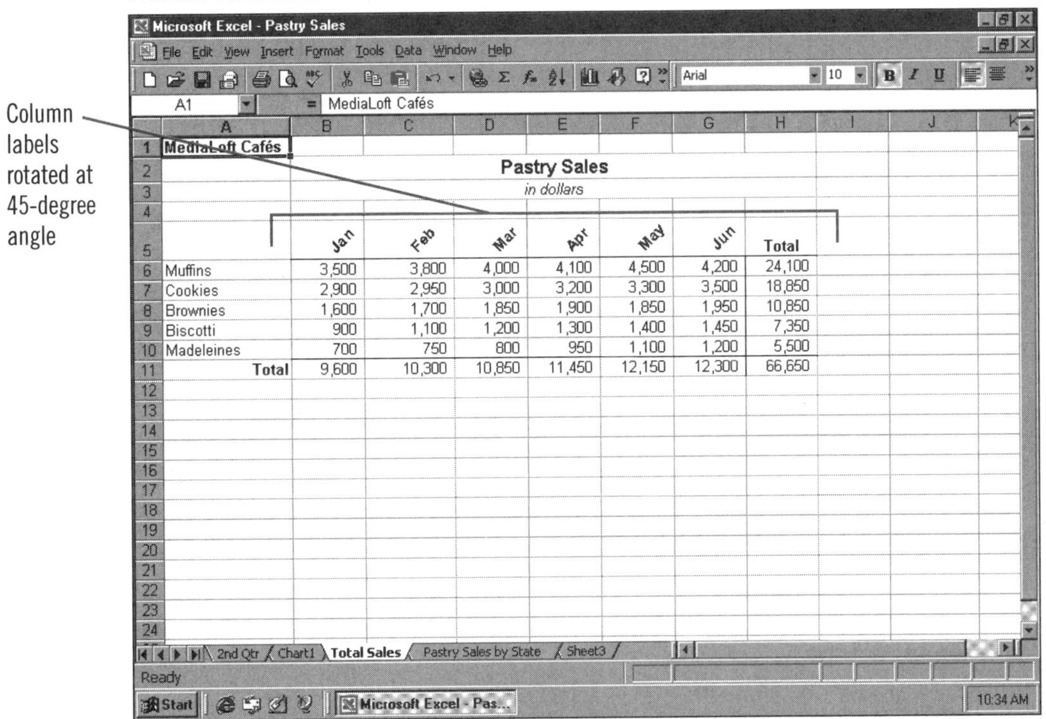

	Jan	Feb	Mar	Apr	May	Jun	Total
Muffins	3,500	3,800	4,000	4,100	4,500	4,200	24,100
Cookies	2,900	2,950	3,000	3,200	3,300	3,500	18,850
Brownies	1,600	1,700	1,850	1,900	1,850	1,950	10,850
Biscotti	900	1,100	1,200	1,300	1,400	1,450	7,350
Madeleines	700	750	800	950	1,100	1,200	5,500
Total	9,600	10,300	10,850	11,450	12,150	12,300	66,650

Rotating chart labels

You can easily rotate the category labels on a chart by using the buttons on the Chart toolbar. First, you select the Category Axis in the Chart Objects list box. Then you click either the Angle Text Downward button or the Angle Text Upward button on the Chart toolbar.

Mapping Data

A **data map** shows geographic features and their associated data. To create a simple data map, arrange your worksheet data in two columns—with the first containing geographic data, such as the names of countries or states, and the second column containing the related data. Jim has compiled detailed sales figures for pastry by state. Now, he wants to create a map that clearly illustrates which states have the highest sales. He begins by selecting the data he wants to map.

Steps 1 2 3 4

1. Click the **Pastry Sales by State sheet tab**, then select the range **A4:B11**
   The first column of data contains the state names and the second contains the sales figures for each state. The column labels in row 4 (which you also selected) will be used in the legend title.
2. Click the **Map button** on the Standard toolbar, drag the **crosshair pointer** from the middle of cell C4 to the lower-right corner of cell H23, then release the mouse button
   The map range is outlined on the worksheet, and the Multiple Maps Available dialog box opens on top.
3. Click **United States (AK & HI Inset) if necessary**, then click **OK**
   The map and the Microsoft Map Control dialog boxes appear.
4. Drag the **Microsoft Map Control dialog box** to the lower-left corner of the screen, then scroll up until most of the map is visible on your screen
   See Figure J-19. Excel automatically divides the sales data into intervals and assigns a different shade of gray to each interval, as the map legend indicates. The rectangular border indicates that the map is in Edit mode.
5. Double-click the **United States (AK & HI Inset) map title**, select the **default text** in the Edit Text Object dialog box, type **MediaLoft Pastry Sales**, then click **OK**
   The new title replaces the default map title. Next, to highlight the sales data more dramatically, you'll change the way values are represented using the Microsoft Map Control dialog box, shown in Figure J-20. You adjust the way data is represented on the map by dragging format buttons into the Format box. You want to change the format from shading to dots of varying density.
6. Click the **Dot Density button** in the Microsoft Map Control dialog box, then drag it over the top of the Value Shading button in the Format box
   When you release the mouse button, the map display changes from shading to dots, with one dot equal to $6,000 in pastry sales.
7. Click **Map** on the Menu bar, click **Features**, under Fill Color click the **Custom option button**, click the **Custom list arrow**, click the **turquoise square**, then click **OK**
   The map's background color changes to turquoise, as shown in Figure J-21. The legend could be more descriptive.
8. Double-click the **map legend**; click the **Legend Options tab** in the Format Properties dialog box if necessary; select the **default text** in the Title box, type **1st and 2nd Quarter**, then click **OK**
9. Press **[Esc]** three times to deselect the map, put your name in the sheet footer, save the workbook, print the worksheet, and exit Excel

Trouble?

If you don't see the Map button, click Tools on the menu bar, click Command, and click Insert. Then under Commands, scroll to the Map icon and drag it to the Standard toolbar.

QuickTip

Click the Map Refresh button to incorporate any changes to the data range into an existing map.

Trouble?

If your map doesn't print, your printer may not have enough memory. Try using another printer.

FIGURE J-19: Newly created map

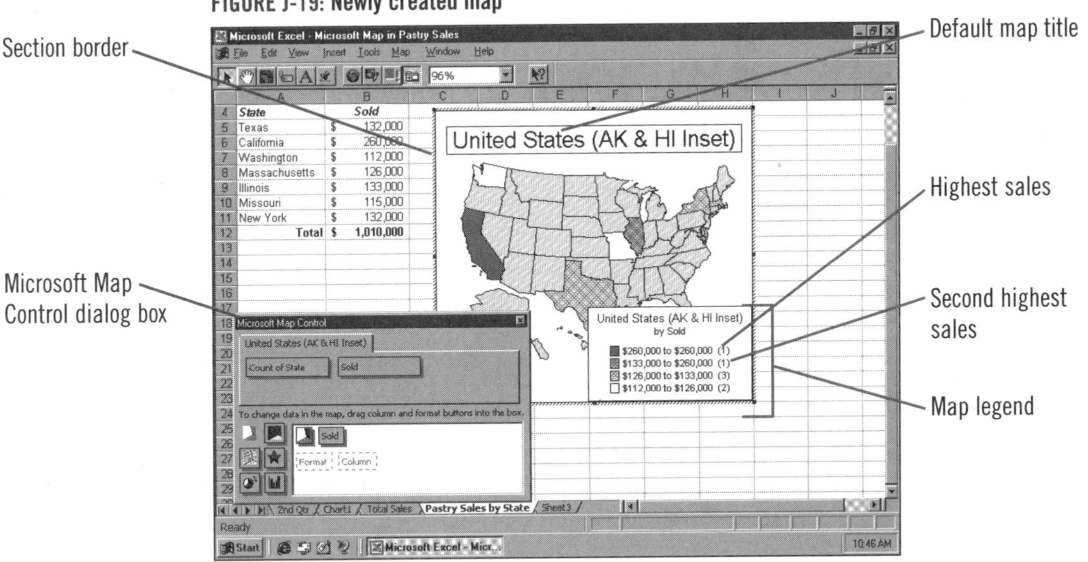

FIGURE J-20: Microsoft Map Control dialog box

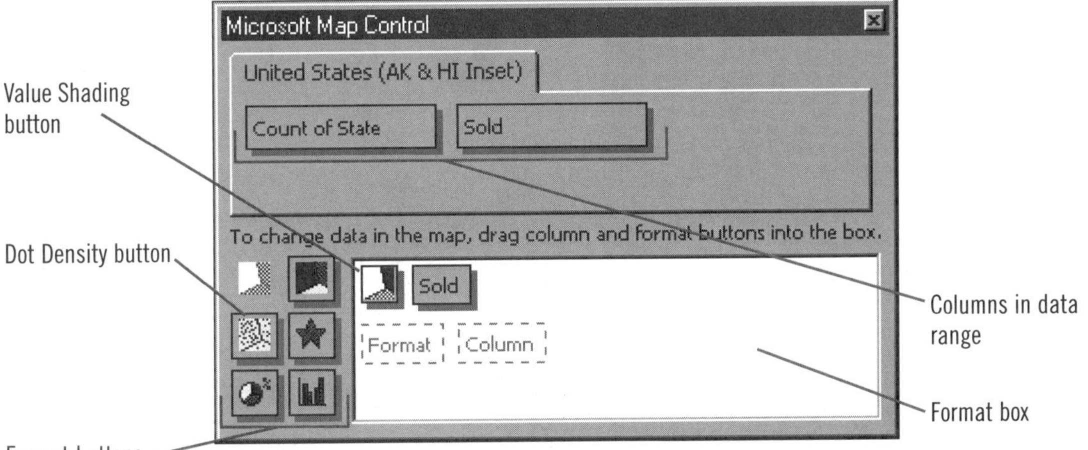

FIGURE J-21: Values formatted as dots

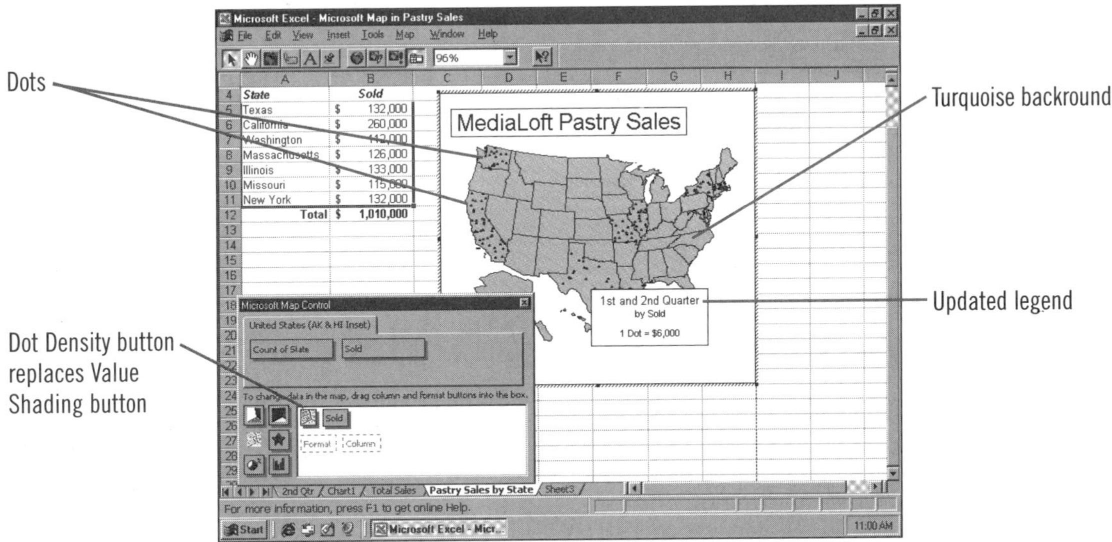

Excel 2000

Practice

► Concepts Review

Label each element of the Excel screen shown in Figure J-22.

FIGURE J-22

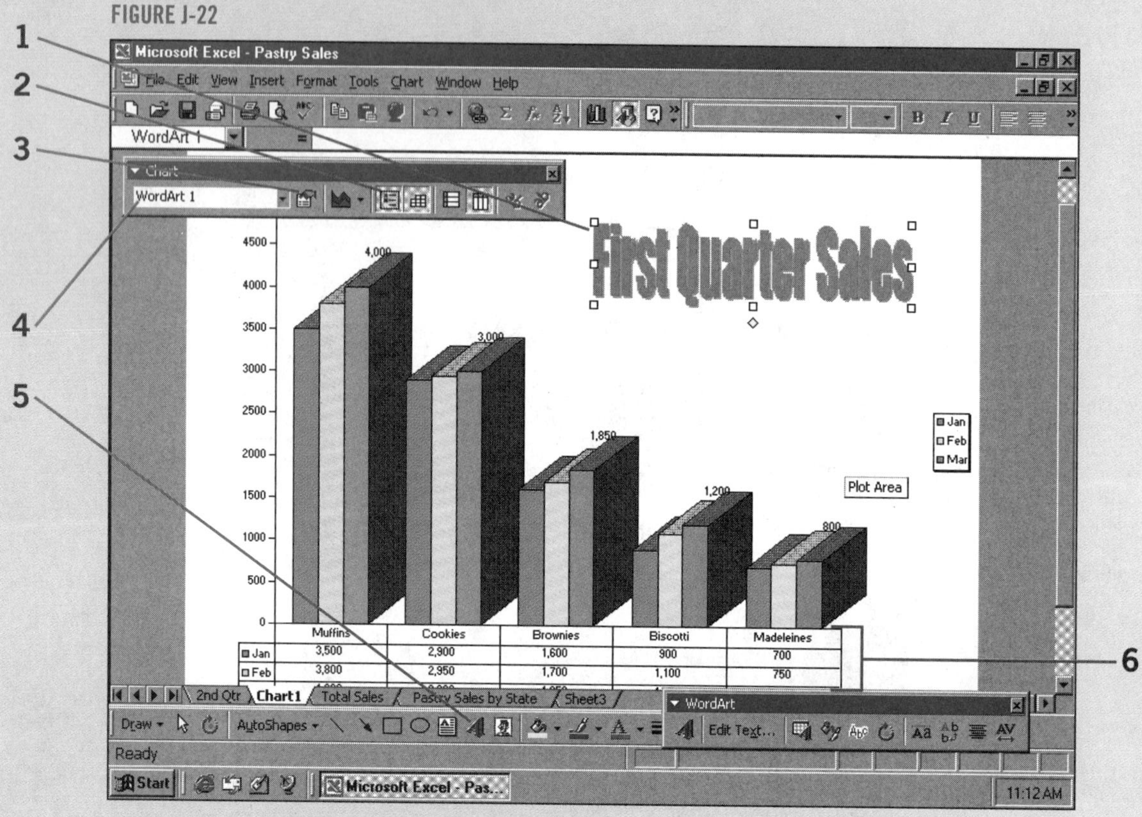

Match each button with the statement that describes it.

7.
8.
9.
10.
11.

a. Opens the WordArt dialog boxes
b. Use to format the selected chart object
c. Use to create a data map
d. Use to change the style of a piece of WordArt
e. Use to display the Drawing toolbar

Select the best answer from the list of choices.

12. A chart's scale

a. Appears on the category (*x*) axis.
b. Displays values on the value (*y*) axis or the value (*z*) axis.
c. Always appears on the value (*y*) axis.
d. Cannot be modified.

13. What is the most efficient method of rotating a 3-D chart?

a. Click Edit on the menu bar, then click Default.
b. Adjust settings in the 3-D View dialog box.
c. Select the chart corners, then drag a corner.
d. Delete the chart, and start over with a new one.

14. How can you change the way data is represented on a map?

a. Drag format buttons in the Microsoft Data Control dialog box.
b. Click Map, then click Data Representation.
c. Click the Map Refresh button.
d. None of the above.

15. Which statement best describes the difference between two- and three-dimensional column charts?

a. Two-dimensional charts have category (*x*) and value (*y*) axes; three-dimensional charts have category (*x*), series (*y*), and value (*z*) axes.
b. Two-dimensional charts show the data in three dimensions.
c. Three-dimensional charts show the data in four dimensions.
d. Two-dimensional charts have a value scale on the *x*-axis, and three-dimensional charts have a value scale on the *z*-axis.

16. What is a data table?

a. A three-dimensional arrangement of data on the *y*-axis.
b. Worksheet data arranged geographically.
c. A customized data series.
d. The data used to create a chart displayed in a grid.

17. A custom chart type

a. Is supplied only by Excel.
b. Can be supplied by Excel or the user.
c. Cannot be saved.
d. All of the above.

18. To rotate text in a worksheet cell,

a. Adjust settings on the Alignment tab of the Format cells dialog box.
b. Click the Rotate button on the Standard toolbar.
c. Select the text, then drag to rotate it the desired number of degrees.
d. Format the text as WordArt, then drag the WordArt.

▶ Skills Review

1. **Select a custom chart type.**
   a. Open the workbook titled EX J-2, then save it as "MediaLoft Coffee Sales".
   b. On the 1st Quarter sheet, select the range A4:B7.
   c. Open the Chart Wizard, and on the Custom Types tab in the Chart Wizard dialog box, make sure the Built-in option button is selected.
   d. Select Blue Pie in the Chart type box.
   e. Go to the Step 2 Chart Wizard dialog box.
   f. Make sure the data range is correct, then go to the Step 3 Chart Wizard dialog box, read the contents, then go to the Step 4 Chart Wizard dialog box.
   g. Make sure the As Object In button is selected, then finish the Wizard.
   h. Drag the chart to a better location in the worksheet.
   i. Put your name in the sheet footer, then save, preview, and print the worksheet data and chart.
2. **Customize a data series.**
   a. On the 2nd Quarter sheet, move the June data in D4:D7 into the chart area.
   b. Select the April data series and display its data labels.
   c. Use the Format Data Series dialog box to change the color of the May data series to the green color of your choice.
   d. Save the workbook.
3. **Format a chart axis.**
   a. Select the value axis.
   b. Set its maximum to 10000 and its minimum to 0.
   c. On the Number tab in the Format Axis dialog box under Category, use the Currency format to add a dollar sign and two decimal places to the values, then close the dialog box.
   d. Save the workbook.
4. **Add a data table to a chart.**
   a. Show the data table.
   b. Use the Location command on the Chart menu to move the chart to its own sheet.
   c. Display the 3rd Quarter sheet tab.
   d. Use the Data Table tab in the Chart Options dialog box to hide the data table.
   e. Remove the chart legend.
   f. Save the workbook.
5. **Rotate a chart.**
   a. On the Chart1 sheet, use the Chart Objects list arrow to select the chart corners.
   b. Drag a chart corner to rotate the chart.
   c. Return the chart to its default rotation using the 3-D View command on the Chart menu.
   d. Change the rotation to 315.
   e. Change the elevation to 13.
   f. Deselect the chart corners.
   g. Save the workbook.

6. **Enhance a chart with WordArt.**
   a. Display the Drawing toolbar.
   b. Open WordArt and select the second style from the right in the second row.
   c. In the Edit WordArt Text dialog box, enter the text "Second Quarter Sales" and format it in italic.
   d. Position the new title above the chart.
   e. Make sure the WordArt is still selected, then use the WordArt Gallery button on the WordArt toolbar to select a new style for the title.
   f. Save the workbook.
   g. Close the Drawing toolbar.
7. **Rotate text.**
   a. On the 1st Quarter sheet tab, select cells B4:D4.
   b. Change the alignment to 45 degrees.
   c. On the 2nd Quarter sheet tab, select the range B4:D4.
   d. Use the rotation indicator on the Alignment tab in the Format Cells dialog box to change the rotation to 45 degrees.
   e. On the 3rd Quarter sheet tab, rotate the Category Axis labels downward.
   f. Save the workbook.
8. **Map worksheet data.**
   a. Make the Mail Order Contacts sheet active.
   b. Select the range A4:B16.
   c. Start Microsoft Map.
   d. Position the map in the range C4:H23, and use the United States (AK & HI Inset) map.
   e. Change the map title to "Western Region Contacts".
   f. Change the map's background color to bright pink.
   g. Change the data formatting to dot density.
   h. Change the legend title to "Mail Order".
   i. In cell B9, change the data for California to 25.
   j. Double-click the map to put it in Edit mode, then click the Map Refresh button on the Map toolbar to update the map.
   k. Put your name in the sheet footer, save the workbook, then select, preview, and print each sheet in the workbook.

► Independent Challenges

1. You are the owner of Sandwich Express, a metropolitan delicatessen. Each week, you order several pounds of cheese: Cheddar, Monterey Jack, Swiss, Provolone, and American. Last month was especially busy, and you ordered an increasing amount of cheese each week in every category except American, which is declining in popularity. Recently, your spouse has joined you in the business and wants to develop a more efficient forecast of the amount of cheese to order each week. To help your spouse analyze last month's cheese orders, you developed a worksheet with a three-dimensional stacked bar chart. Now, you want to enhance the chart by adding data labels, reformatting the value (*z*) axis, increasing the elevation, and adding several titles.

To complete this independent challenge:

a. Open the workbook titled EX J-3, then save it as "Cheese Order Tracking".
b. Customize the data series. Add the data for 8/22 and 8/29 to the chart. Then add data labels to all data markers.
c. Reformat the value (*z*) axis to show values every 40 pounds instead of every 50 pounds.

d. Increase the chart's elevation.
e. Add a WordArt title that reads "Cheese Ordered in August".
f. Move the chart to a chart sheet and add a data table.
g. Put your name in the footer of each sheet, preview and print the worksheet and chart together, then save the workbook.

2. As the owner of Sandwich Express, you meet quarterly with your dairy product salesman, James Snyder, to discuss trends in dairy product usage at your delicatessen. These quarterly meetings seem to take longer than necessary, and you are not always sure he has retained all the information discussed. You decide to use charts to communicate during these meetings. As part of your presentation at the end of the third quarter, you decide to generate an additional chart showing what percentage of the total cheese orders for each month each cheese type represents, starting with August. Because this chart will compare parts of a whole, you create a three-dimensional pie chart. Also, to ensure the intended messages are communicated effectively, you add a few enhancements to the chart and worksheet. First, you need to add totals to the worksheet.

To complete this independent challenge:

a. Open the workbook titled EX J-3, then save it as "Cheese Order Pie".
b. Select and delete the current 3-D bar chart from the worksheet.
c. Add monthly totals in column G that total each cheese type across all five weeks. Then calculate a grand total for the month. (*Hint*: To double-check your monthly total, add totals for each week in row 10. Then insert totals for each week, select the totals in B10:F10, and note the sum in the AutoCalculate box in the Status bar.)
d. Use the Chart Wizard to create a custom chart showing what percentage of the total cheese ordered in August (1,745 pounds) each type of cheese represents. (*Hint*: Use the Control key to select nonadjacent ranges of cheese types and totals to be charted before you open the Chart Wizard.) Place the chart on its own sheet.
e. Add the WordArt title "Sandwich Express—August Cheese Orders".
f. Add an italicized WordArt subtitle that reads "(% of total pounds ordered)".
g. In the August worksheet, rotate the dates in row 4 to a 45-degree angle.
h. Put your name in the footer of each sheet, review and save the workbook, then print the worksheet and the chart.

3. You are a real estate agent for Galaxy Properties, which specializes in residential real estate. In September, you were voted salesperson of the month. Your sales manager has asked you to assemble a brief presentation on your sales activity during September to show to the new agents in the office. You decide to include a chart showing how many properties you closed and their respective dollar amounts in each of three areas: single-family homes, condominiums, and townhouses. Using your own data, create a worksheet and accompanying chart to present the data. Enhance the chart as outlined in the following.

To complete this independent challenge:

a. Create a new workbook, then save it as "September Sales, Galaxy Properties".
b. Enter your own worksheet labels, data, and formulas.
c. Create a custom bar chart showing your September sales activity.
d. Include data labels on the condominium data series.
e. Add a WordArt title.
f. Add new data to the worksheet for rental properties, then add the data series to the chart.
g. Move the chart to a chart sheet and add a data table.
h. Rotate the column labels in the worksheet.
i. Put your name in the sheet footers, preview and print the worksheet and chart, then save the workbook.

4. Maria Abbott of the MediaLoft Sales department has asked you to chart some information from a recent survey of MediaLoft book customers.

To complete this independent challenge:

a. Connect to the Internet, and go to the MediaLoft intranet site at http://www.course.com/Illustrated/MediaLoft. Click the Marketing link, then click the Book Survey Results link. Print the results of the survey. Disconnect from the Internet.
b. Open a new Excel worksheet and save it as "Book Survey". Enter the occupation information in question 5 of the survey, and chart it using a pie chart of your choice on the same sheet. Enlarge the chart to be as large as possible while still fitting on the screen.
c. Move the chart to a separate sheet; name the sheet "Occupation".
d. Reformat one of the pie slices by single-clicking the chart, then single-clicking a slice. Format the area with a new color.
e. Chart the # of children data in question 9 as a horizontal bar chart. Do not add a legend or a title. Place it on a sheet named "Children".
f. Add a WordArt Title to each chart.
g. Rotate the category axis labels on the Children sheet so they point downward and to the right.
h. Put your name in the sheet footers, save the workbook, print all three sheets, then exit Excel.

▶ Visual Workshop

Create the worksheet and accompanying custom chart shown in Figure J-23. Save the workbook as "The Dutch Garden". Study the chart and worksheet carefully to make sure you start with the most appropriate chart type, and then make all the modifications shown. Put your name in the sheet footer, preview, and then print the worksheet and chart together in landscape orientation.

FIGURE J-23

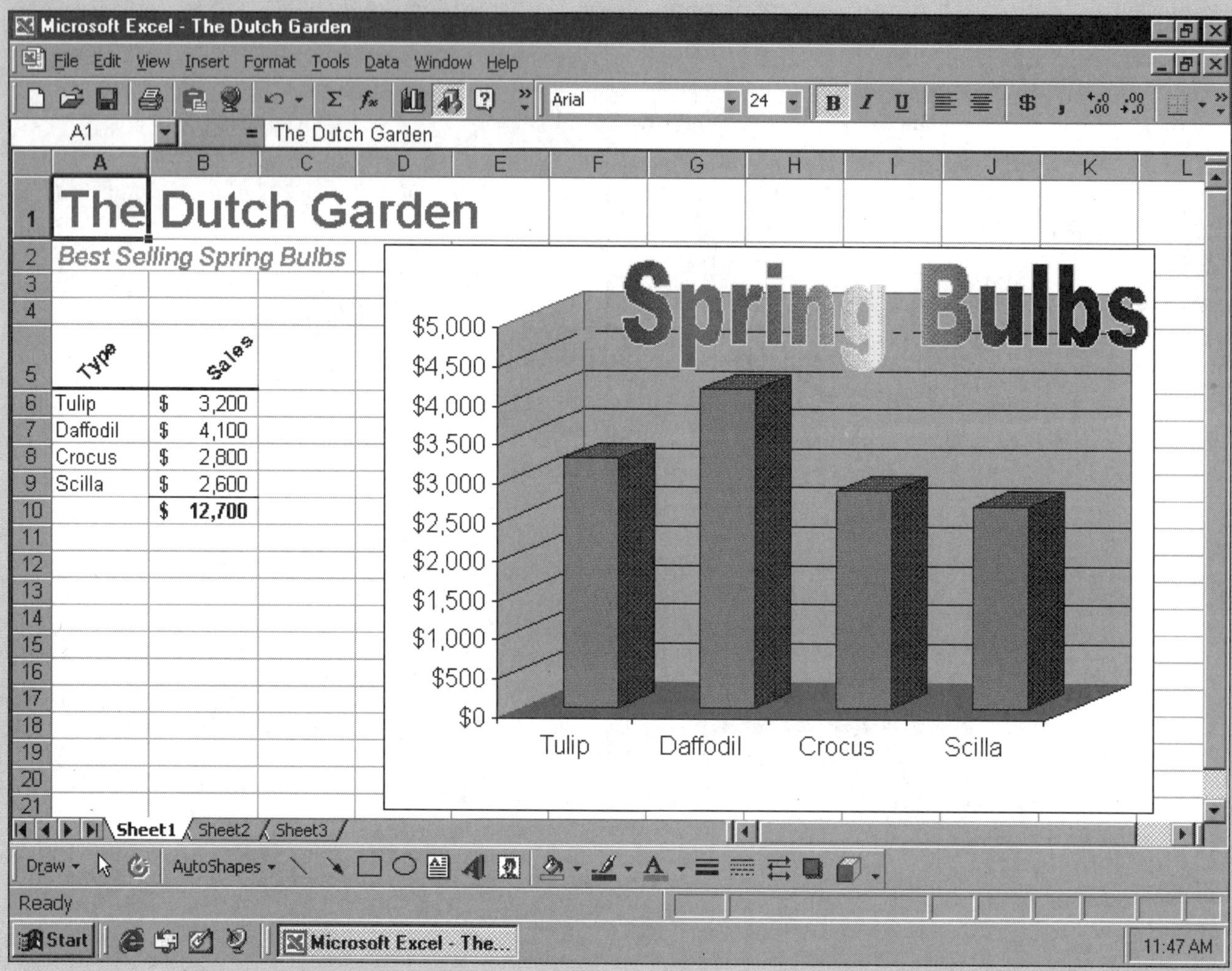

Excel 2000

Unit N

Sharing

Excel Files and Incorporating Web Information

Objectives

- Share Excel Files
- Set up a shared workbook
- Track changes in a shared workbook
- Apply and remove passwords
- Create an interactive worksheet for an intranet or the Web
- Create an interactive PivotTable for an intranet or the Web
- Create hyperlinks between Excel files and the Web
- Run queries to retrieve data on the Web

With the recent growth of networks, company intranets, and the World Wide Web, people are increasingly sharing electronic spreadsheet files with others for review, revision, and feedback. They are also incorporating information from intranets and the World Wide Web into their worksheets. Jim Fernandez has some MediaLoft corporate information he wants to share with corporate office employees and store managers. He also wants to track information on MediaLoft's competitors.

Excel 2000

Sharing Excel Files

Microsoft Excel provides many different ways to share spreadsheets electronically with people in your office, company, or anywhere on the World Wide Web. Users can not only retrieve and review your workbooks and worksheets, but they can modify them electronically and return their revisions to you for incorporation with others' changes. When you share workbooks, you also have to consider how you will protect information that you don't want everyone to see. You can post workbooks, worksheets, or other parts of workbooks for users to interact with on a company intranet or on the World Wide Web. You can also use Excel workbooks to run queries to retrieve data from the Web. Jim considers the best way to share his Excel workbooks with corporate employees and store managers. He also thinks about how to get Web data for use in his workbooks. He considers the following issues:

Details

Allowing others to use a workbook

When you pass on Excel files to others, you could just have them write their comments on a printed copy. But it's easier to set up your workbook so that several users can simultaneously open the workbook from a network server and modify it. Then you can view each user's name and the date the change was made. Jim wants to get feedback on selected store sales and customer information from MediaLoft corporate staff and store managers.

Controlling access to workbooks on a server

When you set up a workbook on a network server, you may want to control who can open and make changes to it. You can do this easily with Excel passwords. Jim assigns a password to his workbook and gives it to the corporate staff and store managers, so only they will be able to open it and make changes.

Distributing workbooks to others

There are several ways of making workbook information available to others. You can send it to recipients simultaneously as an e-mail attachment or as the body of an e-mail message; you can **route** it, or send it sequentially to each user, who then forwards it on to the next user using a **routing slip**, or list of recipients. You can also save the file in HTML format and post it on a company intranet server or on the Web, where people can view it with their Web browsers. Jim decides to make an Excel workbook available to others by putting it on a central company server.

Publishing a worksheet for use on an intranet or the World Wide Web

When you save a workbook in HTML format, you can save the entire workbook or just part of it—a worksheet, a chart, a filtered list, a cell range, or a print area. When you save only part of a workbook, you can specify that you want to make that particular part, or object, **interactive**, meaning that users can make changes to it when they view it in their browsers. They do not have to have the Excel program on their machines. See Figure N-1. The changes remain in effect until users close their browsers. Jim decides to publish part of a worksheet about MediaLoft café pastry sales.

Interactive PivotTables

You can save a PivotTable in HTML format so people can only view it, but the data is much more useful if people can interact with it from their browsers, just as they would in Excel. To make an Excel PivotTable interactive, you need to save it as a PivotTable list. Jim wants corporate staff to explore some sales data using their browsers just as he would with Excel.

Creating hyperlinks to the Web

You can make Web information available to users by creating hyperlinks to any site on the Web. Jim decides to include a hyperlink to a competitor's Web site.

Using an Excel query to retrieve data from the Web

By using Microsoft Query from Excel, you can get data from the Web that you can bring into your workbooks, and then organize and manipulate it with Excel spreadsheet and graphics tools. See Figure N-2. Jim uses a query to get stock information about one of MediaLoft's competitors.

FIGURE N-1: **Interactive worksheet in Web browser**

Toolbar allows users to manipulate worksheet data and format in browser

A:\Managers.htm - Microsoft Internet Explorer

	B	C	D	E	F	G	H
18	Dumont	10/4/86	Corporate Manager	Director of Training	3	68,500	4
19	Stephens	11/3/93	Corporate Manager	Training Manager	3	62,000	4
20	Kimball	5/8/89	Store Manager	Boston Store Manag	3	52,000	4
21	Greenwood	6/2/98	Store Manager	Chicago Store Mana	3	51,500	4
22	Feake	10/9/97	Store Manager	Houston Store Mana	3	47,500	3
23	Hensley	11/19/98	Store Manager	Kansas City Store M	3	43,500	4
24	Manchevski	4/19/97	Store Manager	New York Store Man	3	58,000	3
25	Barradas	12/5/98	Store Manager	San Diego Store Mar	3	55,000	5
26	Martin	5/5/97	Store Manager	San Francisco Store	3	59,000	4
27	Gray	9/26/96	Store Manager	Seattle Store Manag	3	54,500	3
28						=SUM(G2:G27)	

Adding a worksheet total in Internet Explorer

FIGURE N-2: **Retrieving data from the World Wide Web using a Web query**

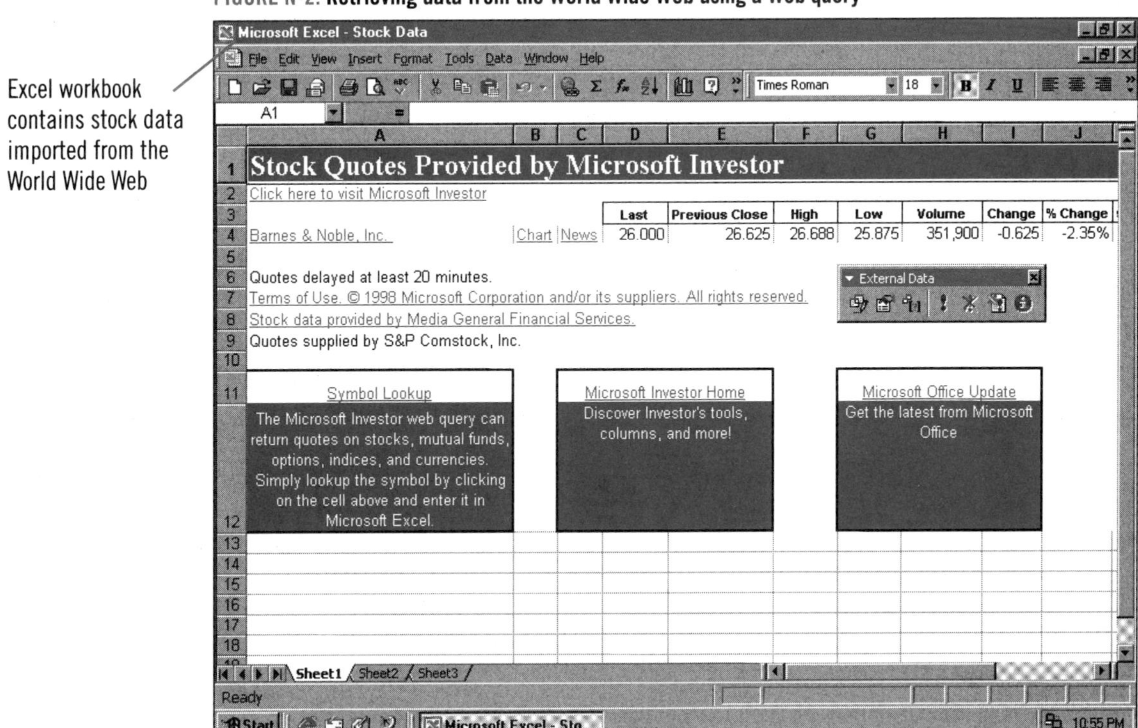

Excel workbook contains stock data imported from the World Wide Web

Excel 2000

Excel 2000

Setting Up a Shared Workbook

You can make an Excel file a **shared workbook** so that several users can open and modify it at the same time. This is very useful for workbooks that you want others to review on a network server. The workbook is equally accessible to all users who have access to that location on the network. When you share a workbook, you can have Excel keep a list of all changes to the workbook, called a **change history**, that you can view and print at any time. Users must have Excel 97 or later to modify the workbook. Jim makes his workbook containing customer and sales data a shared workbook. He will later put it on a network server and ask for feedback from selected corporate staff and store managers before using the information in a presentation at the next corporate staff meeting.

QuickTip

To return personalized toolbars and menus to their default state, click Tools on the menu bar, click Customize, click the Options tab in the Customize dialog box, click Reset my usage data to restore the default settings, click Yes, click Close, then close the Drawing toolbar if it is displayed.

QuickTip

You can remove users from the list by clicking their names and clicking Remove User.

QuickTip

You can easily return the workbook to unshared status. Click Tools, click Share Workbook, and on the Editing tab click to deselect the Allow changes… option.

1. Open the workbook titled **EX N-1**, then save it as **Sales Info**
   The workbook with the sales information opens. It contains three worksheets. The first is the chart of café pastry sales for the first quarter, the second contains the worksheet and map of pastry sales by state, and the third contains a listing of sales for selected stores and sales representatives for the last four quarters.
2. Click **Tools** on the menu bar, then click **Share Workbook**
   The Share Workbook dialog box opens, similar to Figure N-3.
3. If necessary, click the **Editing** tab
   The lower part of the dialog box lists the names of people who are currently using the workbook. You are the only user, so your name (or the name of the person entered as the machine user) appears, along with the date and time.
4. Click to select the check box next to **Allow changes by more than one user at the same time**, then click **OK**
   A dialog box appears, asking if you want to save the workbook. This will resave it as a shared workbook.
5. Click **OK**
   Excel saves the file as a shared workbook. The toolbar now reads Sales Info [Shared]. See Figure N-4. This version replaces the unshared version.

FIGURE N-3: Share Workbook dialog box

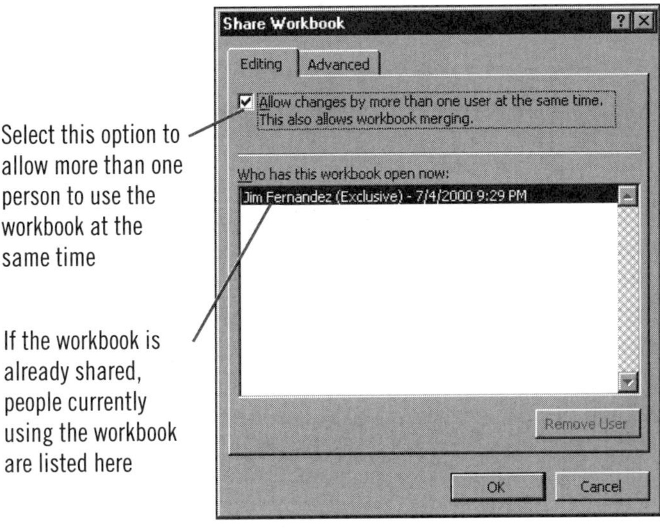

Select this option to allow more than one person to use the workbook at the same time

If the workbook is already shared, people currently using the workbook are listed here

FIGURE N-4: Shared workbook

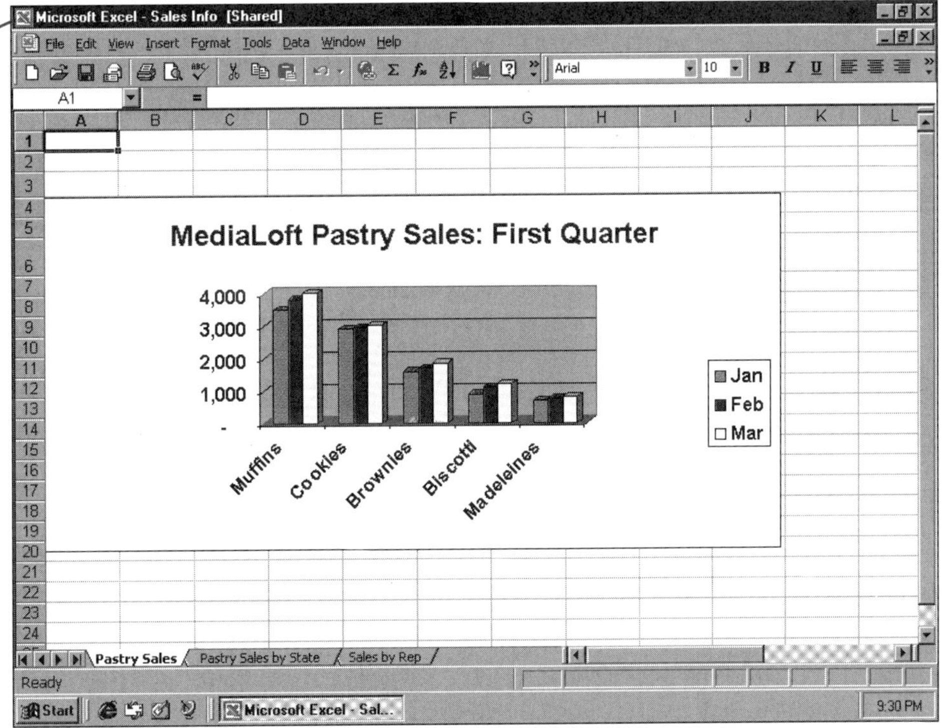

Title bar indicates workbook is shared

Excel 2000

Excel 2000

Tracking Changes in a Shared Workbook

When you share workbooks, it is often helpful to **track** modifications, or identify who made which changes. If you disagree with any of the changes, you can reject them. When the Excel change tracking feature is activated, changes are highlighted in a different color for each user. Each change is identified with the user name and date. In addition to highlighting changes, Excel keeps track of all changes in a **change history**, a list of all changes that you can place on a separate worksheet so you can review them all at once. Jim sets up the shared Sales Info workbook so that all future changes will be tracked. He then opens another workbook that has been on the server and reviews the changes and the change history.

1. Click **Tools** on the menu bar, point to **Track Changes**, click **Highlight Changes**
   The Highlight Changes dialog box opens, allowing you to turn on change tracking, to specify which changes to highlight, and to display changes on the screen or save the change history in a separate worksheet.
2. Click to select **Track changes while editing**, remove check marks from all other boxes except for Highlight changes on screen, compare your screen to Figure N-5, click **OK**, then click **OK** in the dialog box that informs you that you have yet to make changes
   To track all changes, you can leave the When, Who, and Where check boxes blank.
3. Click the **Pastry Sales by State tab**, then change the sales figure for Texas to **133,000**
   A border with a small triangle in the upper-left corner appears around the figure you changed.
4. After you enter the change, move the **mouse pointer** over the cell you just changed, but do not click
   A screen tip appears with your name, the date, the time, and a phrase describing the change. See Figure N-6. Cells that other users change will appear in different colors.
5. Save and close the workbook
   Alice Wegman and Maria Abbott have made changes to a version of this workbook.
6. Open the workbook **EX N-2** and save it as **Sales Info Edits**
7. Click **Tools** on the menu bar, point to **Track Changes**, click **Highlight Changes**, in the Highlight Changes dialog box click the **When** check box to deselect it, click to select **List changes on a new sheet**, then click **OK**
   The History tab appears, as shown in Figure N-7, with a record of each change in the form of a filtered list. Notice that you could, for example, click the Who list arrow in row 1 and show a list of Maria Abbott's changes only.
8. Examine the three sheets, holding the pointer over each change, then click the **History sheet tab**
9. Put your name in the History sheet footer, preview and print the History sheet on one page, then save the workbook, which closes the History worksheet, and close the workbook
   The change history prints, showing who has made which changes to the workbook.

FIGURE N-5: Highlight changes dialog box

Click here so that all changes will be visible on the worksheet

Highlight Changes

Track changes while editing. This also shares your workbook.

Highlight which changes

When: All

Who: Everyone

Where:

Highlight changes on screen

List changes on a new sheet

OK Cancel

FIGURE N-6: Tracked change

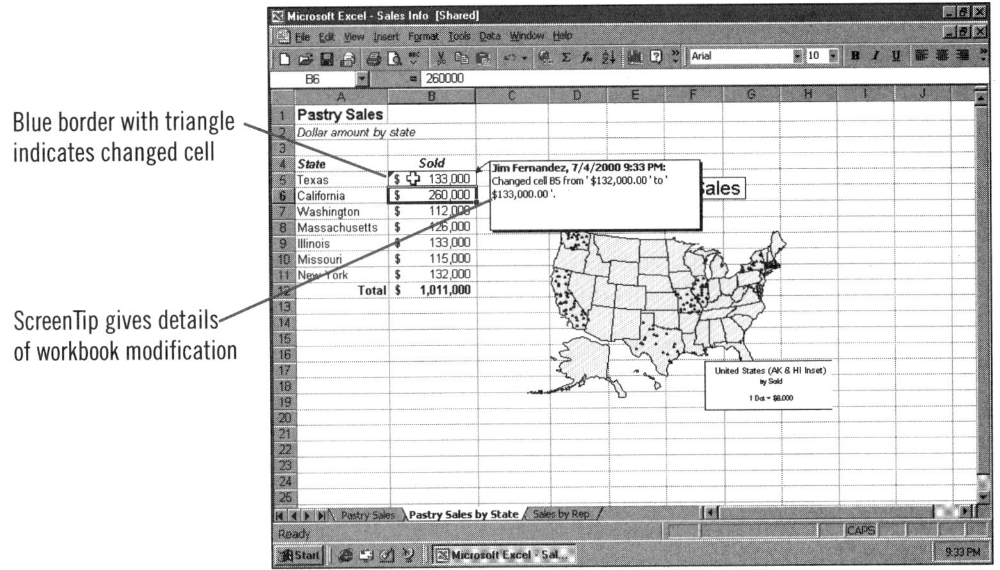

FIGURE N-7: History sheet tab with change history

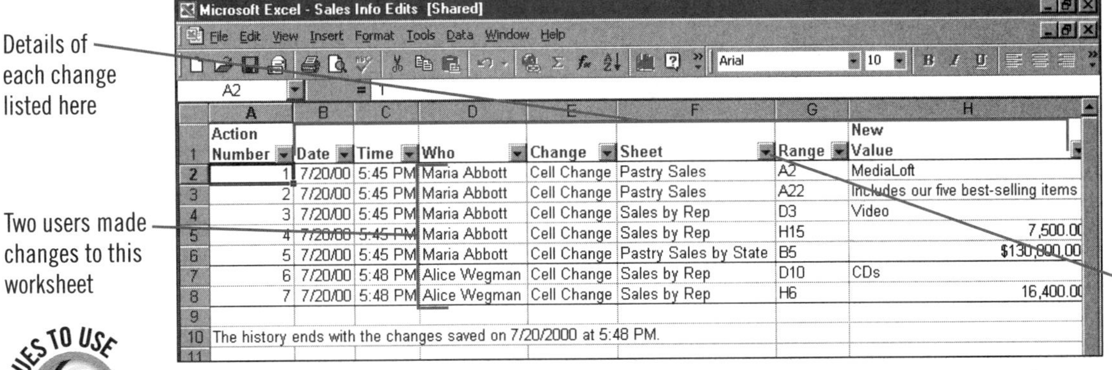

Action Number	Date	Time	Who	Change	Sheet	Range	New Value
1	7/20/00	5:45 PM	Maria Abbott	Cell Change	Pastry Sales	A2	MediaLoft
2	7/20/00	5:45 PM	Maria Abbott	Cell Change	Pastry Sales	A22	Includes our five best-selling items
3	7/20/00	5:45 PM	Maria Abbott	Cell Change	Sales by Rep	D3	Video
4	7/20/00	5:45 PM	Maria Abbott	Cell Change	Sales by Rep	H15	7,500.00
5	7/20/00	5:45 PM	Maria Abbott	Cell Change	Pastry Sales by State	B5	$130,000.00
6	7/20/00	5:48 PM	Alice Wegman	Cell Change	Sales by Rep	D10	CDs
7	7/20/00	5:48 PM	Alice Wegman	Cell Change	Sales by Rep	H6	16,400.00

The history ends with the changes saved on 7/20/2000 at 5:48 PM.

CLUES TO USE

Merging workbooks

Instead of putting the shared workbook on a server, you may want to distribute copies to your reviewers, perhaps via e-mail. Once everyone has entered their changes, you can merge the changed copies into one workbook that will contain all the changes. Each copy you distribute must be designated as shared, and the Change History feature must be activated. Once you get the changed copies back, open your master copy of the workbook, click Tools on the menu bar, click Merge Workbooks, then save when prompted. The Select Files to Merge Into Current Workbook dialog box opens. Click the name of the workbook you want to merge, then click OK. Repeat for all shared workbooks. It's important that you specify that each copy of the shared workbook keep a change history from the date you copy them to the merge date. In the Advanced tab in the Share Workbooks dialog box, set Keep change history for a large number, such as 1,000 days.

Excel 2000

Applying and Removing Passwords

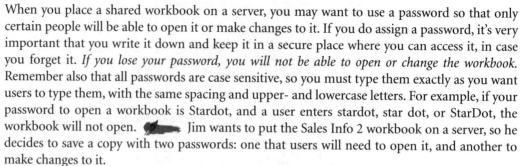

When you place a shared workbook on a server, you may want to use a password so that only certain people will be able to open it or make changes to it. If you do assign a password, it's very important that you write it down and keep it in a secure place where you can access it, in case you forget it. *If you lose your password, you will not be able to open or change the workbook.* Remember also that all passwords are case sensitive, so you must type them exactly as you want users to type them, with the same spacing and upper- and lowercase letters. For example, if your password to open a workbook is Stardot, and a user enters stardot, star dot, or StarDot, the workbook will not open. Jim wants to put the Sales Info 2 workbook on a server, so he decides to save a copy with two passwords: one that users will need to open it, and another to make changes to it.

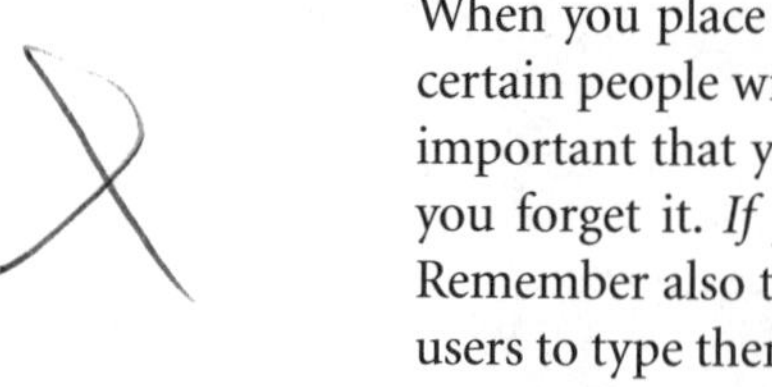

Steps

1. Open the workbook **EX N-1**, click **File** on the menu bar, then click **Save As**
2. In the Save As dialog box, click **Tools**, then click **General Options**
   The Save Options dialog box opens, with two password boxes: one to open the workbook, and one to allow changes to the workbook, similar to Figure N-8.
3. In the Password to open box, type **Saturn**
   Be sure to type the capital S and the rest of the letters lowercase. This is the password users will have to type to open the workbook. Whenever you type passwords, they appear as asterisks (***) so that no one nearby will be able to see them.
4. Press **[Tab]**, then in the Password to modify box type **Atlas**, compare your screen to Figure N-8, then click **OK**
   This is the password users will have to type to make changes to the workbook. A dialog box asks you to verify the password by re-entering it.
5. In the first Confirm Password dialog box, type **Saturn**, then click **OK**; in the second Confirm Password dialog box, type **Atlas**, click **OK**, edit the workbook name so it reads **Sales Info PW**, then click **Save** and close the workbook
6. Reopen the workbook **Sales Info PW**, enter the password **Saturn** when prompted in order to open the workbook as shown in Figure N-9, click **OK**, then type **Atlas** to obtain write access and click **OK**
7. In the Pastry Sales by State worksheet, click cell A-14 and enter **One-year totals**
   You have confirmed that you can make changes to the workbook.
8. Save and close the workbook

FIGURE N-8: **Save options dialog box**

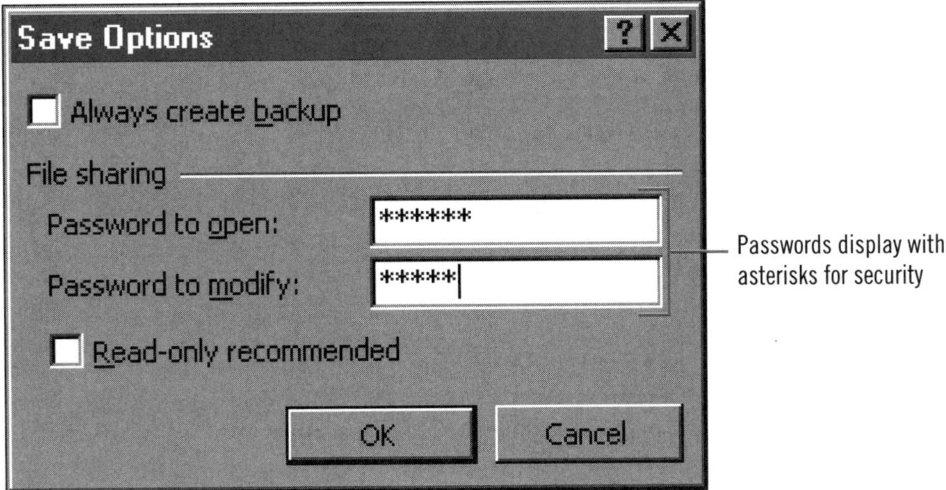

FIGURE N-9: **Password entry prompt**

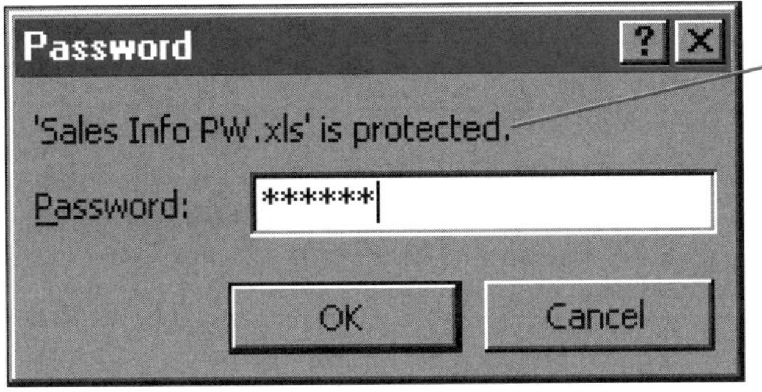

Excel 2000

Removing passwords

You must know a workbook's password in order to change or delete it. Open the workbook, click File on the menu bar, then click Save As. In the Save As dialog box, click Tools, then click General Options. Double-click the symbols for the existing passwords in the Password to open or Password to modify boxes, and press [Delete]. Change the filename if you wish, then click Save.

Excel 2000

Creating an Interactive Worksheet for an Intranet or the Web

You can save an entire workbook in HTML format for users to view. But you can also save part of a workbook—a worksheet, chart, or PivotTable—in HTML format and make it interactive. You cannot save an entire workbook in interactive format. To work with interactive data, users must have installed Internet Explorer version 4.01 or later as well as the Office Web Components. Anyone with Office 2000 will have these. Users do not need to have Excel. Jim decides to save the Pastry Sales by State sheet as an interactive Web page.

Steps 1 2 3 4

QuickTip

Internet Explorer 4.01 or later must be your default browser or you will not be able to use interactive features.

QuickTip

See the Microsoft Excel Help topic "Limitations of putting interactive data on a Web page" for more information about which features might not work or might appear differently on your Web page.

1. Open **EX N-1**, save it as **Sales Info 2**, then click the **Pastry Sales by State sheet**
2. Click **File** on the menu bar, click **Save as Web Page**, then click **Publish**
   The Publish as Web Page dialog box opens.
3. Click the **Choose list arrow** and choose **Items on Pastry Sales by State**, then under Viewing options click to select **Add interactivity with**
4. In the Publish as section, click **Change** and type **Pastry Sales by State**, click **OK**, click **Browse**, make sure your project disk name appears as the Save in location, type the filename **Pastry Sales Web**, then click **OK**
5. If necessary, click to select **Open published Web page in browser** at the bottom of the dialog box, click **Publish**, then maximize your browser window
   After a pause, Internet Explorer opens the HTML version of your data. See Figure N-10. Notice that only the worksheet appears, not the map.
6. Change the Sold number for Washington in cell B7 to **115,000**, press **Enter**, and observe the total update automatically to 1,013,000
   You know the interactive feature is working. Changes you make to the HTML file in your browser remain in effect until you close your browser.
7. Select the range **A5:B11**, click the **Sort Ascending button** on the toolbar above the worksheet, then click **State**
   The data is sorted in a new order according to state name.
8. Select the range **A4:B11**, click the **AutoFilter button**, click the **State list arrow**, click the **Total check mark** to remove it, click **OK**, then click the **Property Toolbox button**
   The total is no longer visible on the worksheet. The Spreadsheet Property Toolbox opens and should look similar to that shown in Figure N-11.
9. Click the **Fill Color list arrow** after Cell format, click the **light green color** in the bottom row, then click the Spreadsheet **Property Toolbox close button** and click outside the selected range
   The range fills with the light green color.
10. Enter your name in any worksheet cell, click **File** on the menu bar, click **Print**, click **OK**, then close your browser

FIGURE N-10: **Pastry Sales worksheet as Web page in Internet Explorer**

Pastry Sales by State - Microsoft Internet Explorer

Address A:\Pastry Sales Web.htm

Pastry Sales by State

	A	B
1	**Pastry Sales**	
2	*Dollar amount by state*	
3		
4	***State***	***Sold***
5	Texas	$ 132,000
6	California	$ 260,000
7	Washington	$ 112,000
8	Massachusetts	$ 126,000
9	Illinois	$ 133,000
10	Missouri	$ 115,000
11	New York	$ 132,000
12	**Total**	**$ 1,010,000**

Spreadsheet toolbar shows that worksheet is interactive and allows users to manipulate data

Map does not appear in Web version

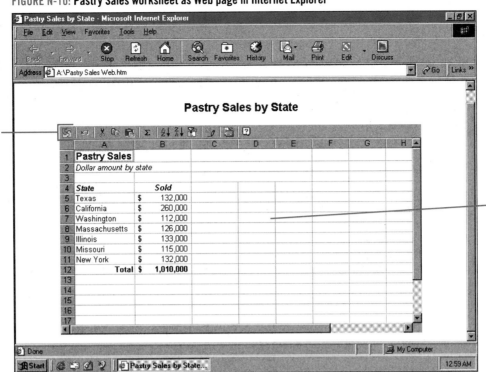

FIGURE N-11: **Spreadsheet Property Toolbox**

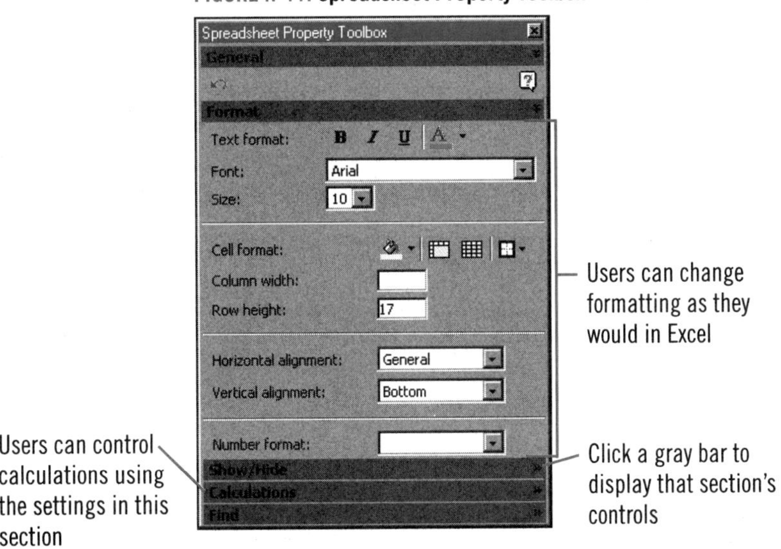

Excel 2000

Clues to Use: Managing HTML files on an intranet or Web site

Once you save your Excel file or item in HTML format, determine the best location for saving your file: an HTTP site, an FTP (File Transfer Protocol) site, or a network server. Check with your system administrator or Internet Service Provider (ISP) to see how your files should be organized—whether they should all be in one folder, whether graphics and other supporting files should be in a separate folder, and the like.

Excel 2000

Creating an Interactive PivotTable for an Intranet or the Web

Not only can you create interactive worksheets that users can modify in their Web browsers, but you can also create interactive PivotTables that users can analyze by dragging fields to get different views of the data. An interactive PivotTable for the Web is called a **PivotTable list**. Users cannot enter new values to the list, but they can filter and sort data, add calculations, and rearrange data to get a different perspective on the information. As the PivotTable list creator, you have complete control over what information is included from the source data, which could be an Excel worksheet, a PivotTable, or external data (for example, an Access database). You can include only selected columns of information if you wish. You can also include charts with your PivotTable data. As with spreadsheets you publish in HTML format, users view PivotTable lists in their browsers, and changes they make to them are retained for only that browser session. The HTML file remains in its original form. Jim has compiled some sales information about sales representatives at selected stores for the last four quarters. He saves it as a PivotTable list so he and selected corporate staff and store managers can review it using their Web browsers.

Steps 1 2 3 4

QuickTip

As with saving spreadsheets in interactive format, you need Office Web Tools and Internet Explorer 4.01 or later to create and use PivotTable lists.

1. In the **Sales Info 2** workbook, click the **Sales by Rep tab**
   Jim will create the PivotTable list directly from the data rather then creating an Excel PivotTable first.
2. Click **File** on the menu bar, click **Save as Web Page**, then click **Publish**
3. Click the **Choose list arrow**, click **Items on Sales by Rep**, then in the Choose list make sure **Sheet All contents of Sales by Rep** is selected
   This will select all the items on the selected PivotTable sheet.
4. Under Viewing options, click **Add interactivity with**, click the **Add interactivity with list arrow**, and click **PivotTable functionality**
   PivotTable functionality will give users the option to move list items around on the PivotTable list as they would move data items on a PivotTable in Excel.
5. Click **Browse**, type **Sales Info PT List**, make sure your Project Disk is selected, click **OK**, make sure **Open published web page in browser** is checked, and compare your screen to Figure N-12

QuickTip

To retain the PivotTable in its original state, click the Address box containing the URL and press [Return]

6. Click **Publish**, then maximize the Internet Explorer window if necessary
   The new PivotTable list opens in Internet Explorer. Its layout looks similar to a PivotTable report in Excel, with row and column fields and field drop-down arrows. As with an Excel PivotTable, you can change the layout to view the data in different ways. In this case, however, there is no PivotTable toolbar; you simply drag the field headings to the desired drop areas.
7. Drag the **Store field** to the Row area, then drag the **Department field** to the Column area
   The layout of the PivotTable list changes, and you now see the data rearranged by region, department, and store. See Figure N-13.
8. Click **File** on the menu bar, click **Print**, then close your browser

FIGURE N-12: Publish as Web Page dialog box

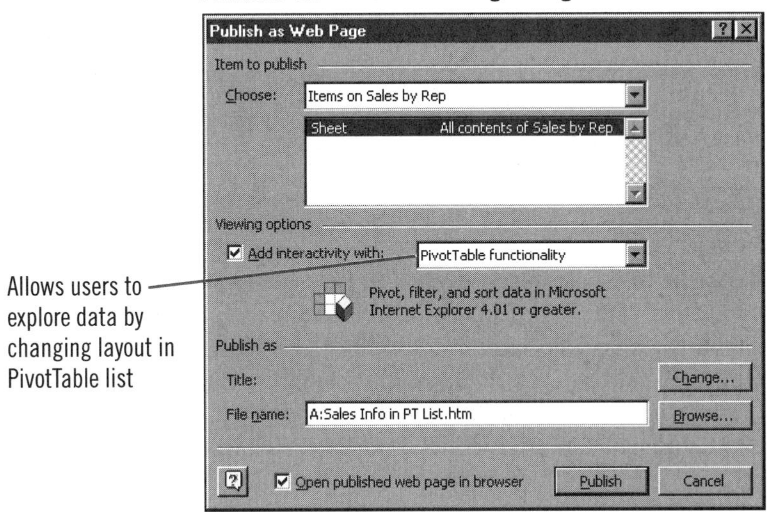

Allows users to explore data by changing layout in PivotTable list

FIGURE N-13: PivotTable list with new layout in Internet Explorer

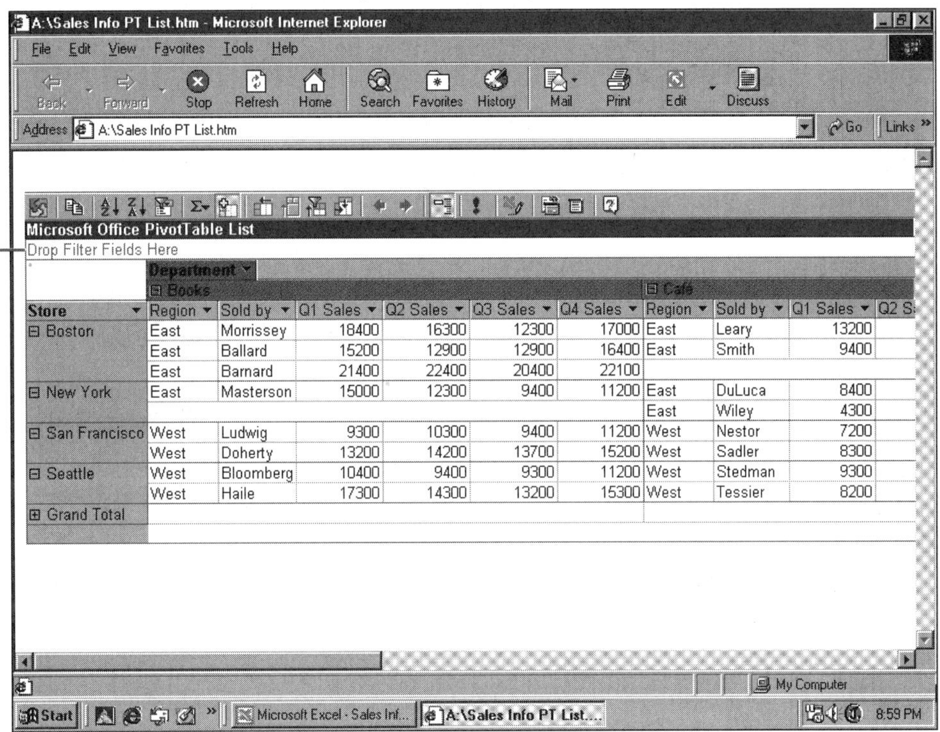

Store	Region	Sold by	Q1 Sales	Q2 Sales	Q3 Sales	Q4 Sales	Region	Sold by	Q1 Sales	Q2 S
Boston	East	Morrissey	18400	16300	12300	17000	East	Leary	13200	
	East	Ballard	15200	12900	12900	16400	East	Smith	9400	
	East	Barnard	21400	22400	20400	22100				
New York	East	Masterson	15000	12300	9400	11200	East	DuLuca	8400	
							East	Wiley	4300	
San Francisco	West	Ludwig	9300	10300	9400	11200	West	Nestor	7200	
	West	Doherty	13200	14200	13700	15200	West	Sadler	8300	
Seattle	West	Bloomberg	10400	9400	9300	11200	West	Stedman	9300	
	West	Haile	17300	14300	13200	15300	West	Tessier	8200	
Grand Total										

User drags fields to drop areas to explore data relationships

Excel 2000

Adding fields to a PivotTable list using the Web browser

You can add filter, data, or detail fields to the PivotTable list to display data. On the toolbar above the PivotTable list, click the Field List button . In the PivotTable Field List dialog box locate the name of the field you want to add. Click the field, and in the lower-right corner of the box, click the area list arrow, then click the section to which you want to add the field: Filter Area, Data Area, or Detail Data. If Add to is not available, the PivotTable creator may have restricted access to it.

Excel 2000

Creating Hyperlinks between Excel Files and the Web

In addition to using hyperlinks to connect related Excel files, you can also create hyperlinks between files created in other Windows programs. You can even use hyperlinks to move between Excel files and information stored on the Web. Every Web page is identified by a unique address called a **Uniform Resource Locator (URL)**. You create a hyperlink to a Web page in the same way you create a hyperlink to another Excel file—by specifying the location of the Web page (its URL) in the Link to File or URL text box in the Insert Hyperlink dialog box. You enter a URL for an intranet site or a site on the World Wide Web using the same method. Jim decides that users of the Pastry Sales worksheet would find it helpful to view competitive information. He decides to include a hyperlink to the URL of one of MediaLoft's competitors, Barnes and Noble, which is also a café bookstore.

Steps 1 2 3 4

1. Activate the **Pastry Sales worksheet**, click cell **A2**, type **Barnes and Noble**, then click the **Enter button** on the Formula bar

2. Click the **Insert Hyperlink button** on the Standard toolbar
   The Insert Hyperlink dialog box opens. This is where you specify the target for the hyperlink, the Barnes and Noble Web site, by entering its URL in the Link to file or URL section of the Insert Hyperlink dialog box.

3. Under Link to, click **Existing File or Web Page**, click in the Type the file or Web page name text box, and type the URL for the Barnes and Noble Web site: **http://www.barnesandnoble.com**
   Your completed Insert Hyperlink dialog box should match Figure N-14. The program will automatically add a slash after the URL, as shown in Figure N-14, if you return to the dialog box and enter a Web address that you've entered previously.

4. Click **OK**
   The Barnes and Noble text is blue and underlined, indicating that it is a hyperlink. You should always test new hyperlinks to make sure they link to the correct destination. To test this hyperlink, you must have a modem, a Web browser installed on your computer, and access to an Internet Service Provider (ISP).

5. Click the **Barnes and Noble** hyperlink in cell A2
   After a moment, the Web browser installed on your computer starts and displays the Barnes and Noble Web page in your browser window.

6. If necessary, click the **Maximize button** on the browser title bar to maximize the browser window

7. Click **File** on the menu bar, click **Print**, click **OK**, then click the **Back button** on the Web toolbar
   Now that you know the hyperlink works correctly, you return to the Sales Info 2 worksheet.

8. Save and close the workbook, then if necessary close your browser, but stay connected to the Internet

Trouble?

If this button does not appear on your Standard toolbar, click the More Buttons button to view it.

QuickTip

Make sure the URL address appears in the text box exactly as shown in Figure N-14. Every Web page URL begins with "http://". This acronym stands for HyperText Transfer Protocol, the method all intranet and Web page data use to travel over the Internet to your computer.

FIGURE N-14: Insert Hyperlink dialog box

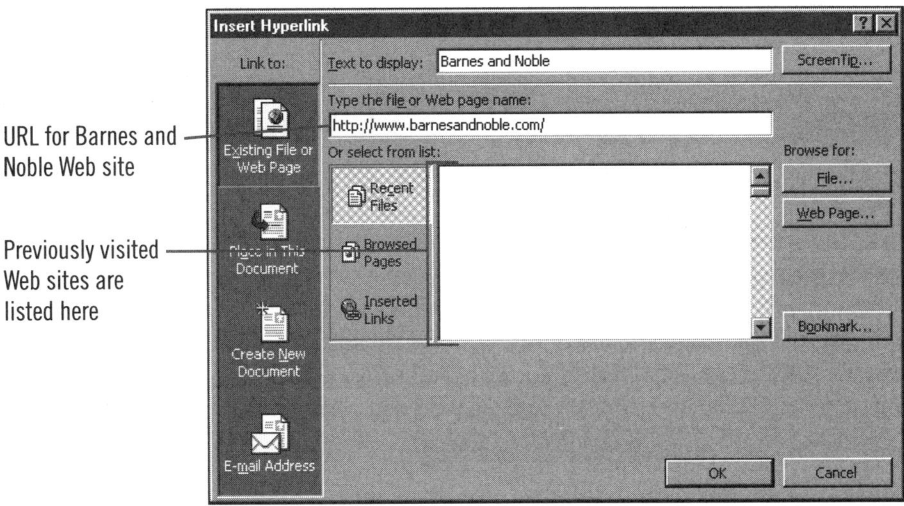

FIGURE N-15: Barnes and Noble Web site in Internet Explorer

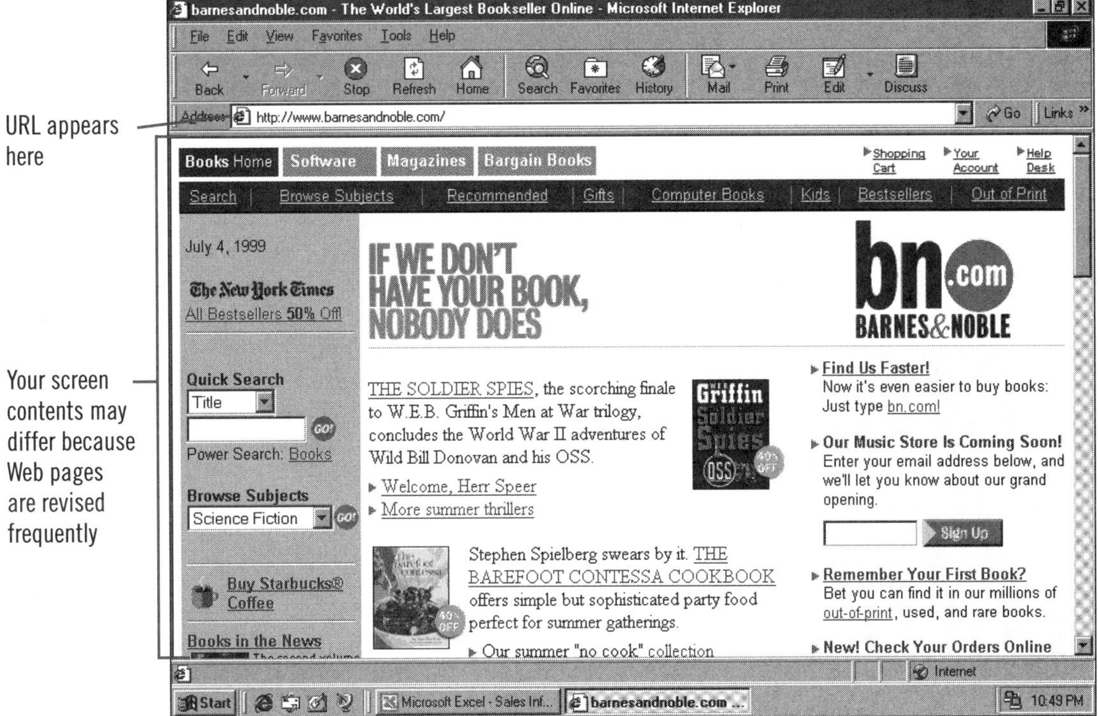

Using hyperlinks to navigate large worksheets

Previously, when you needed to locate and view different sections of a particularly large worksheet, you used the scroll bars, or, if there were range names associated with the different worksheet sections, the name box. You can also use hyperlinks to more easily navigate a large worksheet. To insert a hyperlink that targets a cell or a range of cells at another location in the worksheet or another sheet in the workbook, click the cell where you want the hyperlink to appear, then click the Insert Hyperlink button on the Standard toolbar. In the Insert Hyperlink dialog box, click Place in This Document. Enter the cell address or range name of the hyperlink target in the Type the cell reference text box, or select a sheet or a defined name from the list box below it, then click OK.

Excel 2000

Running Queries to Retrieve Data on the Web

Often you'll want to access information on the Web or the Internet to incorporate into an Excel worksheet. Using Excel, you can obtain data from a Web, Internet, or intranet site by running a **Web query**. You can then save the information as an Excel workbook and manipulate it in any way you choose. As part of a special project for Leilani Ho, Jim needs to obtain stock information on MediaLoft's competitors. He will run a Web query to obtain the most current stock information from the World Wide Web.

Steps

1. Open a new workbook, then save it as **Stock Data**
2. Click **Data** on the menu bar, point to **Get External Data**, then click **Run Saved Query**
   The Run Query dialog box opens, similar to Figure N-16. This is where you select the Web query you want to run from a list of predefined queries.
3. Click **Microsoft Investor Stock Quotes**, then click **Get Data**
   The Returning External Data to Microsoft Excel dialog box opens. This is where you specify the location to place the incoming data.
4. Make sure the **Existing worksheet option button** is selected, then click **OK**
   The Enter Parameter Value dialog box opens, prompting you to enter a stock symbol. The stock symbol for Barnes and Noble is BKS.
5. Type **BKS**, then click **OK**
   Your Internet Service Provider connects to the Web. The Microsoft Investor stock quote for Barnes and Noble appears on the screen. The External Data toolbar also appears, as shown in Figure N-17. Now you have the stock information that Jim can use to research one of MediaLoft's competitor's stock values.
6. Click **File** on the menu bar, click **Print**, then click **Chartlink** on the stock quote page
   A chart appears, showing the stock price and company income for the last year, similar to Figure N-18.
7. Print the chart, close your browser, disconnect from the Internet, save and close the workbook, then exit Excel and your browser

Trouble?

If you don't have a modem and access to the Web through an ISP, check with your instructor or technical support person. If your ISP's connection dialog box opens, follow your standard procedure for getting online, then continue with Step 6.

Finding stock symbols

If you want to check on a stock but don't know its symbol, click the Symbol Lookup hyperlink on the Stock Data worksheet. You may need to download the Microsoft Investor software, which takes about five minutes.

FIGURE N-16: **Run Query dialog box**

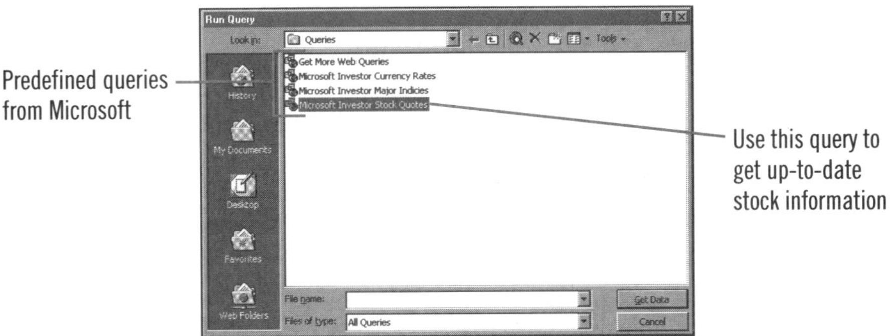

FIGURE N-17: **Stock quote in Stock Data worksheet**

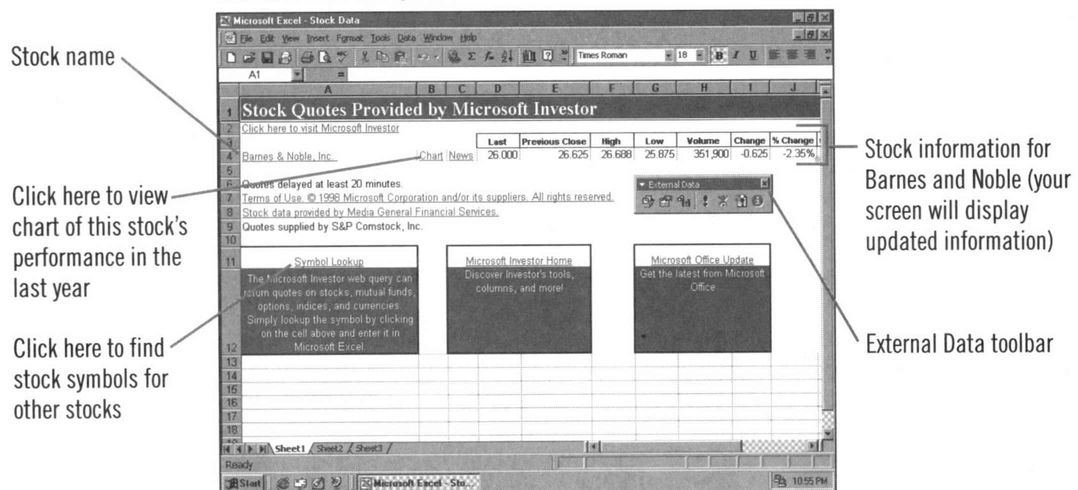

FIGURE N-18: **Stock chart for Barnes and Noble**

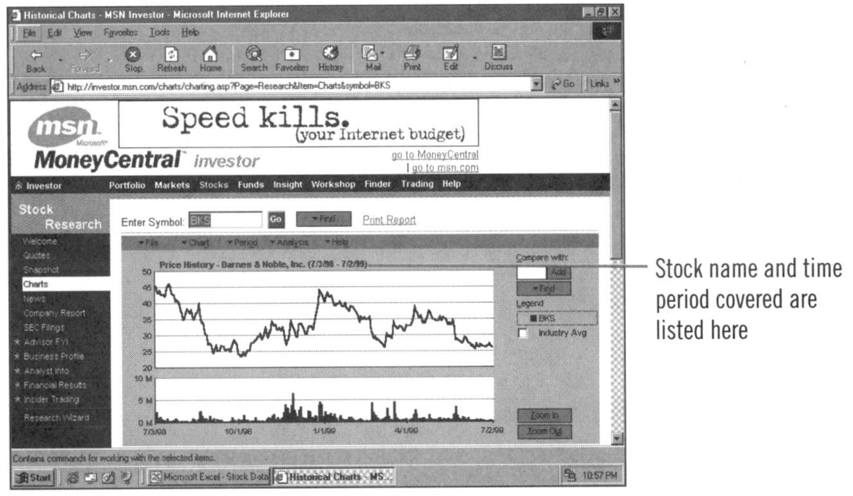

Creating a new query to retrieve Web page data

To retrieve data from a particular Web page on a regular basis, it's easiest to create a customized Web query. Click Data on the menu bar, point to Get External Data, then click New Web Query. In the New Web Query dialog box, click Browse Web to start your browser, go to the Web page from which you want to retrieve data, click the Web page, then return to the dialog box; the address of the Web page will appear in the address text box. Specify which part of the Web page you want to retrieve (for example, only the tables) and how much formatting you want to keep. Click Save Query to save the query for future use with the Run Saved Query command. Then click OK. Specify the location in the worksheet where you want the data, then click OK. The data from the Web page appears in the open Excel worksheet.

Practice

► Concepts Review

Label each of the elements shown in Figure N-19

FIGURE N-19

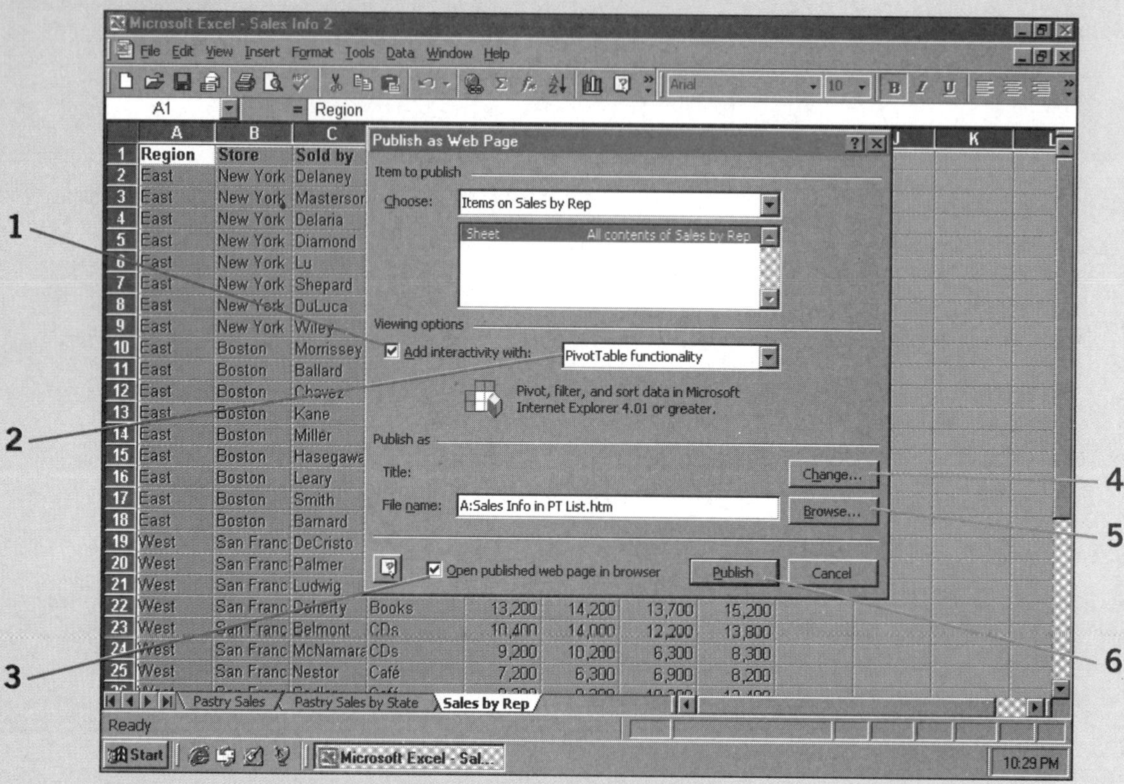

Match each item with the statement that describes it.

7. Web query
8. Change history
9. Shared workbook
10. Interactive worksheet or PivotTable
11. URL

a. A unique address on the World Wide Web
b. Used by many people on a network
c. Can be manipulated using a Web browser
d. Starts the installed Web browser to search the WWW
e. A record of edits others have made to a worksheet

12. A ____________ is a list of recipients to whom you are sending a workbook sequentially.
   a. PivotTable
   b. Hypertext document
   c. Routing slip
   d. Shared workbook

13. Which of the following can be saved in HTML format, placed on a server, and then manipulated on an intranet or Internet using a Web browser?
   a. A worksheet
   b. A PivotTable
   c. A workbook
   d. a and b only

14. Which of the following allows you to obtain data from a Web or intranet site?
   a. Web Wizard
   b. PivotTable
   c. Data query
   d. Web query

15. A shared workbook is a workbook that
   a. Has hyperlinks to the Web.
   b. Is on the World Wide Web.
   c. Several people can use at the same time.
   d. Requires a password to open.

16. In an interactive worksheet or PivotTable,
   a. You can make changes and they are saved to the HTML file.
   b. You can make changes but they are not saved to the HTML file.
   c. You can change formatting but not perform calculations.
   d. You can perform calculations but not change formatting.

▶ Skills Review

1. **Set up a shared workbook**
   a. Open the file EX N-3 and save it as Ad Campaigns.
   b. Set up the workbook so that more than one person can use it at one time.
   c. On the Advanced tab, specify that the change history should be maintained for 1,000 days.

2. **Track changes in a shared workbook**
   a. Specify that all changes should be highlighted. Changes should be both highlighted on the screen and listed in a new sheet.
   b. In the Ads Q1 All Stores worksheet, change the Billboards totals to $600 for each month.
   c. Save the file.
   d. Display and print the History sheet. (If the History worksheet does not appear, reopen the Highlight Changes dialog box and reselect the options for All and List changes on a new sheet.)
   e. Save and close the workbook.

3. Apply and remove passwords

- **a.** Open the file EX N-3, open the Save As dialog box, then open the General Options dialog box.
- **b.** Set the password to open as Marsten and the password to modify as Spring.
- **c.** Resave the password-protected file as Ad Campaigns PW.
- **d.** Close the workbook.
- **e.** Reopen the workbook and verify that you can change it, using passwords where necessary.

4. Create an interactive worksheet for an intranet or the Web.

- **a.** Save the Ads Q1 All Stores worksheet as an interactive Web page, with spreadsheet functionality.
- **b.** Set the title bar to read Ad Campaign Forecast, automatically preview it in Internet Explorer, if that is your Web browser, and save it to your Project Disk using the filename Ad Campaigns. If you use a different Web browser, don't use the automatic preview option.
- **c.** If you can open the HTML file in Internet Explorer, do so.
- **d.** In Internet Explorer, add totals for each month in B11:D11, then add a grand total to cell E11.
- **e.** In F3, enter a formula that calculates the percentage newspaper ads are of the grand total. (*Hint:* You will need to type in the formula instead of clicking cells, and use the Property Toolbox to change the number format to a percent.)
- **f.** Use the Property Toolbox to fill the range B11:E11 with yellow.
- **g.** Sort the list in ascending order by ad type. You might need to reenter the percentage formula.
- **h.** Print the worksheet from Internet Explorer, then close Internet Explorer.

5. Create an interactive PivotTable for an intranet or the Web.

- **a.** In the Ad Campaigns PW workbook, save the worksheet Ad Detail as an interactive PivotTable with PivotTable functionality. Make the title Ad Forecast 4 Stores, and save it as Ads4Stores. Open the file in Internet Explorer.
- **b.** Drag fields to analyze the data by Region, Ad Piece, Store, and Department.
- **c.** Print the page showing changed data.

6. Create Hyperlinks between Excel files and the Web.

- **a.** On the Ads Q1 All Stores worksheet, enter the text "American Ad Foundation" and make it a hyperlink to the American Ad Foundation at http://www.aaf.org in cell A13.
- **b.** Test the hyperlink and print the Web page.
- **c.** Save and close the workbook.

7. Run queries to retrieve data on the Web.

- **a.** Open a new workbook and save it as Stock Quotes.
- **b.** Use the Run Saved Query command to locate Microsoft Investor Major Indices.
- **c.** Specify that you want to return the data to cell A1 of the current worksheet.
- **d.** After the stock quotes appear, click one of the stock indices listed and print the results.
- **e.** Display a chart for one of the indices, then print the chart. (*Hint:* If you are prompted to download MSN Money Central and you are unable to download software at your site, continue with step f.)
- **f.** Preview and print the Stock Quotes sheet, then save and close the workbook.
- **g.** Open a new workbook and save it as MediaLoft Products.
- **h.** Create a new Web query that retrieves the following page from the MediaLoft intranet site: www.course.com/illustrated/MediaLoft/Product.html. Import the entire page with full HTML formatting, and save the query as MediaLoft Products on your project disk.
- **i.** Test the hyperlinks on the imported Web page, use the Back arrow to return to the workbook, then save and close the workbook.

▶ Independent Challenges

1. Blantyre Consulting helps small businesses attain and maintain profitability by monitoring their sales and expense information. The company makes it a practice to hold a monthly phone conference with clients to discuss strategy. There are 10 consultants in the organization, and they share information via the company intranet. They have adopted a team approach to their accounts, so five consultants work on each account. You are setting up the information for a new client, Boston Touring Company, which specializes in giving trolley and bus tours in Boston, Massachusetts, and the surrounding area. You are preparing the workbook to be placed on the company intranet so that only the consultant group for that account can view the information.

To complete this independent challenge:

a. Open the file EX N-4 and save it as Boston Touring.
b. Format the workbook so it is more attractive and the information is easy to read.
c. Make the workbook shared so that all consultants can access it.
d. Set up the workbook so that all changes will be tracked. Make two changes to the worksheets as a test and print the change history.
e. Password protect the workbook for both opening and editing, and write down the passwords you have chosen.
f. Save and close the workbook, then reopen it, using passwords as necessary.
g. Save the Q1 Sales worksheet as an interactive worksheet with spreadsheet functionality. Make the browser title bar read "Boston Touring Company" using the filename Boston Touring - Web.
h. Open the worksheet in Internet Explorer, then calculate the percentage that half-day tours of Cambridge are of the total.
i. Add the heading Total over the column of totals and format it in a different text color.
j. Print the interactive worksheet, then close the browser.
k. Save and close the Boston Touring worksheet.

2. The First Southern Bank has a Web page containing information about its current rates and procedures for opening an account. The bank would like to expand the site in order to help customers find answers to more of the questions the Customer Service line receives. Customers frequently call in asking for the bank's Mortgage Calculator, a printed table that shows various mortgage amounts and interest rates, and lets customers look up what their monthly payments would be. John Barnes, the Customer Service Manager, has asked you to set up an Excel worksheet for their Web site that will allow customers to enter various mortgage amounts and interest rates, and automatically see what their monthly payments, total payments, and total interest would be. He wants you to make the worksheet both attractive and easy to use.

To complete this independent challenge:

a. Open the file EX N-5 and save it as Mortgage Calculator.
b. Add the bank's name and any other marketing-oriented information that will identify what the worksheet is and how to use it.
c. Format the worksheet with colors, fonts, or other formats to make it attractive for public use.
d. Save the worksheet in HTML format with interactive spreadsheet functionality and an appropriate title in the title bar.
e. Open the HTML file in Internet Explorer, then test the calculator. Enter various mortgage amounts and interest rates and make sure the payment information changes appropriately.
f. Close Internet Explorer, the Mortgage Calculator worksheet, and Excel, saving as necessary.

3. Tuckerman Teas is a tea import and export firm with offices in Tokyo and London that distributes teas to shops in the United States and Canada. Tuckerman wants the officers in both offices to be able to analyze sales data, but because of incompatible software, they must rely on their Web browsers. They have asked you to help them set up a file that they will all be able to access on their intranet site.

To complete this independent challenge:

a. Open the file EX N-6 and save it as Tuckerman Teas.
b. Format the worksheet using fonts and colors to make it more attractive.
c. Save the file as a Web page with PivotTable functionality. Assign the title bar an appropriate title.
d. Open the file in Internet Explorer and manipulate the data to determine the following:
   - How do shipments of the flavored afternoon blends compare to the flavored breakfast blends?
   - Considering only blends, flavored, and Japanese teas, what is the total kilos shipped for afternoon and breakfast teas?
   - Which category consistently did better than the others during the quarter?
e. Explore any other data relationships you wish.
f. Return to the Tuckerman Teas worksheet, and on a blank sheet, write three or four sentences summarizing your conclusions.

4. Jim Fernandez, MediaLoft's office manager, has been asked by the Accounting department to examine CD sales trends. Assuming that a higher stock price reflects higher sales, he has decided to compare MediaLoft CD sales patterns to the stock price of Amazon.com, which also sells CDs, to see if both display seasonal trends, particularly the higher sales at the end of the calendar year. You will get sales information from the MediaLoft intranet site, retrieve stock data on Amazon.com, then create charts that illustrate trends of each one for easy comparison.

To complete this independent challenge:

a. Connect to the Internet, and go to the MediaLoft intranet site at http://www.course.com/Illustrated/MediaLoft. Click the Accounting link, then click the CD Sales Analysis link. Print the page and disconnect from the Internet.
b. Open a new workbook, then enter the total figures for CD sales for each of the four quarters. Save the workbook as Trend Analysis.
c. Create a line chart of the figures on the same worksheet as the sales figures, assigning the chart an appropriate title.
d. Name the sheet Trends.
e. Run a Microsoft Investor Stock Quote Web query to obtain a stock quote for Amazon.com, stock symbol AMZN, placing the data in a new worksheet.
f. Display the chart of this data by clicking Chart.
g. On the File menu above the chart, select Export Data. The data will appear in Excel in a separate workbook called AMZN.
h. In the new workbook, delete all the rows of data except the row representing the earliest date for each month. Generally, this will be the first of the month, unless that falls on a weekend, in which case it might be the second or third of the month. You should end up with one row of data for each month, showing the High, Low, Close, and Volume. If any line is blank, use the date nearest to it that has data.
i. Delete the columns for High, Low, and Volume, leaving the Date and Close columns.
j. Sort the rows in ascending order by date, then copy the data into the Trends sheet in the Trend Analysis workbook.

k. Create a line chart of the Amazon data, and assign it an appropriate title. Place it on the same sheet as the MediaLoft chart. Use any Excel features to point out similarities or differences you see. Do both rise toward the end of the year?

l. On the chart sheet, create a hyperlink to Amazon.com.

m. Save and close the Trend Analysis workbook, close the AMZN workbook without saving, then close Internet Explorer.

► Visual Workshop

Create the interactive Web page shown in Figure N-20. Use Excel to create the company name, product listing, and the sales figures for each quarter, all in black text. Save and print the worksheet. Save the worksheet in interactive HTML format, using the title bar text shown. Use Internet Explorer to obtain totals for each quarter and to apply formatting to totals, column headings, and the company name. (*Hint:* If you have any trouble with AutoSum, try formatting the figures using the Number format.) Print the HTML worksheet with your modifications applied.

FIGURE N-20

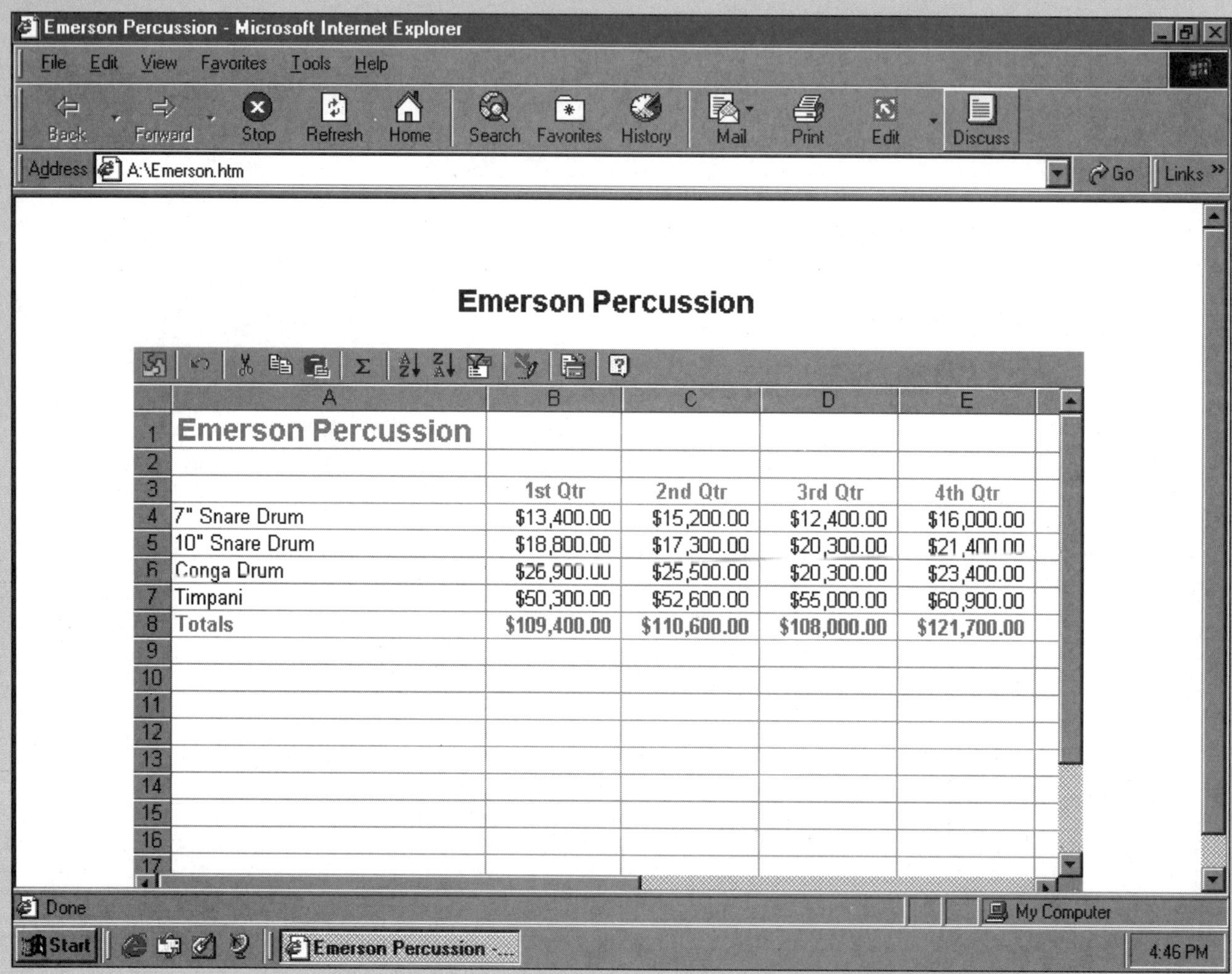

Excel 2000 MOUS Certification Objectives

Below is a list of the Microsoft Office User Specialist program objectives for Core and Expert Excel 2000 skills showing where each MOUS objective is covered in the Lessons and the Practice. This table lists the Core and Expert MOUS certification skills covered in the units in this book. For more information on which Illustrated titles meet MOUS certification, please see the inside cover of this book.

MOUS standardized coding number	Activity	Lesson page where skill is covered	Location in lesson where skill is covered	Practice
XL2000E.3	**Using multiple workbooks**			
XL2000E.3.1	Using a workspace	Excel F-11	Clues to Use	
XL2000E.3.2	Link workbooks	Excel F-14	Steps 1–2	Skills Review 7, Independent Challenge 4
		Excel F-7	Clues to Use	Skills Review 3
XL2000E.5	**Printing workbooks**			
XL2000E.5.2	Use the Report Manager	Excel F-10	QuickTip	
XL2000E.6	**Working with named ranges**			
XL2000E.6.2	Use a named range in a formula	Excel I-14	Steps 2–3	Skills Review 6
XL2000E.6.3	Use Lookup Functions (Hlookup or Vlookup)	Excel I-13 (HLOOKUP)	Clues to Use	
		Excel I-12 (VLOOKUP)	Steps 1–8	Skills Review 5, Independent Challenge 3
XL2000E.7	**Working with toolbars**			
XL2000E.7.1	Hide and display toolbars	Excel G-16	QuickTip	
XL2000E.7.2	Customize a toolbar	Excel G-16	Steps 1–8	Skills Review 7, Independent Challenges 1, 2
XL2000E.7.3	Assign a macro to a command button	Excel G-16	Steps 1–8	Skills Review 7, Independent Challenges 1, 2
XL2000E.8	**Using macros**			
XL2000E.8.1	Record macros	Excel G-4	Steps 1–8	Skills Review 1
XL2000E.8.2	Run macros	Excel G-6	Steps 1–8	Skills Review 2
XL2000E.8.3	Edit macros	Excel G-8	Steps 1–6	Skills Review 3
XL2000E.10	**Displaying and Formatting Data**			
XL2000E.10.2	Perform single and multi-level sorts	Excel H-12	Steps 1–6	Skills Reviews 4, 5, Independent Challenges 1–3
		Excel H-14	Steps 1–6	Skills Review 5, Independent Challenges 1–3

MOUS standardized coding number	Activity	Lesson page where skill is covered	Location in lesson where skill is covered	Practice
XL2000E.10.3	Use grouping and outlines	Excel I-10	Steps 1–7	Skills Review 4
XL2000E.10.4	Use data forms	Excel H-6	Steps 1–8	Skills Review 2, Independent Challenge 2
XL2000E.10.5	Use subtotaling	Excel I-10	Steps 1–7	Skills Review 4, Independent Challenge 3
XL2000E.10.6	Apply data filters	Excel I-2, 4, 6	Steps 1–7, 1–7, 1–5	Skills Reviews 1–3, Independent Challenges 1, 3
XL2000E.10.7	Extract data	Excel I-8	Steps 1–5	
XL2000E.10.9	Use data validation	Excel I-16	Steps 1–7	Skills Review 7, Independent Challenges 1, 3
XL2000E.11	**Using analysis tools**			
XL2000E.11.7	Create interactive PivotTables for the Web	Excel N-12	Steps 1–7	Skills Review 5, Independent Challenge 3
XL2000E.11.8	Add fields to a PivotTable using the Web browser	Excel N-13	Clues to Use	
XL2000E.12	**Collaborating with workgroups**			
XL2000E.12.2	Apply and remove worksheet and workbook protection	Excel F-8	Steps 1–8, QuickTip	Skills Review 4
XL2000E.12.3	Change workbook properties	Excel F-9	Clues to Use	Independent Challenge 3
XL2000E.12.4	Apply and remove file passwords	Excel F-8 Excel N-8 Excel N-9	Table F–1, QuickTip Steps 1–6, Clues to Use Clues to Use	Skills Review 3, Independent Challenge 1
XL2000E.12.5	Track changes (highlight, accept, and reject)	Excel N-6 (Highlight)	Steps 1–2, 7	Skills Review 2, Independent Challenge 1
		Excel N-6 (Accept and Reject)	QuickTip	Skills Review 2
XL2000E.12.6	Create a shared workbook	Excel N-4	Steps 1–5	
XL2000E.12.7	Merge workbooks	Excel N-7	Clues to Use	

Glossary

3-D references A reference that uses values on other sheets or workbooks, effectively creating another dimension to a workbook.

Analyze To manipulate data, such as a list, with Excel or another tool.

Change history A worksheet containing a list of changes made to a shared workbook.

Consolidate To add together values on multiple worksheets and display the result on another worksheet.

Criteria range A cell range containing one row of labels (usually a copy of column labels) and at least one additional row underneath it that contains the criteria you want to match.

Custom chart type A specially formatted Excel chart.

Data entry area The unlocked portion of a worksheet where users are able to enter and change data.

Data form In an Excel list (or database), a dialog box that displays one record at a time.

Data label Descriptive text that appears above a data marker in a chart.

Data map An Excel chart that shows information plotted on a map with symbols representing data points.

Data series The selected range in a worksheet that Excel converts into a graphic and displays as a chart.

data series The numbers or values that Excel plots on a chart.

Database An organized collection of related information. In Excel, a database is called a list.

External reference indicator The exclamation point (!) used in a formula to indicate that a referenced cell is outside the active sheet.

Extract To place a copy of a filtered list in a range you specify in the Advanced Filter dialog box.

Field In a list (an Excel database), a column that describes a characteristic about records, such as first name or city.

Field name A column label that describes a field.

Filter To hide data in an Excel list that does not meet specified criteria.

Footer Information that prints at the bottom of each printed page; on screen, a footer is visible only in Print Preview. To add a footer, use the Header and Footer command on the View menu.

Freeze To hold in place selected columns or rows when scrolling in a worksheet that is divided in panes. See also *panes.*

Header Information that prints at the top of each printed page; on screen, a header is visible only in Print Preview. To add a header, use the Header and Footer command on the View menu.

Hide To make rows, columns, formulas, or sheets invisible to workbook users.

HTML Hypertext Markup Language, the format of pages that a Web browser such as Internet Explorer or Netscape Navigator can read.

Hyperlink An object (a filename, a word, a phrase, or a graphic) in a worksheet that, when you click it, will display another worksheet, called the target.

Interactive Describes a worksheet saved as an HTML document and posted to an intranet or Web site that allows users to manipulate data using their browsers.

Internet A large computer network made up of smaller networks and computers.

Intranet An internal network site used by a particular group of people who work together.

Linking A method of connecting data in a source document with a destination document; the data is not pasted in the destination document, but a represtation of the data appears there. When you double-click the linked object, you open the actual source document; any changes you make affect the source document and its representation in the destination document.

Linking The dynamic referencing of data in other workbooks, so that when data in the other workbooks is changed, the references in the current workbook are automatically updated.

List The Excel term for a database, an organized collection of related information.

Lock To secure a row, column, or sheet so that data there cannot be changed.

Macro A set of instructions, or code, that performs tasks in the order you specify.

Module In Visual Basic, a module is stored in a workbook and contains macro procedures.

Object A chart or graphic image that can be moved and resized and contains handles when selected. In object linking and embedding (OLE), the data to be exchanged between another document or program.

Panes Sections into which you can divide a worksheet when you want to work on separate parts of the worksheet at the same time; one pane freezes, or remains in place, while you scroll in another pane until you see the desired information.

PivotTable list An interactive PivotTable on a Web or intranet site that lets users explore data relationships using their browsers.

Plot area The area of a chart that contains the chart itself, its axes, and the legend.

Print title In a list that spans more than one page, the field names that print at the top of every printed page.

Record In a list (an Excel database), data about an object or a person.

Route To send an e-mail attachment sequentially to each user in a list, who then forwards it to the next user on the list.

Routing slip A list of e-mail users who are to receive an e-mail attachment.

Search criterion The specification for data that you want to find in an Excel list, such as "Denver" or "is greater than 1000."

Shared workbook An Excel workbook that several users can open and modify.

Sort keys Criteria on which a sort, or a reordering of data, is based.

standard chart type A commonly used column, bar, pie, or area chart in the Excel program; each type has several variations. For example, a column chart variation is the Columns with Depth.

Target The location that a hyperlink displays after you click it.

Template A workbook containing text, formulas, macros, and formatting you use repeatedly; when you create a new document, you can open a document based on the template workbook. The new document will automatically contain the formatting, text, formulas, and macros in the template.

Track To identify and keep a record of who makes which changes to a workbook.

Uniform Resource Locator (URL) A unique address for a location on the World Wide Web; www.course.com is an example.

View A set of display or print settings that you can name and save for access at another time. You can save multiple views of a worksheet.

Web query An Excel feature that lets you obtain data from a Web, Internet, or intranet site and places it in an Excel workbook for analysis.

World Wide Web A structure of documents, called pages, connected electronically over a large computer network called the Internet.

Index

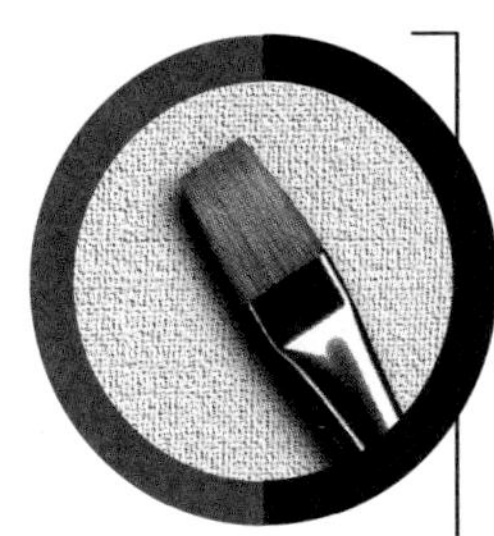

special characters

' (apostrophe)
indicating numbers as text with, EXCEL H-2, EXCEL H-4
* (asterisk) wildcard, in custom filters, EXCEL I-4
! (exclamation point), external reference indicator, EXCEL F-6
? (question mark) wildcard, EXCEL H-9
in custom filters, EXCEL I-4

▶A

Advanced Filter dialog box, EXCEL I-6–7, EXCEL I-8
advanced filters
creating, EXCEL I-6–7
criteria range for, EXCEL I-6–7, EXCEL I-8–9
extracting list data with, EXCEL I-8–9
alignment
of text in cells, EXCEL J-14–15
analysis, of list data, EXCEL I-1–17
Advanced Filter for, EXCEL I-6–7
AutoFilter for, EXCEL I-2–3
custom filters for, EXCEL I-4–5
data validation for list entries, EXCEL I-14–15
extracting list data, EXCEL I-8–9
looking up specific values, EXCEL I-12–13
subtotals for, EXCEL I-10–11
summarizing list data, EXCEL I-14–15
And condition
in custom filters, EXCEL I-5
apostrophe (')
indicating numbers as text with, EXCEL H-2, EXCEL H-4
prefacing code comments with, EXCEL G-9
ascending order sorts, EXCEL H-12–13, EXCEL H-14
Assign Macro dialog box, EXCEL G-14
asterisk (*) wildcard, in custom filters, EXCEL I-4
attachments
e-mailing workbooks as, EXCEL F-17
AutoFilter, EXCEL I-2–3
AutoFilter button, EXCEL N-10
AutoFit Selection, EXCEL H-4
AVERAGE function,
creating subtotals with, EXCEL I-10
axes, for charts
formatting, EXCEL J-6–7

▶B

blank lines
inserting in macro code, EXCEL G-9
borders
for field names, EXCEL H-4
built-in custom chart types, EXCEL J-2–3

▶C

case
matching, in searches, EXCEL H-8–9
Category (x) axis, EXCEL J-6–7
cell pointer
returning to cell A1, EXCEL F-2
cells
deleting contents of, EXCEL G-6
deleting formatting of, EXCEL G-6
hiding, EXCEL F-8–9
locking, EXCEL F-8–9
protecting, EXCEL F-8–9
rotating text within, EXCEL J-14–15
unlocking/relocking, EXCEL F-9
change history
for shared workbooks, EXCEL N-4, EXCEL N-6–7
chart axis
formatting, EXCEL J-6–7
chart labels
rotating, EXCEL J-15
Chart Options dialog box, EXCEL J-8–9
charts, EXCEL J-1–17
adding data table to, EXCEL J-8–9
legends for, EXCEL J-5
rotating, EXCEL J-10–11
Word Art in, EXCEL J-12–13
Chart toolbar, EXCEL J-2, EXCEL J-15
chart types
custom, EXCEL J-2–3
standard, EXCEL J-2
user-defined, EXCEL J-3
Chart Wizard dialog box, EXCEL J-2–3
Col_index_num
for VLOOKUP function, EXCEL I-12
column headings
printing, EXCEL H-16
column labels
improving appearance of, EXCEL H-12
sorting and, EXCEL H-12
columns
freezing, EXCEL F-2–3
hiding/unhiding, EXCEL F-9
Columns with Depth chart, EXCEL J-2–3
column width
adjusting for field names, EXCEL H-4
comments
adding to macro code, EXCEL G-9
Confirm Password dialog box, EXCEL N-8
consolidating data
with 3-D references, EXCEL F-6–7
with linking, EXCEL F-7
copying
active worksheet, EXCEL F-4
list data, to another location, EXCEL I-8–9
Copy to another location option
for extracting list data, EXCEL I-8–9
COUNT function,
creating subtotals with, EXCEL I-10
criteria
for deleting records, EXCEL H-10–11
for finding records, EXCEL H-8–9, EXCEL I-2
Criteria data form, EXCEL H-8–9
criteria range
for advanced filters, EXCEL I-6–7, EXCEL I-8–9
defining in Advanced Filter dialog box, EXCEL I-9
crosshair pointer, EXCEL J-16
Custom AutoFilter dialog box, EXCEL I-3–4
Custom Buttons
for Macros toolbar, EXCEL G-16–17
custom chart types
creating, EXCEL J-3
selecting, EXCEL J-2–3
sizing handles for, EXCEL J-2
custom filters
creating, EXCEL I-3–4
Customize dialog box, EXCEL G-16–17
custom sort order, EXCEL H-15
custom views
saving, EXCEL F-10–11
Custom Views dialog box, EXCEL F-10–11
custom Web queries, EXCEL N-17

▶D

data
consolidating, with 3-D references, EXCEL F-6–7
databases
defined, EXCEL H-1 (*See also* lists)
vs. lists, EXCEL H-3
data entry area
locking cells outside of, EXCEL F-8
data form
adding records to lists with, EXCEL H-6–7
data labels, EXCEL J-4
data maps, EXCEL J-16–17
data series
customizing, EXCEL J-4–5
defined, EXCEL J-4

Index

data tables
 adding to charts, EXCEL J-8–9
data validation
 for list entries, EXCEL I-16–17
DCOUNTA function, EXCEL I-14–15
defaults
 macros names, EXCEL G-4
Delete button, EXCEL H-10–11
deleting
 macros, EXCEL G-6
 ranges, EXCEL H-10
 records, EXCEL H-10–11
 worksheets, EXCEL F-4–5
descending order sorts, EXCEL H-12, EXCEL H-14
details
 showing or hiding in outlines, EXCEL I-11
Drawing toolbar, EXCEL J-12
DSUM function, EXCEL I-14–15
dynamic page breaks, EXCEL F-12

▶E

Edit Text Object dialog box, EXCEL J-16–17
Edit WordArt Text dialog box, EXCEL J-12–13
e-mail
 sending workbooks via, EXCEL F-17
Enter Parameter Value dialog box, EXCEL N-16
entry order sorts, EXCEL H-12
Excel Macro Recorder
 recording macros with, EXCEL G-4–5, EXCEL G-8
exclamation point (!)
 external reference indicator, EXCEL F-6
External Data toolbar, EXCEL N-16
external reference indicator, EXCEL F-6
extracting list data, EXCEL I-8–9
extract range
 defining in Advanced Filter dialog box, EXCEL I-9

▶F

field names
 adjusting column widths for, EXCEL H-4
 borders for, EXCEL H-4
 defined, EXCEL H-2
 guidelines for, EXCEL H-5
 planning, EXCEL H-2
fields
 defined, EXCEL H-2
 planning, EXCEL H-2
 sorting lists by, EXCEL H-12–13
file(s)
 HTML, EXCEL F-16–17, EXCEL N-10–11
 hyperlinks between, EXCEL F-14–15
 posting to Web, EXCEL F-16
 saving as HTML files, EXCEL F-16–17
 sharing, EXCEL N-2–3
filtering
 with advanced filters, EXCEL I-6–7
 with custom filters, EXCEL I-3–4
 defined, EXCEL I-2
 using AutoFilter, EXCEL I-2–3
finding
 records in lists, EXCEL H-8–9
 text, EXCEL F-2
 with wildcards, EXCEL H-9
folders
 creating, EXCEL F-16
footers
 specifying, EXCEL F-5
Format Axis dialog box, EXCEL J-6
Format Cells dialog box
 Alignment tab, EXCEL J-14–15
Format Data Series dialog box, EXCEL J-4–5
formatting
 chart axis, EXCEL J-6–7
 data series, EXCEL J-4–5
 deleting, EXCEL G-6
 legends, EXCEL J-5
 numbers, EXCEL H-2
Formatting toolbar, EXCEL H-4
Freeze panes command, EXCEL F-2
freezing
 rows and columns, EXCEL F-2–3

▶G

graphics
 inserting, EXCEL F-15
gridlines
 printing, EXCEL H-16
grouping
 creating subtotals using, E[illegible] I-10–11

▶H

headers
 specifying, EXCEL F-5
Hide Details button, EXCEL I-11
HLOOKUP function, EXCEL I-13
HTML files
 saving Excel files as, EXCEL F-16–17, EXCEL N-10–11
hyperlinks
 creating between Excel files, EXCEL F-14–15
 creating to Web URLs, EXCEL N-14–15
 navigating large worksheets with, EXCEL N-15
Hypertext Markup Language. *See* HTML files

▶I

indenting
 labels, EXCEL H-12
Insert ClipArt window, EXCEL F-15
Insert Hyperlink dialog box, EXCEL F-14–15, EXCEL N-14–15
inserting
 blank lines, in macro code, EXCEL G-9
 pictures, EXCEL F-15
 worksheets, EXCEL F-4–5
interactive PivotTables
 creating for intranet or Web, EXCEL N-12–13
 publishing on intranet or Web, EXCEL N-2–3
interactive worksheets
 creating for intranet or Web, EXCEL N-10–11
 publishing on intranet or the Web, EXCEL N-2–3
Internet, EXCEL F-16. *See also* World Wide Web
Internet Explorer
 viewing interactive PivotTables in, EXCEL N-12–13
 viewing interactive worksheets in, EXCEL N-10–11
intranets, EXCEL F-16
 creating interactive PivotTables for, EXCEL N-12–13
 creating interactive workbooks for, EXCEL N-10–11
 managing HTML files on, EXCEL N-11
 publishing interactive workbooks and PivotTables to, EXCEL N-2–3

▶L

landscape orientation
 printing worksheets in, EXCEL H-16
legends
 inserting, formatting, and removing, EXCEL J-5
 for maps, EXCEL J-16–17
linking
 consolidating data with, EXCEL F-7
list data
 analyzing, EXCEL I-1–17
 analyzing with Advanced Filter, EXCEL I-6–7
 analyzing with AutoFilter, EXCEL I-2–3
 analyzing with custom filters, EXCEL I-4–5
 data validation for list entries, EXCEL I-14–15
 extracting, EXCEL I-8–9
 looking up specific values, EXCEL I-12–13
 subtotals for, EXCEL I-10–11
 summarizing list data, EXCEL I-14–15
lists, EXCEL H-1–17
 adding records with data form, EXCEL H-6–7
 creating, EXCEL H-4–5
 databases *vs.*, EXCEL H-3
 defined, EXCEL H-1
 finding records in, EXCEL H-8–9
 maintaining quality of information in, EXCEL H-5
 number formatting for, EXCEL H-2
 PivotTable, EXCEL N-12–13
 planning, EXCEL H-2–3
 printing, EXCEL H-16–17
 row and column content guidelines, EXCEL H-3
 size and location guidelines, EXCEL H-3
 sorting, by multiple fields, EXCEL H-14–15
 sorting by one field, EXCEL H-12–13
Locked check box, EXCEL F-8
locking selected cells, EXCEL F-8–9
logical conditions
 in custom filters, EXCEL I-5

▶M

macros, EXCEL G-1–17
adding as menu items, EXCEL G-14–15
adding blank lines to, EXCEL G-9
adding comments to code, EXCEL G-9
creating toolbars for, EXCEL G-16–17
default names for, EXCEL G-4
defined, EXCEL G-1
deleting, EXCEL G-6
descriptions of, EXCEL G-2–3
disabling, EXCEL G-3
editing, EXCEL G-8–9
enabling, EXCEL G-3
naming, EXCEL G-2
Personal Macro Workbook, EXCEL G-12–13
planning, EXCEL G-2–3
recording, EXCEL G-4–5
running, EXCEL G-6–7
shortcut keys for, EXCEL G-10–11
stopping, while running, EXCEL G-6
storing, EXCEL G-2, EXCEL G-8
uses of, EXCEL G-1
viruses and, EXCEL G-3
mapping data, EXCEL J-16–17
Match case box, EXCEL H-8–9
creating subtotals with, EXCEL I-10
menu(s),
adding macros to, EXCEL G-14–15
merging
workbooks, EXCEL N-7
Microsoft Clip Gallery, EXCEL F-15
Microsoft Investor, EXCEL N-16
Microsoft Investor Stock Quotes, EXCEL N-16–17
Microsoft Map Control dialog box, EXCEL J-16–17
MIN function
creating subtotals with, EXCEL I-10
modules
storing macros in, EXCEL G-8
Multiple Maps Available dialog box, EXCEL J-16

▶N

navigating worksheets
with hyperlinks, EXCEL F-14, EXCEL N-14–15
New Toolbar dialog box, EXCEL G-16–17
numbers
formatting, EXCEL C-2–3, EXCEL H-2

▶O

Or condition
in custom filters, EXCEL I-5
for extracting list data, EXCEL I-8
outlines
creating subtotals using, EXCEL I-10–11
showing or hiding details in, EXCEL I-11

▶P

Page Break command, EXCEL F-12
Page Break Preview, EXCEL F-13, EXCEL H-17
page breaks, EXCEL F-12–13
dynamic, EXCEL F-12
horizontal, EXCEL F-12–13
vertical, EXCEL F-12
page numbering, EXCEL F-12–13
Sheet tab, EXCEL H-16–17
panes
defined, EXCEL F-2
splitting worksheets in, EXCEL F-3
password entry prompt, EXCEL N-8–9
passwords
applying, EXCEL N-8–9
removing, EXCEL N-9
Paste function button, EXCEL I-12
Personal Macro Workbook, EXCEL G-1, EXCEL G-12–13
perspective
of 3-D charts, EXCEL J-10–11
pictures. *See also* Graphics
inserting, EXCEL F-15
PivotTable Field List dialog box, EXCEL N-13
PivotTable lists
adding fields to, using Web browser, EXCEL N-13
defined, EXCEL N-12
publishing to the Web, EXCEL N-12–13
PivotTables
interactive, creating for the intranet or Web, EXCEL N-12–13
interactive, creating for the intranet or the Web, EXCEL N-12–13
plot area, EXCEL J-6
pointers
cell, EXCEL F-2
posting files to the Web, EXCEL F-16
print areas
clearing, EXCEL H-17
setting, EXCEL H-17
Print dialog box, EXCEL A-12–13, EXCEL H-17
Print Preview, EXCEL G-14, EXCEL H-16–17
for page breaks , EXCEL N-13
print title, EXCEL H-16
printing
lists, EXCEL H-16–17
more than one worksheet, EXCEL H-16
multiple ranges, EXCEL H-16
selected areas of worksheets, EXCEL H-16–17
Property Toolbox button, EXCEL N-10
protection, of worksheets areas, EXCEL F-8–9
Protection tab, EXCEL F-8–9
Publish as Web Page dialog box, EXCEL N-10, EXCEL N-12–13

▶Q

queries
retrieving data from Web with, EXCEL N-2–3, EXCEL N-16–17
question mark (?) wildcard, EXCEL H-9
in custom filters, EXCEL I-4

▶R

ranges
deleting, EXCEL H-10
printing multiple, EXCEL H-16
Record Macro dialog box, EXCEL G-4–5
EXCEL G-10–11, EXCEL G-12–13
recording macros, EXCEL G-4–5
records
defined, EXCEL H-2
deleting, EXCEL H-10–11
finding in lists, EXCEL H-8–9
restoring, EXCEL H-11
retrieving, with AutoFilter, EXCEL I-2–3
references
creating, EXCEL F-6
external reference indicators, EXCEL F-6
3-D, EXCEL F-6–7
Relative Reference button, EXCEL G-10–11
Replace All option, EXCEL H-8–9
Replace dialog box, EXCEL H-8–9
Replace option, EXCEL H-8–9
Report Manager, EXCEL F-10
restoring records, EXCEL H-11
restricted cells
entering data in, EXCEL I-16–17
Returning External Data to Microsoft Excel dialog box, EXCEL N-16
rotating chart labels, EXCEL J-15
rotating charts, EXCEL J-10–11
rotating labels, EXCEL H-12
rotating text, EXCEL J-14–15
row headings
printing, EXCEL H-16
Row_index_num
for HLOOKUP function, EXCEL I-13
rows
freezing, EXCEL F-2–3
hiding/unhiding, EXCEL F-9
running macros, EXCEL G-6–7
Run Query dialog box, EXCEL N-16

▶S

Sample box
in Chart Wizard dialog box, EXCEL J-2–3
Save As dialog box, EXCEL F-16–17
creating folder in, EXCEL F-16
Save Options dialog box, EXCEL N-8–9

Index

saving
  custom views, EXCEL F-10–11
  as HTML files, EXCEL F-16–17
ScreenTips
  tracking changes to shared workbooks with, EXCEL N-6–7
shared workbooks, EXCEL N-2
  applying and removing passwords, EXCEL N-8–9
  change history for, EXCEL N-4
  defined, EXCEL N-4
  issues, EXCEL N-2–3
  setting up, EXCEL N-4–5
  tracking changes in, EXCEL N-6–7
Share Workbook dialog box, EXCEL N-4–5
shortcut keys, for macros, EXCEL G-10–11
Show Details button, EXCEL I-11
sizing handles
  for custom charts, EXCEL J-2
sort buttons, EXCEL H-12
Sort command, EXCEL H-12
Sort dialog box, EXCEL H-14–15
sorting
  ascending order, EXCEL H-12–13, EXCEL H-14
  custom sort order, EXCEL H-15
  descending order, EXCEL H-12, EXCEL H-14
  entry order, EXCEL H-12
  lists, by multiple fields, EXCEL H-14–15
  lists, by one field, EXCEL H-12–13
sort keys, EXCEL H-14–15
splitting worksheets, EXCEL F-3
Spreadsheet Property Toolbox, EXCEL N-10–11
standard chart types, EXCEL J-2
stock symbols, EXCEL N-16
Stop Recording button, EXCEL G-4–5
Stop Recording toolbar, EXCEL G-4–5, EXCEL G-10–11
subtotals
  creating with grouping, EXCEL I-10–11
  creating with outlines, EXCEL I-10–11
Subtotals dialog box, EXCEL I-10–11
SUM function
  creating subtotals with, EXCEL I-10
summarizing list data, EXCEL I-14–15
Symbol Lookup hyperlink, EXCEL N-16

▶T

targets
  hyperlinks to, EXCEL F-14–15
templates
  creating workbooks with, EXCEL G-5
text
  rotating, EXCEL J-14–15
three-dimensional (3-D) charts
  rotating, EXCEL J-10–11
3-D references, EXCEL F-6–7
3-D View dialog box, EXCEL J-10–11
titles
  printing, EXCEL H-16
toolbars
  Chart, EXCEL J-2, EXCEL J-15
  creating for macros, EXCEL G-16–17
  Drawing, EXCEL J-12
  External Data, EXCEL N-16
  Formatting, EXCEL H-4
  Stop Recording, EXCEL G-4–5, EXCEL G-10–11
Top 10 AutoFilter dialog box, EXCEL I-2
tracking changes
  in shared workbooks, EXCEL N-4, EXCEL N-6–7

▶U

Undo command
  restoring deleted records with, EXCEL H-11
Unfreeze panes command, EXCEL F-2
Uniform Resource Locators (URLs)
  creating hyperlinks to, EXCEL N-14–15
User-defined chart types, EXCEL J-3

▶V

values
  looking up in a list, EXCEL I-12–13
Value (y) axis, EXCEL J-6–7
Value (z) axis, EXCEL J-7
VBA code
  Vertical Lookup function. *See* VLOOKUP function
views
  custom, saving, EXCEL F-10–11
viruses
  macros and, EXCEL G-3
VLOOKUP dialog box, EXCEL I-12–13
VLOOKUP function, EXCEL I-12–13

▶W

Web. *See* World Wide Web
Web browsers
  adding fields to PivotTable lists with, EXCEL N-13
  viewing interactive PivotTables in, EXCEL N-12–13
  viewing interactive worksheets in, EXCEL N-10–11
Web Page Preview, EXCEL F-16–17
wildcards
  for searches, EXCEL H-8–9
Word Art
  in charts, EXCEL J-12–13
workbooks, EXCEL F-1–17
  applying and removing passwords, EXCEL N-8–9
  consolidating data from, with linking, EXCEL F-7
  creating hyperlinks between, EXCEL F-14–15
  creating with templates, EXCEL G-5
  deleting worksheets from, EXCEL F-4–5
  distributing to others, EXCEL N-2
  inserting pictures in, EXCEL F-15
  inserting worksheets in, EXCEL F-4–5
  merging, EXCEL N-7
  protecting, EXCEL F-9
  saving as HTML documents, EXCEL F-16–17
  sending via e-mail, EXCEL F-17
  on server, controlling access to, EXCEL N-2
  setting up, EXCEL N-4–5
  shared, EXCEL N-2
  specifying headers and footers for, EXCEL F-5
  tracking changes in, EXCEL N-6–7
Worksheet menu bar
  adding macros to, EXCEL G-14–15
worksheets
  copying, EXCEL F-4
  deleting, EXCEL F-4–5
  enhancing, EXCEL J-1
  hiding areas of, EXCEL F-8–9
  inserting, EXCEL F-4–5
  interactive, creating for intranet or Web, EXCEL N-10–11
  interactive, publishing on intranet or the Web, EXCEL N-2–3
  navigating with hyperlinks, EXCEL F-14, EXCEL N-15
  page breaks and page numbering, EXCEL F-12–13
  printing, EXCEL H-16–17
  printing more than one, EXCEL H-16
  printing selected areas of, EXCEL H-16–17
  protecting areas of, EXCEL F-8–9
  publishing on intranet or the Web, EXCEL N-2–3
  saving as HTML documents, EXCEL F-16–17
  splitting into multiple panes, EXCEL F-3
workspaces, EXCEL F-11
World Wide Web
  creating interactive PivotTables for, EXCEL N-12–13
  creating interactive workbooks for, EXCEL N-10–11
  customized queries on, EXCEL N-17
  managing HTML files on, EXCEL N-11
  preparing workbooks for publishing on, EXCEL F-14–17
  publishing interactive workbooks and PivotTables to, EXCEL N-2–3
  running queries on, EXCEL N-2–3, EXCEL N-16–17
Wrap Text, EXCEL H-4

▶Z

Zoom box, EXCEL F-10